Advanced Praise for *The Puppy Whisperer*

"I've known Paul personally for many years and have faithfully followed his training advice with wonderful results. He has a great and gentle touch with animals, as I've seen firsthand from the many times he's come over to the house to help me train my dogs. I've given his books and DVDs to several friends. Paul's new book, *The Puppy Whisperer,* allows everyone to see what his positive, reward-based training is all about. I can't recommend him highly enough."

—*Jeff Probst, host of* Survivor

"*The Puppy Whisperer* offers dog lovers a perfect combination of wisdom and compassionate guidance in a humane, loving approach to training your kindred spirit. The inclusion of mind/body medicine, mindfulness, and consciousness offers a comprehensive, integrated approach. Combined with critical practical care information, *The Puppy Whisperer* is a blessing to both you and your canine companion. Read it and enjoy your lives together at a whole new level!"

—*Allen M. Schoen, DVM, author of* Kindred Spirits:
How the Remarkable Bond Between Humans and Animals
Can Change the Way We Live *and editor of* Veterinary
Acupuncture: Ancient Art to Modern Medicine

"This book, like its predecessor, is a delight—filled with practical, useful, and important information about obtaining the right puppy, keeping her happy and healthy, and sharing a meaningful life together."

—*W. Jean Dodds, DVM, president, Hemopet,*
Santa Monica, CA

"With his usual compassion, good humor, and dedication to gentle training methods, Paul Owens offers puppy owners everything they need to get their pups off on the right paw. No puppy owner should be without this book!"

—*Nicole Wilde, author of* Help for Your Fearful Dog *and*
So You Want to Be a Dog Trainer

"The positive training principles presented by Paul Owens and his coauthors in *The Puppy Whisperer* are a gift to all of us who want to experience a relationship of mutual respect and lifelong joy with our dogs. Based on love, compassion, and kindness, this book celebrates and helps us to enhance the unique bond between humans and animals."

—*Michael Bernard Beckwith, featured in* The Secret *and*
author of Inspirations of the Heart

THE PUPPY WHISPERER

A Compassionate, Nonviolent Guide to Early Training and Care

Paul Owens and Terence Cranendonk

with Norma Eckroate

Avon, Massachusetts

Published by Adams Media, a division of F+W Media, Inc.
57 Littlefield Street
Avon, MA 02322
www.adamsmedia.com

ISBN 10: 1-59337-597-2
ISBN 13: 978-1-59337-597-3

Library of Congress Cataloging-in-Publication Data
is available from the publisher.

Printed in the United States of America.
J I H

This publication is designed to provide accurate and authoritative information with regard to the subject matter covered. It is sold with the understanding that the publisher is not engaged in rendering legal, accounting, or other
professional advice. If legal advice or other expert assistance is required,
the services of a competent professional person should be sought.
—From a *Declaration of Principles* jointly adopted by a Committee of the
American Bar Association and a Committee of Publishers and Associations

Many of the designations used by manufacturers and sellers to distinguish
their product are claimed as trademarks. Where those designations appear
in this book and Adams Media was aware of a trademark claim, the designations have been printed with initial capital letters.

All photos by Brian Stemmler of Stemmler Photography, Los Angeles,
California; except photos on pages 62, 217, and 218 by
Marianne Goebel; and pages 37, 104, and 112 by Christine Lee.

This book is available at quantity discounts for bulk purchases.
For information, please call 1-800-289-0963.

Contents

Acknowledgments

There are many people who assisted greatly in the process of creating this book. We'd have to put our agent Lisa Hagan at the top of the list with special thanks. Thanks to Adams Media, especially: Kate Epstein, who persuaded us to write this book; Shoshanna Grossman and Jennifer Kushnier, the editors who succeeded Kate and took such wonderful care of us; and Meredith O'Hayre, project manager, for her great attention to detail.

For their valuable professional input, we are greatly indebted to Nancy Scanlan, DVM; Mary Brennan, DVM; Pam Reid, PhD; and Nicole Wilde.

We're grateful to our photographers: Brian Stemmler at Stemmler Photography in Los Angeles, whose professionalism and patience are incomparable; Marianne Goebel for the photos shot in Akron, Ohio; and Christine Lee, who provided us with additional shots.

And what would a puppy book be without gorgeous puppies? Special thanks to those friends whose furry sidekicks came out to strut their stuff and demonstrate how it is done: Joan and Lauren Asarnow with Layla, ten weeks; Kerry and Haley Witzeman with Homer, four months; Ronda Bingham and Brian Nemes with Sparky, five months; George and Randy Austin with Blitz, six months; Barbara Holliday with Bozley the Beagle; Carol Cupp with Rocket; and Christine Lee and Peggy Larkin with Caydee, Ellie, and lots of adorable puppies.

In addition, Paul would especially like to thank: the Owens's clan; Pam, Peg, Pat and Tom, Jennifer Mielziner, Jenina Schutter, Carol and Richard Cupp, Carol and Terry Boyer, Christine Lee,

Peggy Larkin, Barbara Holliday and Bozley the Beagle, Jim and Keelin O'Neill, Nicole Walder, and the incomparable Molly and Grady. Your support and faith made it all possible. And blessings to my awesome coauthors: "That was easy."

Terry would like to thank:
My mother, Elisabeth Cranendonk, my sister, Yolande McNeely, and my late father, John Cranendonk, who fostered in me a love for all animals.

My wife Debora and daughter Viola for their patience with the continual refrain, "Daddy's working on the book," and Magoo, for starting me on this whole adventure—if I only knew then what I know now.

All the staff and volunteers at the Humane Society of Greater Akron, especially Richard Farkas, Kathy Romito, Sarah Aitken, and Chalan Geul for supporting my work all these years. Special thanks to Humane Society volunteer and puppy socializer extraordinaire Marianne Goebel.

Ken McCort, who is always ready to talk shop.

Finally, Paul and Norma, with whom destiny has thrown me together in a most glorious and amazing fashion.

And, last but not least, Norma would like to thank:
Meryl Ann Butler, who is like a sister to me, and is always ready to share her amazing creative input. I'm also very grateful for the inspiration of Rev. Dr. Michael Beckwith; Esther and Jerry Hicks; Rev. Nirvana Gayle; Bruce Lipton, PhD; Gary Craig; John Sarno, MD; Kathleen McNamara; Dr. Maisha Hazzard; and Mathew Howard-Houston. I send special thanks to Joseph Sciabbarrasi, MD, and Ronald Andiman, MD, for being their amazing, supportive selves, and Charles Livingstone Fels, who is surely keeping the heavens laughing. And, last but not at all least, special thanks to Paul and Terry for a wonderful co-creative process. Even though it sometimes seemed as though it was an unending process, writing this book with you was a fun ride and an honor.

Preface by Paul Owens

Several puppies attacked my shoelaces as I entered the room but my eyes were attracted to a little brown ball of fuzz huddled against the wall. The breeder saw me focusing on this puppy and said, "She's a bit timid. You might want to choose one of these other puppies. I think there's something wrong with her." I didn't hesitate. "No," I said. "I think I'll choose her." And so began a journey and a partnership that I celebrate to this day.

Molly is a Portuguese water dog. As of this writing, she has gracefully aged into her twilight years, although a genetic eye disease gradually took her sight. She's been blind as a bat for more than seven years. Molly can no longer jump into my van through the window. And she isn't up to many of her old tricks anymore. One of her favorites was answering the phone by picking up the receiver in her mouth. Then when I told her, "It's a bill collector," she would ceremoniously drop it in the wastebasket.

However, Molly still happily chews away at carrots held between her paws—even though the chewing takes a bit longer than it used to. And she still jumps on the bed with ease when it's time to sleep—although these days she more often than not lands on one of the other dogs already lying there. When we recently moved to a new home, she still had all circuits firing as she learned to navigate her way back into the house from the yard. It took her three weeks, but she doggedly persevered until she memorized the new layout. Not bad for a blind, sixteen-year-old dog.

When Molly came into my life, I had been training dogs for many years using the standard methods of the time, which included jerking, shocking, and pinning a dog to the ground. In

1990 something inside me switched gears. I could no longer use these methods. I realized that physical punishment and aversive training were not necessary.

Martin Luther King Jr. once said, "If our goal is peace, then our means must be peaceful." Well, jerking, hitting, and pinning a dog to the ground do little to promote peace. Positive dog training fosters safety, patience, kindness, and compassion for humans and the family dog. Over the years, many dog trainers have adopted these kinder, gentler, and yes, more peaceful, methods.

In my first book, *The Dog Whisperer, A Compassionate Nonviolent Approach to Dog Training*, and my DVD of the same title (*www.dogwhispererdvd.com*), I've tried my best to foster and promote these nonviolent concepts. And the message of this book, geared for puppies, remains the same. When you see and experience the power of nonviolent dog training, you will be empowered and encouraged to use positive methods with animals and even with the people around you. Molly says so.

Preface by Terence Cranendonk

More than ten years ago, I rescued a puppy that a coworker had picked up off the streets of Cleveland, Ohio—a brown and white charmer with touches of black, who was found huddling and frightened under a car in a parking lot. I estimated his genetic background as collie/terrier mix, promptly dubbed him a "collier," and gave him the name Magoo, based on his big, round, and often sad eyes. This was before I was a professional dog trainer and I had no idea what I was getting into! I just knew that I loved this puppy and that I was looking forward to having a great time with him.

I took books out of the library, which all advised me to "be the pack leader," and to "not let my puppy get away with bad behavior." I was also instructed to teach my puppy to heel, as if this would somehow magically imbue me with leadership status and he would stop behaving in ways I didn't want him to. I was told to jerk him by his collar and shake him by the scruff of his neck, which I instinctively found abhorrent. Much to my frustration, none of the suggestions worked. I quickly abandoned these methods.

Fortunately, I finally had the good sense to seek out a professional trainer and found Paul Owens, who was practicing in Cleveland in those days. It was there that Paul's patience, humor, and compassion initially enticed me into the dog training world. Paul's philosophy and approach, viewing dogs as actual living, breathing beings who are worthy of respect, were unique to me at that time. Plus, the training worked!

I apprenticed as a trainer with Paul and over the years continued my education with other great trainers and behaviorists from around the country and world. A scruffy street puppy literally changed my life. Not only did Magoo lead me to a career as a dog trainer and behavior consultant, but he also opened my eyes to the amazing power of positive training. I learned that treating him with simple generosity, kindness, and fairness was the foundation for a happy relationship. And this holds true whether the relationship is between a dog and human, a human and human, or indeed, between any two animals.

When I first adopted Magoo, I desperately looked for answers. I needed a book that provided two things—precise instructions for positive, reward-based training, and a detailed plan for the early socialization of my puppy. A book like this was not to be found. I hope that with *The Puppy Whisperer*, Paul and I have filled a need and, in a small way, helped to create a beacon of light for those who are searching for answers like I once did.

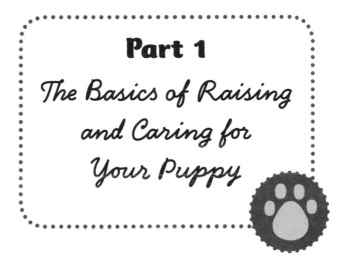

Part 1

The Basics of Raising and Caring for Your Puppy

Chapter 1

Are You Ready for a Puppy?

Repeat this ten times as fast as you can: "Pretty perspicacious puppies pick to play and party." (They also pee and poop, but we couldn't figure out how to fit these words into the phrase.) Introducing a puppy into your life can be one of the most fun, rewarding, and even inspiring experiences you will ever have. Puppies remind us of innocence and freedom. Their carefree joy, unabashed curiosity, and fearless explorations trigger our own primal joy and sense of freedom. Together, you and your puppy will grow old, dancing hand-in-paw through this glorious thing called life. Tra-la-la-la-la! It's all true!

But just like anything else, real life often butts heads with ephemeral dreams, and the stress of raising a puppy can open our other, not-so-pleasant emotional trap doors. One client was aghast that his new puppy had destroyed his $29,000 oriental rug. "Twenty-nine thousand dollars!" he repeated over and over again with the emphasis (for dramatic effect) always being on the "*Twenty-nine* thousand. . ."! He really resented this little puppy. It was as if the puppy was responsible for shattering his dreams and gloriously envisioned expectations of the perfect human-canine household. He hadn't done his homework and then he blamed the puppy. Accidents do happen but it's our goal with this book to give you the tools you'll need to set up an environment for success and safety so there will be fewer of them.

Puppies teach us patience. Puppies teach us how to physically handle a living, breathing, feeling machine without breaking its parts. Puppies teach us to give more of ourselves and hence, not

3

be so selfish. Puppies teach us responsibility. Isn't it wonderful that puppies give us the opportunity to better ourselves? The key to a happy, healthy human-puppy relationship begins with preparedness, realistic expectations, patience, and consistency. If this is your first puppy or the first puppy you've lived with in many years—get ready. Your daily life is about to change. If you're ready, all will be well. If you're not ready, not so much.

As wonderful as those moments are when you feel all warm and happy inside watching your puppy chew her toy, slide across the kitchen floor, and pounce on your shoelaces, there are the other times. The same teeth that chewed the toy might destroy your slippers, newspapers, and—horror of all horrors—the television remote! The same carefree energy the puppy displayed while romping through the yard will also be released on the plants in your carefully tended garden. And the same curious nature that you found so cute when you first brought your puppy home can also lead to illness and injury if cabinets aren't locked, sharp objects picked up, and doors kept closed. So before adopting a puppy, it's very important that you consider the commitment you are making and whether or not this is the right time to bring a puppy home.

Is It Puppy Time?

Adopting a dog of any age, whether a puppy or an adult, is a commitment for the life of the dog. Your puppy will have to go through his own equivalents of childhood and adolescence, just like humans do. Dogs reach maturity somewhere between eighteen months and three years of age. These early growth stages can get to be a tad stressful for the typical family, so before you get a puppy, take a step back. Consider your financial situation, your physical capabilities, the size of your home, how physically active you are, how much you travel, your health, and, if you have a family, the size, age, and temperaments of your children.

Here are just some of the factors to consider when you bring a puppy into your house:

Annual Costs: $1,500 to $5,000. Annual costs include veterinary care, food, training, grooming, treats and toys, and a dog sitter or doggie daycare when you're away. Injuries and illnesses add to the total.

Scheduling Meals and Potty Training: A puppy must be fed three to four times a day and provided frequent trips outside for elimination purposes.

Human Stress Factors: It can be frustrating having dog hair on all of your clothes and stressful dealing with common problems that crop up such as a flea infestation, skunk spray, "accidents" on the carpet, or any medical emergencies.

Neutering and Spaying: As a responsible dog guardian, you'll want to neuter or spay your puppy unless you are willing and able to accept responsibility for the lives of more puppies.

Long-Term Commitment: There's a great quote: "A dog is not just for the holidays." You'll be making a long-term commitment to care for a dog, for better or for worse, for the dog's entire life. It's a big commitment to adopt a living, breathing being who is totally dependent on you.

Consider a Mature Dog: If the requirements of a puppy seem overwhelming to you, you might want to consider adopting an adolescent or even an older dog since they aren't as time-intensive. While there are many benefits of raising a dog from puppyhood, in most cases those who adopt older dogs find wonderful companions that are as close to them as any dog that was adopted as a puppy.

Still think a puppy's for you? Great! Read on. . . .

Where to Get Your Puppy

One of the best methods of finding your new puppy is through networking. Ask your relatives, friends, coworkers, your veterinarian, and even the people you meet at a dog park where they got their dog and if they were happy with the adoption process. The options for finding the right puppy include shelters, rescue organizations, breeders, private individuals, pet stores, and sometimes veterinary clinics. Let's look at each of these possibilities.

Adopting from an Animal Shelter

Adopting a homeless puppy at an early age puts you in a position of tremendous influence over her behavior, which far offsets any disadvantage you face in not knowing your puppy's ancestry. The greatest influence you will have on your dog's behavior is the environment you provide. And, by adopting from a shelter, you will be putting your two cents of goodness into the universal pot!

Most animal shelter staffs try to get a thorough history on dogs when they are surrendered. If the puppies were born at the shelter or brought to the shelter with their mother, the staff may be able to share some information about her disposition and tendencies. In addition, adopting a puppy from a shelter or rescue organization helps fight the terrible problem of dog overpopulation. With literally millions of homeless dogs in the United States, and local humane society shelters bursting from overcrowding, adopting a shelter puppy prevents a canine life from being wasted, as up to 50 percent of all dogs turned into shelters are euthanized due to overcrowding.

If the shelter doesn't have a puppy who is right for you, check back. Some shelters keep waiting lists and will let you know when a puppy arrives who meets your particular criteria—be it breed or size or temperament. The Humane Society of the United States estimates that 25 percent of shelter animals are purebred, occasionally including purebred puppies. Many local shelters now have Web sites where they post the photos of the animals that are available for adoption. The animal shelter in your area might be referred to as "animal control," the "humane society," or "animal services," so check the phone directory to locate the one nearest you.

Adopting from a Breed-Specific Rescue Organization

Some rescue organizations are devoted to finding homes for specific breeds. These dedicated individuals often foster the animals in their own homes until a suitable home is available. The neat thing about breed-specific rescue organizations is that the fostering family really gets to know the puppy's personality and can give you a pretty good assessment of her temperament.

Animal shelters often turn purebred dogs over to these groups, knowing that the animal is in good hands and may be more likely to find a home among the aficionados of the breed. Rescue organizations usually charge minimal fees, similar to those charged by animal shelters. Most rescue organizations have Web sites with postings of available animals.

Adopting from Breeders, Private Individuals, and Pet Stores

Breeders range in size from small family operations that breed dogs in their homes to large kennels. Some are extremely reputable but, sadly, a large percentage of purebred puppies, including many that are sold in pet stores, come from breeding facilities that are referred to as puppy mills. Puppy mills are dog breeding operations that mass produce puppies, often in unsanitary conditions where dogs are kept in cages and continuously bred without a break between pregnancies. These facilities often lack even basic veterinary care, food, water, and socialization. These breeders are responsible for inbreeding that causes genetic problems leading to health and behavioral abnormalities. They sell puppies to brokers and pet stores across the country; however, they also sell directly to the public, often through Internet sites or newspaper ads.

Humane animal organizations oppose the sale of puppies and dogs from these mass-breeding establishments and warn the public to beware. But how do you know if you're getting a puppy that came from one of these deplorable places? It's not an easy thing to figure out since unscrupulous breeders can appear to be gentle and humane.

A reputable breeder, whether a professional who is breeding purebred dogs or a friend or neighbor whose mixed-breed dog had puppies, is probably as concerned about finding a puppy a good home as you are about finding the right puppy. That breeder will want to interview you to assure himself that you will provide for all of the puppy's needs and that you are ready, willing, and able to take on the responsibility of a new puppy for as long as that dog lives. The American Society for the Prevention of Cruelty to Animals has produced a terrific set of guidelines to find a reputable breeder. Their "Responsible Breeder Position Statement" can be found on their Web site at *www.aspca.org*.

The bottom line for adopting: Do your research, ask questions, and meet the puppy's parents if possible.

Chapter 2

The Right Puppy for You

Many of us have preconceived notions of what "the perfect dog" might look and behave like. Visions come to mind of a golden retriever romping playfully through a field or a loyal shepherd walking stoically by the handler's side. But too many times a humane, caring person brings home a puppy only to find that, "Gee, this isn't at all what I expected."

Each dog is an individual with his own abilities, personality, stress-management thresholds, and so on, just as each human family has its own special desires, needs, and abilities. So how can you tell which puppy is for you? Sometimes life happens and a stranded puppy ends up on your doorstep and Mother Nature makes the decision for you. Otherwise, when you adopt a puppy, here are a few considerations to keep in mind:

- Health (both the puppy's and your family's)
- Personality and temperament (including energy level)
- Breed-specific needs and characteristics, including grooming considerations
- Size
- Climate considerations
- Exercise needs
- Other animals in the house
- Children in the family and their ages

In addition to this list of considerations, we'll add two more—chemistry and intuition.

The Puppy's Health and the Human Family's Health

Before you bring a puppy into your home, it is important to consider health issues.

The Health of the Puppy

Before adopting a puppy, get a clean bill of health from the shelter, rescue, or breeder. If the puppy shows signs of listlessness; has sores or wounds on her body; has any discharge coming from her nose, eyes, or mouth; has areas of hair missing; or is coughing or sneezing, bring these concerns to the staff's attention, of course, and seriously consider whether this is the puppy for you. Ask for a written report as to any vaccinations the puppy has had, whether she is being treated for parasites or worms, and her overall health. Reputable breeders go to great lengths to provide the ultimate care for their litters, as their reputation depends on healthy puppies.

Family Members' Health Issues

The health of the human family also should be considered, especially because some people have allergies to dogs. If a family member has an allergy, it can often be resolved by adopting a breed that is hypoallergenic. These breeds shed less and hence throw out less dander and other allergens. However, since all dogs carry small amounts of allergens and they also can pick up outside allergens in their fur, there's no guarantee that any specific dog will be hypoallergenic. Another thing to consider is that one hypoallergenic breed might not trigger an allergic reaction but another will. Experimentation is necessary by meeting the dog first before adopting.

You can also keep the allergy risk low by bathing and grooming your dog frequently. On the flip side, overbathing removes natural oils from the coat, which can cause the skin to flake and potentially lead to allergic reactions. If allergies among family members are a problem, one way to keep the allergens low is to have your dog wear a T-shirt in the house. A high-quality air purifier can also be helpful. In extreme situations, humans can get allergy shots, but it's always preferable to avoid the problem rather than having to treat the individual.

The following breeds are considered to be hypoallergenic:

Hypoallergenic Breeds
- Airdale Terrier
- American Hairless Terrier
- Basenji
- Bedlington Terrier
- Bichon Frisé
- Border Terrier
- Cairn Terrier
- Chinese Crested (hairless)
- Havanese
- Kerry Blue Terrier
- Maltese
- Miniature Schnauzer
- Portuguese Water Dog
- Puli
- Shih-Tzu
- Soft-Coated Wheaten Terrier
- Spanish Water Dog
- Standard Poodle
- Standard Schnauzer
- Tibetan Terrier
- Toy Poodle
- West Highland White Terrier
- Wirehaired Fox Terrier
- Yorkshire Terrier

A Puppy's Personality and Temperament

Ultimately, there are three major factors that influence personality and temperament:

1. The genetic components

2. The amount of socialization that the puppy has had in the first sixteen weeks of life through positive exposure to many different people, animals, and environments
3. The puppy's continuing training and life experiences to date

It bears repeating that every puppy has to be evaluated as an individual with his own personality and temperament, which includes energy level and degree of sociability. By sociability, we mean how much he seeks out human or canine companions and desires to interact with them in a friendly way. These factors are more important than breed-linked behaviors like retrieving, herding, digging, pulling, or chasing to most people. We want to emphasize the importance of adopting based on temperament first, and breed and beauty second.

People often assume that a particular breed will guarantee a particular degree of sociability. For example, Labrador and golden retrievers, generally speaking, have been bred to have a high threshold of tolerance for myriad sight, sound, and tactile stimuli. As a result, they tend to adapt to the changeable nature of life, are generally much easier to socialize, and are considered "friendly" or "highly sociable" dogs. But this is not true of all Labradors and goldens, as some are prone to aggressive behavior and require a lot of behavior modification. This is generally due to traits inherited within a single family line and/or a lack of early socialization.

Paul sees more aggression problems in retrievers than any other breed, but that's only because he is closely aligned with retriever rescue organizations and gets called in to help when aggression is a problem. Trainers aligned with boxer rescues would say the same thing about boxers . . . as would those who work closely with German shepherd, Newfoundland, and cocker spaniel rescues. These breeds are all considered "good with kids," nevertheless, there are some individuals within the breed who growl, bare their teeth, and/or bite people. Clients often express bewilderment when they see such behaviors appear in their "known-to-be-friendly breed" dog and seem to feel they have been cheated.

Conversely, other breeds are stuck with the perception that aggressive tendencies are a given. The belief that some breeds are automatically dangerous has made them the target of breed-specific legislation and bans by insurance agencies, cities and townships, and homeowners' associations. The bottom line is that every dog is an individual, no matter the breed or mixture of breeds. We recommend that you visit potential puppies, as several times the sociablility they exhibit may change—in either direction—depending on the circumstances surrounding your visit. (See the following section, "Evaluating a Puppy.")

So how do you determine a puppy's temperament? We place a high degree of trust in the opinions of the staff at shelters and rescue organizations and with breeders. Many of these professionals can evaluate personalities and temperaments pretty well, especially when it comes to aggression or fear. However, you can't always trust the information you receive. And, in many cases, a puppy's genetic background and early socialization, both of which influence behavior, are totally unknown. So let's look at how you might hedge your bets and, to the best of your ability, find a puppy who is a perfect fit.

Evaluating a Puppy

Many professionals in the dog world have developed "temperament tests," hoping to use a puppy's current behavior to predict the way he will behave as an adult. But do these methods really help? Unfortunately, the scientific evidence indicates that these "puppy tests" are not very reliable. The fact is that the many variables in any given situation make it virtually impossible to detect any significant behavior pattern from a single observation or even a handful. For example, a puppy's reaction to unexpected sounds or to being stroked and petted may vary from one visit to another.

So should we discard temperament tests altogether? Well, not so fast. There may be some value to these tests, particularly if a puppy exhibits extreme aggressive tendencies. Research by Margaret Young of the College of Veterinary Medicine at North Carolina State University found that puppies who growled or barked in an overtly aggressive way during temperament testing were likely to continue to display aggressive behaviors as adults. However, as Young followed these puppies, she also found that some who did not display aggressive behavior when they were puppies became aggressive later in life.

What does all this mean for you? Although these tests may not prove infallible, the use of a temperament evaluation may help you to hedge your bets, especially if a puppy displays extreme behavior. Here is a modified temperament test to help you evaluate any puppies you are considering.

Puppy Evaluation Guidelines
- Ask the breeder or shelter staff for their input.
- Don't wear heavy perfume or accessories such as dangling jewelry.
- Be cool, friendly, and calm.
- Be sure that all of the puppies you are considering are healthy.
- Visit the puppy three times if possible, at various times of the day, to see if he responds the same way, or close to it, each time.
- Ask the breeder or shelter if you can separate the puppy from the rest of the litter and then take him to a different area.
- Each time you visit the puppy, evaluate him in a different environment—outside, inside, with other people, alone, and so on.

Puppy Evaluation Procedure

Your goal is to determine how the puppy will interact with you, how shy or outgoing he will be, and how he'll respond to stimuli such as touch, sound, and motion. There are six evaluation procedures or "experiments" below. Your decision about the puppy's temperament should be based on the results of all of the experiments, not just the way he reacts or responds to one or two of them. If a puppy regularly responds with an extreme reaction to any of these experiments, he will probably require rehabilitation—and that requires additional time, energy, effort, and financial resources. Extreme reactions include biting, intensely aggressive behavior, ignoring you completely, cowering, or showing no interest in toys or food treats.

What Does the Puppy Do When You:

1. Enter the room.

When you enter the room, most puppies will run to greet you, possibly attack your shoelaces, and want to play. Some may pause before interacting with you as if they're making sure that you're a "safe" person. These puppies will soon warm up to you with a little encouragement. An extreme reaction would be cowering in the corner and refusing to interact no matter how encouraging you are or how quiet you remain.

2. Clap your hands.

Kneel down to the puppy's level and try to call her over to you using hand claps and "kissy" sounds. Don't make your hand clap too loud or too soft. Then gently hold out your flat palm to see if she will touch it. Most puppies will happily engage with you and actually climb all over you. Extreme reactions include cringing, running away, or urinating.

3. Offer treats.

Offer small treats to see if the puppy will take something from your hand. Most puppies will show an interest in the treat and lick or mouth your hand in an effort to get the treat. A puppy who attacks and repeatedly bites so hard that he draws blood illustrates a lack of bite inhibition. This is a concern, especially if you have young children. Depending on the severity of the puppy's aggressiveness, it may take some extra effort to teach him not to use his mouth on you. (See more on mouthing on page 272.)

4. Stroke gently.

Starting at the top of the puppy's head, stroke with your hand all the way to the tail. If a puppy bites you, cowers, or shivers and shakes whenever you gently stroke him, and continues that behavior for the length of all your visits, you may be facing fear and anxiety problems down the line.

5. Lift the puppy.

Gently lift any puppies who have shown enough confidence and interest to seek out your touch. If a puppy gives frenzied growls and tries to bite your hand when you lift him, he may tend to react aggressively to being handled and touched later on in life. If you get an aggressive reaction like this on your first attempt, make sure to repeat this step on a future occasion. It is a good sign if the puppy becomes more and more tolerant of handling on each new attempt. If, however, the reaction stays the same or worsens, the puppy may require special help (see Figure 2-1).

Figure 2-1

When holding a puppy, put one hand underneath the chest and the other hand around the body so the puppy feels secure.

6. Throw a toy or ball.

Throw a ball or a toy a short distance. Most puppies will chase it and play with it. Some may even bring it back to you. If the puppy shows absolutely no interest in the toy or in you, factor that independent behavior into your evaluation.

Breeds and Mixed Breeds

Should individual breed tendencies be considered in your decision about which puppy to adopt? Sure. Why not? Maybe you saw someone with a really obedient shepherd and that, in turn, evoked memories of favorite old movies in which the shepherd's awesome abilities were depicted. Or maybe your grandfather had a shepherd and therefore the breed is associated with the fond memories of that beloved relative. Sportsmen adopt and raise specific breeds for their purposes. And what would the world of dog shows be without aficionados of each specific breed? Similarly, the typical family often adopts a specific breed primarily because of some established emotional attachment. This is not a bad thing. That is, unless the person starts comparing his new beagle with a beagle he had when he was young. Or to Snoopy. It isn't fair or healthy to compare one dog with another—or one child with another, or one significant other with another.

"Breeds" are groups of dogs who look similar and, in certain ways, behave similarly to each other, due to being selectively bred for certain behavioral and physiological traits. The American Kennel Club (AKC) officially recognizes more than 150 such breeds, but in reality thousands of these distinct groupings have been purposely created all over the world. All dogs have more in common with each other as "dogs" than they have differences as "breeds." Different breeds are not different species. In other words, in the big picture, the Great Dane and the Chihuahua have more in common with each other than either one of them have in common with, say, a fox.

This is not to say, however, that there aren't demonstrable similarities in size, appearance, and behavioral patterns that are fairly predictable among dogs of the same breed. But a "breed description" or list of "breed traits" is not a guarantee of what your dog will look like and how she will behave. Yes, your puppy brings certain genetic material with her into the world that will affect her health, behavior, personality, and temperament. But your puppy's behavior will be significantly impacted by the environment in which you raise her, the training you provide, and, especially, her socialization experiences.

To use a computer analogy, you might think of a dog's genetic tendencies or hardwired reflexes as his "hard drive." As an example, let's look at the "chase" impulse. All normal dogs are born with a visual sensitivity to the appearance of small, quickly moving objects, which tend to trigger an impulse to chase. This is one of the reasons so many dogs enjoy chasing balls or toys. This sensitivity to motion is heightened, however, in some breeds. For example, the greyhound has been selectively bred to respond faster to quickly moving objects. Greyhounds sprint after the object sooner, with more intense focus, and at a greater speed than most other breeds. Again, most dogs have the tendency to chase, but compared with most other dogs, a greyhound's visual sensitivity and response time is more finely tuned. It is on what we might call a "hair trigger." However, even though dogs of the same breed share many characteristics, there is always a variability of behavior patterns within the breed. Not all greyhounds will respond to a particular stimulus with the same degree of quickness and intensity.

Another example is the Border collie, which is selectively bred for herding—a pattern of stalking and chasing animals such as sheep. In other words, they bunch them together and move them in the same direction. Again, dogs of all breeds have the genetic capability of at least some stalking and/or chasing behavior, no matter how unpronounced or undeveloped that disposition may be. But even among Border collies, there are individual differences, as some dogs will have a higher threshold for triggering their special pattern of stalking and chasing. That is, some Border collies won't be triggered by the sheep as quickly or intensely as the majority of Border collies. There may even be a small number of Border collies who show no interest in sheep at all. And then there will be Border collies who react more intensely to sheep than the majority of other Border collies—even to the point of trying to bite and kill the sheep. If all Border collies displayed exactly the same type of ideal herding behavior, there would be no need to select the best herders for breeding, which of course there is.

So what does all this mean for you in deciding which puppy to choose? Well, in addition to the basic size and appearance of the dog, the breed or mixture of breeds can give you some idea of tendencies to certain behavior patterns. This can be helpful particularly in understanding the likely activity levels of your puppy. If you have a Border collie, it's likely that you will be throwing a ball around a lot more than if you have a Shih Tzu. And you will probably need to schedule a lot more time for running if you have a Jack Russell terrier than if you have a Saint Bernard. Remember that these are only probabilities and tendencies, not guarantees.

Mixed Breeds

What about mixed breeds? We have spent years helping out in shelters and have seen up close the suffering that dogs who never find a home go through. There are millions of homeless dogs throughout the United States, so we strongly advocate adopting from shelters. Besides the enormous sense of gratification you'll get for saving a life, there are other advantages, such as the low cost of a shelter adoption and the fact that mixed-breed dogs are not as prone to many of the congenital diseases that are sometimes found in purebreds. These congenital diseases are primarily due to in-breeding or linebreeding, the practice of refining certain desired traits within the breed relating to size, coat color, physical features, and disposition. Reputable breeders do their best to avoid these congenital problems. That's why it's so critical to do your homework when selecting a breeder. (See "Adopting from Breeders" in Chapter 3.)

Size Considerations

Selecting the right size puppy is also important as it affects your finances (the big guys eat a lot), safety (the big guys knock stuff over pretty easily, and a swoop of the tail can easily send granddaughter Amy flying through the air), and space. Predicting a dog's future size when dealing with purebred dogs like Newfoundlands, mastiffs, Great Danes, Bernese mountain dogs, and Saint Bernards is easy. But remember that although these larger breed puppies start out cute and cuddly, they get big and take up a lot of space quickly. When adopting from a shelter, you are a little more challenged in trying to guesstimate how big the puppy will grow to be. However, seasoned shelter workers get pretty good at this and a veterinarian can usually give a pretty accurate evaluation.

Size of Dog Checklist

🦴 Do you live in a house or a small apartment? Consider how physically comfortable your fully grown dog will be in the amount of space you have to offer.

🦴 Do you have young children? A puppy of a large breed will quickly grow and if the puppy is overly energetic (what puppy isn't?) the children will often find themselves on their behinds. So, you might want to consider a smaller dog.

🦴 What size dog are you physically capable of handling? Size relates to strength. Any dog weighing more than forty pounds can really be a handful. The eighty-five-pound big guys can be unhandleable, and those who weigh more than 100 pounds have unbelievable strength. Grady, Paul's 110-pound golden retriever, once actually bent the plus-sized, reinforced clip attached to the end of his leash. The bottom line is: A friendly, lovable, big dog is no fun if she pulls you to the ground on walks or knocks you over in greeting when you come home or when she decides to chase a squirrel. Although these issues can be addressed with training and managed in the meantime with specialized collars and leashes, if you are petite, elderly, or physically challenged in any way, a small dog might be the better fit. On the other hand, the giant breeds like Great Danes tend to need less exercise. So, if you prefer fewer walks, you might want to consider a giant breed.

Climate Considerations

It's important that you consider seasonal temperatures—not just for your dog's comfort but also for his well-being. Some breeds are more comfortable in climates similar to the region of the world to which they are native. For example, short-haired dogs might have problems in extremely cold climates, while dogs with extremely thick coats may have difficulty adapting to a hot climate.

Exercise Needs and Activity Level

There's no exact recipe for the amount of exercise your dog will need when he reaches adulthood. If a dog doesn't get enough exercise, he'll have excess energy to burn, which may manifest in digging in the yard, barking, or tearing up your house. A good rule of thumb for any dog is to provide a bare minimum of twenty to thirty minutes of exercise twice a day. The exercise should include brisk walks or jogging, swimming, fetch, find it, and hide-and-seek.

However, exercise requirements aren't always related to the dog's size, as some small breeds such as terriers are extremely active and require a good deal of exercise, while giant breeds tend to need less exercise. If you are a runner or are physically active outdoors, you'll want to select a puppy who is built to keep up with you.

Grooming Needs

Do a little research. Some breeds require special care due to long hair or thick coats and some have undercoats that can easily become matted. For these dogs, grooming may be a daily requirement. Ask the breeder, shelter, or other professional about a specific puppy's grooming needs and consider the time and cost. There is an upside to daily grooming . . . if you learn to groom your puppy yourself you can use this time to bond with him, and grooming is also a part of socialization.

Other Dogs in the House

If you already have one or more dogs living in your household, they will all be making adjustments when the new guy arrives. If possible, take your dog(s) to meet the puppy that you are considering before you make your final decision. This step is particularly helpful if the puppy is more than five months old. Does your dog tolerate the puppy's play and his jumping, mouthing, and chasing? The best response is that they start to play with each other. But you might hear some low-intensity growling as your dog tells the puppy to go away. The two will probably sort out their differences and soon start playing. If they don't, and your dog gets really grouchy, the chemistry between them may be off and a different puppy would be a better choice. A shelter worker can help read the language—or you might take a professional trainer along to translate. If your dog is really aggressive toward a puppy, separate them immediately. If the problem is with your dog, call a professional trainer who can evaluate him, identify the causes of the aggression, and set up a behavior modification program to resolve the aggression problem before you adopt.

Your evaluation isn't just focused on whether or not the puppy will be safe. You also have to consider your dog. A puppy who hasn't learned to socialize with other dogs is very difficult for other dogs to deal with.

In Chapter 5, "Bringing Your Puppy Home," we offer some tips for introducing a new puppy to your dog (or dogs) when you bring him home.

Adopting Two Puppies

Of course, you might not have a dog already, but decide to adopt two puppies. Raising two puppies at the same time provides an excellent opportunity to teach them how to share affection, attention, play, and food with another dog. But don't be fooled into thinking that they will "take care of each other." Two puppies mean twice as much work. There will be twice as many potty accidents, twice as much training time, twice as many walks (or twice as much pull if walked together), twice as much food to buy, and twice as many headaches. However, for those who enjoy a multi-dog household, there are at least twice as many benefits.

Note: There is some evidence that aggression occurs more often between two female siblings than other pairings, such as a brother or sister or two brothers. In our experience, this seems more prevalent with siblings that come from rescue organizations rather than reputable breeders and would seem, therefore, to be related to early socialization or a lack thereof. If you are considering adopting two female siblings, please be aware of the extra effort you may have to use and call a professional dog trainer if the puppies exhibit behaviors that go beyond play aggression. (See "Play Aggression" in Chapter 6.)

Children in the Family

If you have children under the age of twelve, think small. Your puppy will grow more quickly than your child—within a year of puppyhood, your large breed or mix of breeds will be practically full grown, while your child will still be a child. Imagine a six-month-old, sixty-pound Saint Bernard playfully charging and knocking over your sixty-pound eight-year-old. You can and should, of course, teach any puppy good manners, including respecting play boundaries. Obviously, a Great Dane poses more of a knockdown risk than a Cairn terrier.

Another consideration is that children are extremely active and loud. A puppy who seems hypersensitive to sound and motion is a bad candidate for a household in which children and their friends will be running in and out, screaming and yelling. (Review "A Puppy's Personality and Temperament" earlier in this chapter.) Children, particularly one- to five-year-olds, are prone to rough handling of dogs and puppies. Teaching children to handle a puppy gently is a priority. This means no pulling of ears, tugging of tails, or riding like a horsey. All puppies will nip and mouth to a certain extent, but be wary of a puppy who repeatedly bites, especially if he draws blood. This puppy will need concerted bite inhibition training.

First, evaluate puppies without your child present. Then, when you have identified a candidate for adoption, if possible, take your child with you to see the puppy. Some shelters require that you bring your children to meet the puppy before sending him home with you, while other shelters prohibit children from their premises. All interactions between children and puppies should be closely supervised in an environment managed for safety to make sure neither the child nor the puppy gets rough. Never leave a child of any age and a puppy together unsupervised.

Regardless of how friendly a puppy might behave toward your child, if your child is afraid or resentful of a particular puppy, or puppies in general, you will probably face problems in your family dynamic somewhere down the line. The bonding process between the child and the puppy is your responsibility and entails teaching compassionate and positive give and take.

The bottom line is this: If your child has an abiding and generalized fear or dislike of all dogs, you'll need to resolve those issues before bringing a puppy into your home. Plopping a new puppy into your family won't suddenly "cure" a child's fear of dogs. Bringing children and dogs together is a lot of fun when done properly. In Chapter 5 we will explain how to introduce your new puppy to your child when you take the puppy home.

Some Thoughts About Breed-Specific Legislation

Some dogs, such as American pit bull terriers, or "pit bulls," have gained a reputation for being "vicious" or "dangerous" simply by virtue of their breed. The American Society for the Prevention of Cruelty to Animals (ASPCA), which offers pit bulls for adoption at its shelters, reminds us on their Web site, *www.aspca .org,* that "a well-bred, well-socialized, and well-trained pit bull is one of the most delightful, intelligent, and gentle dogs imaginable." They point out that, historically, dogs of this breed were nicknamed the "nursemaid's dog" because they were so reliable with young children. Unfortunately, over time, pit bulls became known as dangerous dogs because they were commonly used in the "sport" of dog fighting. This reputation lingers among those who consider the pit bull to be macho. The fact is that while a dog's breed contributes to his temperament, breed alone cannot be used to predict whether a puppy will grow up to be a danger to his community. We have trained many pit bulls and feel these are some of the greatest examples of the ultimate human–dog friendship. Along with the ASPCA, we agree that the pit bull can make a wonderful family dog. It's never the breed of dog that causes problems; it is the individual dog and, often, the line to which that dog belongs. By "line," we mean the parents and grandparents who also had these tendencies and passed them along.

The fact is that dogs of any breed can be selectively bred for aggressive tendencies. A ban on pit bulls or rottweilers or any other breed would not stop the problems of aggression and dog bites. In other words, if a backyard breeder wants a "fighting dog" he can find plenty of individual dogs who like to fight from breeds other than pit bulls, and breed them. If he continues to select the most aggressive offspring for breeding, he will most likely have created a new "aggressive breed" in a few generations.

The Humane Society of the United States (HSUS) suggests that a better strategy for reducing dog attacks and bites would be to pass legislation that punishes the owner of a dangerous dog rather than punishing all dogs of a certain breed. In fact, HSUS points out that two decades ago the Doberman pinscher was being vilified while pit bulls and rottweilers, the breeds most often targeted today, attracted little to no public concern. They also point out the case of a San Francisco woman who died as the result of an attack by a little-known breed, the Perro de Presa Canario. According to HSUS as reported on About.com: "Now that breed [the Presa Canario] is being sought by individuals who desire the new 'killer dog.' Unfortunately, the 'problem dog' at any given time is often the most popular breed among individuals who tend to be irresponsible, if not abusive, in the control and keeping of their pets. Simply put, if you ban one breed, individuals will just move on to another one. Banning a breed only speeds up the timetable."

The attitude that all dogs within some breeds are aggressive by nature betrays a lack of understanding of the relationship between genetics, breed, environment, and upbringing. The truth of the matter is that all dogs have the genetic capability for friendly, fearful, or aggressive behavior. Such adaptability of behavior is essential for survival. And while different dogs have different thresholds of tolerance for different stimuli in their environment, much of that tolerance level is a result of upbringing and experience. In addition, while patterns of sociable, fearful, or aggressive behavior are certainly influenced by genetic factors, breed is not necessarily a good indicator of those factors. Size, appearance, and activity levels tend to be more consistent adoption guidelines than general breed temperament.

Chapter 3

The Stuff You'll Need

Be prepared. Before you take your puppy home, have everything ready. You'll need to puppyproof your home and purchase equipment, toys, food, and a collar and leash. You'll also need to line up professionals, including a veterinarian, groomer, and trainer, and make arrangements for puppy care when you're not home. Also, post the number of the emergency veterinarian on your refrigerator. Finally, be sure to have your best friend's number on speed dial so she can comfort you as you sob, "What have I gotten myself into?!"

If you haven't done the prep work outlined in this chapter, wait until you have before introducing puppy to the new digs.

Safety Issues

"She's just a 'Devil Dog!'" the obviously distraught woman told Terry over the phone. It seems her new puppy, Munchkin, was out of control. "She chews everything. I just came home and the sofa is ripped, the kitchen table is chewed, and my brand new Pradas are torn to shreds." The woman started to cry and said, "I really love her but I think I have to give her up. She even sneaks away and chews things when I'm home." Terry consoled the woman and asked how old the puppy was. "Four months," she replied. "And where do you keep her while you're away?" Terry queried. "Oh, she has free run of the house. I think it's cruel to keep a dog locked up."

This is an all-too-common scenario. It dramatically illustrates the need for puppy supervision, prevention, and management, particularly the importance of puppyproofing the home. Puppies chew. Puppies are curious and explore with their mouths. Just as you would lock cabinets and keep forbidden or harmful objects out of a child's reach, you must keep all but appropriate toys out of your puppy's reach.

Minimize the potential for accidents by removing or locking up chewable and toxic objects; practice good management by putting your puppy in a kennel, behind baby gates, or in an exercise pen so he can't get to "illegal" objects; and, finally, practice prevention by putting off-limits objects like the kitchen wastebasket in a safe place where he can't get to them.

Here's a list of some of the more common dangers to your puppy's safety. You can also consult your veterinarian or the Animal Poison Control Center on the Web at *www.aspca.org/apcc* or call their hotline at 888-426-4435 for more specific information.

Chemically treated lawns: Anything that your puppy's paws come in contact with can be absorbed through the skin or ingested when the paws are licked.

Hazards during walks: Watch for broken glass and other hazards. In the winter, if salt has been used to melt snow and ice, be sure to wipe your puppy's paws when you take her inside. Otherwise, she may ingest too much sodium from the salt.

Dangers when traveling in a car, van, or truck: Don't allow your puppy to hang his head out the window. This can be dangerous for a couple of reasons—stones can be thrown from the pavement by passing cars and cut your puppy's head or eyes, or insects can get in the eyes. Don't allow your puppy to ride loose in the back of a pick-up truck. This seems like a commonsense notion, but Paul has actually witnessed a dog being flipped out of a truck and has seen others trying to keep their balance as if they are holding on for dear life. (See the following section, "Kennel or Carrier.") Purchase a doggy seat belt to secure your puppy in a vehicle.

Foods—chocolate, grapes, raisins, onions, greasy foods, and cooked bones: Chocolate, grapes, raisins, and onions can be harmful or even fatal to some (though not all) dogs. Too many greasy foods can cause pancreatitis. Cooked chicken and turkey bones can cause choking. Make sure your puppy can't get into the trash bin to retrieve any forbidden foods or bones. (**Note:** Uncooked poultry bones do not splinter like cooked ones and are therefore not as dangerous.)

Plants, plant bulbs, and plant water (including Christmas tree water): There's a long list of plants that are toxic and/or can cause gastrointestinal upsets. Refer to the ASPCA Web site.

Medicines and household cleaners: Keep your cabinets locked. A small prescription bottle could seem like a fun toy that rattles but if your puppy cracks it open, the medication inside could be extremely harmful.

Household and office items: Plastic bags, plastic ties, balloons, rubber bands, electrical cords, tinsel, string, paper clips, needles, pens, pencils, and any sharp object could be dangerous if your puppy bites it or ingests it.

Children's and puppy's toys: Some toys can be dangerous, particularly if a puppy could tear or chew off a part and choke on it. Keep squeaky toys out of reach unless supervised, as puppies can chew the toy and choke on the squeaker. Avoid rawhides, pig's ears, and hooves, which are also choking hazards if a piece breaks off.

Electric wires and cords: A puppy could be injured if he chews on a wire or cord.

Tablecloths: A puppy could pull on an overhanging table-cloth and be injured by a falling object.

Antifreeze: Dogs find the taste of antifreeze appealing but it can be deadly. If your puppy ingests even a small amount of antifreeze, call your veterinarian immediately. A safer type of antifreeze is available; ask your veterinarian about this.

Rat poison: Rat poison is a toxic and deadly substance that dogs have been known to ingest. If you suspect your puppy has ingested rat poison, call your veterinarian immediately.

Toilet bowl cleaners: Don't use a toilet bowl cleaner that is placed in the tank. The toxic chemicals can cause illness if your dog should happen to drink from the toilet.

Disposable diapers: Dogs sometimes like to eat soiled diapers, but the chemicals in the absorbent material can be harmful. Make sure to put diaper baskets and garbage cans where your puppy can't get them.

Keeping Your Puppy Safe

- Keep your puppy in a kennel or exercise pen or behind a baby gate while you're away.
- Keep your puppy tethered to you or the furniture while you're home until she is reliably trained and you trust her to roam through the house without supervision.
- When a puppy is given free time to explore throughout the house, let her drag a leash around with her in case you need to retrieve her quickly to keep her out of trouble. Always keep her in sight.
- Lock all cabinets and closets, especially those with cleaning supplies.
- Pick up all shoes, children's toys, pens, pencils, plants, and any small objects that your puppy could chew or swallow.

🦴 Remove tablecloths or keep them from overhanging the table.

🦴 Leave appropriate puppy stuff for your puppy to chew on, including Kongs, Nylabones, chicken strips, bully sticks, balls, and so on.

🦴 Provide plenty of exercise so your puppy has less energy and less motivation to want to chew.

🦴 Teach the "leave it" behavior (see page 247).

Puppy Equipment

Let's look at the individual pieces of equipment that you will need and how to choose the right equipment for your puppy's size and behavioral requirements.

🦴 Kennel or carrier

🦴 Baby gates

🦴 Exercise pen for indoors

🦴 Dog run or fence for your yard (if applicable)

🦴 Bed

🦴 Toys

🦴 Food and dishes

🦴 Collars, halters, and harnesses

🦴 Tethers and leashes

🦴 Identification tags and microchip IDs

🦴 Grooming aids

Kennel or Carrier

Kennels and carriers, also called cages and crates, come in sizes to fit breeds from the smallest to the largest. There are two basic types. Some are open, like the wire cage kennels, and others are closed, with either soft sides or solid plastic walls.

A high-quality wire cage kennel, made with zinc bars, has the advantage of being sturdy and durable and may very well last for your dog's lifetime. The open sight lines of a wire cage also allow your puppy a 360-degree view of her surroundings, which helps her remain a part of the social activity in the household.

This element can be particularly helpful when kenneling your puppy at night, since she can see, hear, and smell stimuli outside of the kennel, which helps to keep her from getting bored or feeling entirely isolated. Even though she is not curled up to her mother and siblings, your nearby presence will be reassuring to her. If she is sensitive and the environment is over-stimulating, you can place a cover over the kennel, especially during naptime and at night. If you will be moving the kennel around the house frequently, you might want to purchase a folding cage. These cages fold down flat for easy transport without any disassembling and are easy to set up. A closed kennel or carrier may be a better choice if your puppy tends to get overly excited or aroused by outside sights and noises. You might want to buy both types of kennels. The wire cage can be used at home, while the soft-sided or plastic one can be used for safe car travel.

Figure 3-1

Closed crate and wire kennel.

Whichever type of kennel you choose, pick one that will allow your puppy, when full grown, to stand without stooping and lie down without curling her body. If your dog is a mixed breed, ask your veterinarian approximately how large your puppy will be as an adult before picking a kennel. While she's still small, block off part of the interior of a larger-sized kennel so she doesn't have room to eliminate in it. Do this by putting a cardboard box in the back of the kennel, or buy a special divider designed to adjust the interior size of the kennel. Then, as your puppy gets bigger, simply remove the barrier.

The kennel is an item you will be keeping for years and years. It will become your dog's "safe spot." So it's worth it to buy a quality kennel that will last. Cheaply made kennels can cause injuries if a nail is caught on the wire or a paw is cut—or if a head gets stuck.

When your puppy is riding in the car with you, safety is the number one issue. Loose dogs can injure themselves and you. There are several options to safely transport your puppy:

Doggy seat belts: Specially designed seat belts will protect your puppy from injury in case of accident or sudden braking.

Figure 3-2

Doggy seat belts will help protect your puppy from injury.

Vehicle barriers: Pet stores sell special barriers that can be installed in the back of the vehicle to create a separate space for dogs. However, if you use a barrier, we recommend that you use it along with a doggy seat belt.

Kennel or carrier: Unless your dog is one of the larger breeds, his kennel will probably fit in your vehicle. This is a safe way to transport him.

Baby Gates

Until your puppy is acclimated to his kennel, keep him behind baby gates in the kitchen or laundry room to keep him safe and out of trouble. Baby gates come in three-, four-, and five-foot heights, with prices ranging from $30 for the inexpensive wooden ones to custom-made models that cost $300 to $400. If you have a puppy who can leap tall buildings with a single bound, get a tall one.

There are two basic styles of baby gates: compression and fixed. Compression gates are installed by adjusting the guides at the top and bottom of the gate to extend their length so that they fit snugly between the doorjambs. Higher-quality compression gates are really sturdy and have doors within them that can be easily opened to walk through. Fixed gates must be attached to the doorjambs with brackets and screws. They are impossible to knock down and are recommended if your puppy happens to be a Bernese mountain dog or other strong breed.

Note: Be sure to puppyproof any room your puppy is in. Lock cabinet doors. Pick up cleaning supplies or any "chewable" items and put them out of reach.

Exercise Pen for Indoors

Exercise pens are hinged panels made of steel. They usually come in sixteen-foot lengths with panels that are two feet wide and are available in heights of two, three, and four feet. The cost of these pens runs from $100 to $150. An exercise pen works on the same principle as baby playpen, so you can set it up in your living room or other social area and let the puppy chill with you and the family. It's also a good idea to set one up as a barrier outside the door of your house as an added protection for escape artists. Then, if you forget to check where your puppy is before answering the door, the exercise pen will be there to keep your puppy from darting into the street.

Figure 3-3

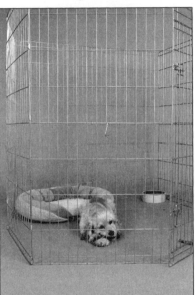

Exercise pens keep your puppy safe.

Dog Run or Fence for Outdoors

Dog runs are sold in modular units made of chain-link fencing. Each section is four feet wide and they are available in heights of four, five, or six feet. You can build a run as big as you want simply by adding more sections. A dog run is great for those times when you want to do some gardening or entertaining and have your puppy outside with you. Of course you can also tether your dog, but dog runs, if used correctly, help your puppy acclimate to being confined. Give your puppy great treats while she is in the run and, throughout the week, play with her and train her inside the run so she looks at it as a great place to be.

Fences give you a terrific opportunity to let your puppy off leash for play and exercise outdoors. A fence is an actual physical barrier like a chain-link or wooden privacy fence.

Note: Many dogs learn to open a fence gate by flipping the latch. For safety, we recommend having two latches on the gate or remembering to lock the gate each time you pass through it.

Electronic fences have two components: a collar receiver and a transmitter. They are designed to keep dogs from leaving the yard by shocking them if they approach the boundary. In positive training, we do not advocate the use of electronic fences for four reasons:

1. They shock the dog to keep him in the yard.
2. They are not 100 percent reliable.
3. If the dog does get out, he can't get back in without once again getting shocked.
4. They do not keep your puppy safe from other animals who are able to enter your yard, since only animals wearing the collar receiver receive the shock.

Many people purchase electronic fences because they want the freedom to play with their puppies safely outside. Some can't afford to install a chain-link or privacy fence, and others live in communities that forbid the building of fences for "aesthetic" reasons. If you find yourself in such a situation, we recommend an aerial dog run. This is a device that consists of two sturdy wire cables: One cable is stretched between two posts, two trees, or the side of the house and a post or tree, just like an outdoor clothesline; the other cable attaches to a pulley on the aerial cable and to your puppy's collar. The result is that your puppy can move back and forth the entire length of the cable without choking or jerking himself. The aerial cable should be at least eight feet off the ground and can be as long as 100 feet. An aerial dog run is inexpensive and allows your puppy to run and catch Frisbees and balls safely without any shock or pain.

Your puppy should always be supervised when tethered to anything, including an aerial dog run. Don't leave her alone!

Bed

Your puppy's bed can range from a simple mat to a plush, cushiony throne with his name embroidered in gold. We recommend beds with a slipcover that can be easily washed. Use mild soap as harsh detergents can cause skin reactions in some dogs. For those puppies who are prone to chewing, you can purchase bed covers that are more durable and able to withstand the onslaught of little puppy teeth. Depending on the size of the kennel, you may want a second bed or cushion that fits inside to make it comfortable.

Figure 3-4

Dog beds come in all shapes, sizes, and prices.

Once you teach your puppy the behavior "go to your spot" (see Chapter 18) the bed can serve double duty as a "safe spot" representing security and comfort anywhere around the house or anyplace you go with your puppy.

Toys

There are several types of toys that you will want to provide to your puppy to keep him occupied and mentally stimulated.

"Smart" Toys

"Smart" toys like the Kong are hollow toys made of durable rubber or plastic and are filled with food treats. Unlike Nylabones and other similar types of chewies, smart toys are mentally stimulating, highly motivating, and challenging because your puppy must figure out how to manipulate the toy in order to dislodge the food treats inside. This motivates your puppy so he will spend time solving the problem presented to him. Kongs come in two types—durable (the red ones) and super durable (the black ones)—and various sizes.

We suggest filling the Kong with a cornucopia of goodies such as peanut butter, cheese cubes, dry kibble, small pieces of chicken or turkey or pieces of a cooked hamburger, and good quality freeze-dried treats. Instead of putting just one type of treat into the smart toy, you can use several treats from this list, making the adventure of chewing on it, bouncing it, and digging into it with his tongue even more exciting. A well-stuffed smart toy can keep a puppy occupied for up to an hour. In addition, you can freeze the toy after stuffing it, making it even more time consuming to finish.

A simpler version of a smart toy is a hard, baked beef bone that you can buy at pet stores, specially prepared so that it does not chip or break. These bones can be stuffed in the center with peanut butter and other goodies in much the same way as a Kong. Other types of smart toys are large plastic cubes or balls, such as the Buster Cube, and are designed to be filled with dry kibble rather than soft foods. With these toys, your puppy learns to push the ball or cube around with his nose as the kibble comes out intermittently, a piece at a time.

The Kong company also makes a machine that dispenses up to four toys at timed intervals throughout the day. The company refers to this dispenser as "doggie daycare in a box." Treat-filled Kongs that intermittently appear during the day give your puppy even more to look forward to when you're away—and that's a good thing.

The key to making smart toys work is the balance between the degree of difficulty the puppy has in obtaining the food that's stuffed within the toy and the puppy's desire to overcome the difficulty. Make it too difficult and your puppy will give up on the toy quickly. On the other hand, if it's too easy, your goal of keeping your puppy occupied for a period of time will be thwarted.

Chew Toys

In addition to smart toys, there are other chewies that you will probably find useful, such as Nylabones, chicken strips, and bully sticks. They do not present as much variation as smart toys, but they are still good outlets for puppy chewing.

Interactive Toys—Tennis Balls, Frisbees, and Rope Tug Toys

Interactive toys like tennis balls, soft Frisbees, and rope tug toys are excellent for teaching your dog how to give and take cooperatively in play. Tennis balls and soft Frisbees are great for running, catching, and fetching. Rope tug toys are also great for this purpose; however, there are some rules for their safe use, which are covered in the "take it" and "drop it" behaviors in Chapter 18. Terry particularly likes the kind of cloth Frisbee that can be folded and stuck in a pocket. Squeaky toys are also fun, but be sure that you supervise your puppy while she plays with them, since many dogs love to tear out the squeaky, which is a choking hazard.

Food and Dishes

It is important to carefully consider what you will be feeding your puppy before you take her home and have an ample supply of food on hand. (See Chapter 8, "A High-Quality Diet.") You'll also want to have your doggy dishes ready for serving it up. Puppies chew everything and plastic food and water dishes are especially susceptible. Ceramic food and water bowls are durable and do not easily slide around the floor while your puppy is eating. They are available in many different colors and designs. Other options are heavy-duty glass bowls or stainless steel bowls with rubber rings at the base to prevent sliding.

Collars, Halters, and Harnesses

There are several different types of collars, halters, and harnesses that are acceptable for nonviolent puppy management and training. These are divided into everyday use collars and anti-pulling collars or harnesses.

Everyday Use Collars

The basic type of acceptable collar is the flat buckle collar, with either a metal or plastic snap buckle. The collar should be adjusted so it is snug but not tight and fitted so it won't slip off. These collars are usually designed with a "D" ring that provides a convenient place to attach identification tags. We prefer buckle collars made from nylon, which are durable, light, and nontoxic. Martingale-style collars are also acceptable. They are flat and made from nylon but, instead of having a buckle, they are designed to slip over your puppy's head. When attached to the leash and properly adjusted, this collar will close so that your puppy cannot slip out of it. It will not, however, tighten so much that it will choke your puppy.

For walking your puppy, we're big fans of body harnesses as they take pressure off the dog's neck and throat. A regular body harness is pretty easy to slip on your puppy and can be used in addition to your puppy's everyday collar.

Note: Traditional collars like buckle or martingale collars are not designed to discourage your dog from pulling. For that, you'll need an anti-pulling collar.

Anti-Pulling Collars

Anti-pulling collars are particularly recommended for puppies who fall into one of the following four categories:

1. Heavy pullers;
2. Puppies who chase bicycles, motorcycles, cars, joggers, rollerbladers, or skateboarders;
3. Puppies with aggressive behaviors toward other dogs or people; or,
4. Puppies who are so active and rambunctious that it is difficult to control them when on leash.

For larger, stronger puppies, we highly recommend an anti-pulling harness called the Easy Walk Harness by Premier (see Figure 3-5) It is easy to put on and ingenious in its design as the leash attaches to a ring on the dog's chest. When the dog pulls, he is easily guided to the side, re-directing his forward motion.

Figure 3-5

The Easy Walk anti-pulling harness attached to a bungee leash.

Another style of anti-pulling collar is the head halter. There are several different brands, including the Halti style and the Gentle Leader, that all operate on the same basic principle— leading your dog by the head rather than the neck. They have a nose strap across the top of the puppy's snout and another strap that goes high up around the back of his head, just behind the ears. The leash then attaches to the halter below the chin. This principle is similar to that used in guiding a horse—where the head goes, the body follows.

Note: Take a few days to acclimate your puppy to a head halter. Many puppies dislike the feeling of a strap around the nose and may try to fight the head halter by pawing it off the nose. If your puppy reacts this way, simply hold the halter in one hand and a treat in the other hand. Then have your puppy reach her nose through the strap to eat the treat. After several sessions, your puppy will associate the strap with something positive (the food treat). Then you can take her for a walk with the head halter on. No one collar or harness works for every dog, so choose the one that works best for you. If you don't notice any lessening of pulling with one collar, try another type.

Figure 3-6

Get your puppy used to a head halter by having her reach her nose through the strap to eat a treat.

As important as a collar is, if there's another dog in the household the collar can present a danger when the two play together. We've seen unfortunate tragedies that resulted when one dog's jaw was caught in another's collar. If you have more than one dog or puppy and they like to grab each other when they play, as many do, take off their collars whenever you leave them alone. This creates a "Catch-22" because the ID tag on the collar is important in case your puppy gets lost. So the best solution is to keep collars on your dogs and supervise all play between them. Set up your environment with the same degree of supervision you would use with a child. We also recommend "breakaway" collars that release when twisted as they lessen the possibility of injury to puppies who like to continuously grab another dog's throat when playing.

Choke collars, also known as choke chains, slip collars, or training collars, are intended for use in training methods that use physical punishment and are not acceptable in positive, nonviolent training. These collars, made of chain or nylon, are designed to slip over your puppy's head like a noose and used to discourage or suppress behavior as the handler jerks or yanks the leash attached to the collar around the dog's neck. Prong collars, also known as pinch collars, are also unacceptable. These collars are made of metal, with removable links, and have sharp prongs on the inside that "pinch" the dog's neck when he pulls on the leash. Although, in practice, prong collars tend to do less physical damage than choke collars, they are still based on the infliction of pain to stop unwanted behaviors.

Finally, shock collars, also known as electronic collars, are unacceptable for positive training. Some trainers recommend them, contending that they are sophisticated training tools that can be regulated to inflict only minor shocks as "corrections." However any electrical shock, when used as a correction, is effective only due to the infliction of physical punishment, pain, and the resulting fear. Therefore, it is antithetical to the principles of nonviolent training.

The fact is that any piece of equipment can be used violently and, conversely, many pieces of equipment designed to be used violently can be used nonviolently. But doing this requires perfect timing, perfect intensity, perfect consistency, and constant monitoring of the dog's reactions. These qualities take years to develop even for a professional trainer. Our position is that collars should be used only for identification and as a management tool, not as a training tool.

We recommend that you use equipment designed to minimize physical stress and discomfort for your puppy. You have the responsibility to gauge how your puppy is reacting to any piece of equipment and to make sure that you are not causing her any pain or emotional distress.

Leashes and Tethers

We recommend "bungee" leashes for everyday walks. These leashes are elastic and don't hang as low to the ground as regular leashes, reducing the likelihood of the puppy getting tangled. Regular six-foot, nylon leashes are also good choices.

The term *tether* is used for a leash or cable that holds a dog in place. If you hook one end of a leash to your belt or a piece of furniture and the other end of the leash to the puppy, your puppy is tethered. Since most puppies chew a lot, a wire chew-proof cable is recommended as a tether. Indoor tethers are generally four to six feet in length. These lengths are difficult to find in pet stores but can be purchased via the Internet at *www.dogwhisperer dvd.com*.

We don't recommend retractable "extension leashes"—the type with a cord that pulls out of a little plastic box as the dog moves forward. It is more difficult to control your puppy with an extension leash, especially if the puppy tries to give chase. Extension leashes should definitely not be used:

1. If you live in an area where there are loose dogs or coyotes roaming around;

2. If there is any possibility that a squirrel or cat might run by; or,

3. If your dog weighs twenty pounds or more.

Identification Tags and Microchip IDs

Even with the most careful attempts at supervising and managing your new puppy, it is possible that he will get away from you and not find his way home. The simplest and least expensive identification method is a tag that attaches to your puppy's collar. Identification tags give your phone number and might also include your puppy's name, your name, and your street address. Custom-made tags can usually be ordered or made at a pet store while you wait or your veterinarian's office.

Another identification method is the microchip ID. These IDs are grain-sized chips injected under a puppy's skin that contain all of your dog's pertinent information. If your dog is lost, a shelter or veterinarian can read the chip with a scanner and contact you. Many shelter dogs are automatically microchipped as a part of the adoption process. That being said, there is controversy about the possibility of health problems if the chip migrates through the body. While the evidence is not conclusive, some veterinarians report that when chips were removed, a health problem disappeared. However, others point out that thousands of dogs are reunited with their owners because of the microchip, especially during natural disasters such as earthquakes and hurricanes. So, consider your options.

Note: If you also have cats, some veterinarians warn that a cat's body can react to the microchip as a "foreign body," resulting in chronic inflammation and even, on occasion, cancer.

Grooming Aids

Grooming will be an integral part of your puppy's health care, and getting her used to grooming equipment is best done as early as possible (see Chapter 10 on socialization).

Brushes

If your puppy has a long-haired coat, or will have one as an adult, your best choice is a wire "slicker" brush or a wire "pin" brush with a curved head. A slicker brush has very fine, pointy wire bristles, usually arranged in a rectangular shape. A pin brush uses wire bristles that are a little thicker and that are topped with a little round head, like a sewing pin. These pin bristles are usually arranged in an oval shape.

If your puppy has a medium-length coat, like a German shepherd or a Siberian husky, a wire slicker brush with a flat head is the best choice. For short coats use a rubber-bristled curry that you hold in your palm or a grooming mitt that actually slips over your hand like a glove.

Since wire bristles may feel painful to a young puppy's sensitive skin, especially under the age of twelve weeks, you may want to get her used to the feel of a brush by using a soft, nylon-bristled brush, similar to the ones we humans use ourselves. So, for all coat types, you can start using a soft-bristled brush in the early weeks and then shift over to one of the other brushes when your puppy is more used to the grooming routine.

Shampoos

You will have a stunning array of choices when it comes to puppy shampoos. We recommend choosing one that doesn't contain harsh detergents, medications, or insecticides. Avoid "flea" shampoos that use anything other than herbal ingredients or extracts such as d-limonene, pennyroyal oil, or eucalyptus. Also avoid sulfur tar shampoos, dandruff suppressors, or any other synthetic chemicals. We especially advise you to find a mild "no tears" shampoo, so that any accidental dripping of shampoo into your puppy's eyes will not cause any pain or physical damage. Human shampoos should not be used on puppies.

Nail Clippers

There are two types of doggy nail clippers: the "guillotine" type and the "wire cutter" type. The guillotine type has a little hole through which you place your puppy's toenail. When you squeeze the clipper handles, what looks like a small guillotine comes down through the hole and cuts off the point of the nail. The wire cutter type looks just like a wire cutter, and cuts your puppy's nail in a scissoring motion. Either type of clipper is fine—it depends most on what makes you feel comfortable when you clip. Depending on your puppy's size, however, you may want to start out with a plain old human nail clipper, particularly for a puppy under the age of twelve weeks. Young puppy nails tend to be soft and don't need the force of adult-style clippers. Once your puppy is acclimated to nail clipping (see Chapter 10 on socialization) you can switch over to one of the clippers designed specifically for dogs.

You may also want to use a file or emery board to file down roughly cut nails. Or you can use an electric rotary file, such as one made by Dremel, in place of clippers altogether. The electric file is more time consuming, but it frequently eases anxiety about clipping a puppy's nails, since you are filing down rather than cutting. Note, however, that you will still need to go through the process of getting your puppy used to the sound and feel of the electric file, just as you would get her used to the regular clippers (again, see Chapter 10).

Chapter 4

The People and Services You'll Need

In addition to procuring the right equipment before your puppy comes home, you will want to investigate caregivers, facilities, and services. If you have other animals at home, it's vital that you have the new puppy examined by a veterinarian before taking him home to get a clean bill of health and be assured of the absence of fleas, ticks, or disease. If a problem does exist, treatment can begin right away and your veterinarian can tell you if your other animals are at risk and how to handle it.

Choosing a Vet

We suggest finding a vet who practices both standard Western veterinary medicine and alternative or "holistic" medicine. Alternative veterinary medicine includes such modalities as chiropractic, acupuncture, homeopathy, herbal remedies, and nutritional supplements, which are often very effective and are less invasive than Western medical treatment. Holistic veterinarians also tend to be more focused on a high-quality diet and promote foods that contain only human-grade ingredients.

If possible, get referrals and visit several vets before making your final choice. You can also find a holistic vet through one of the following professional organizations: the American Holistic Veterinary Medical Association (*www.ahvma.org*), the International Veterinary Acupuncture Society (*www.ivas.org*), and the American Veterinary Chiropractic Association (*www.animal chiropractic.org*). Your puppy's veterinarian will play an important role in his life. It is imperative that you feel comfortable with your choice.

Your regular veterinarian will deal with common health issues such as skin problems, digestive system problems, or urinary tract concerns. Most veterinary clinics are not open on nights and/or weekends, so you'll also need to have your vet's recommendation of an emergency care clinic in the event of an accident or sudden illness.

Veterinarian Checklist

- Ask for a tour of the facility and discuss the types of problems the clinic is able to handle.
- Is the clinic available for night or weekend emergencies?
- Does the vet practice or advocate holistic methods of treatment?
- Does the facility make you feel safe and comfortable?
- Do the doctors and staff seem helpful, patient, and ready to answer your questions?

Pet Emergency Numbers

Make a list of the following numbers and put it on your refrigerator or in another easily accessed place:

- Veterinarian
- Emergency animal clinic
- Poison control center

Grooming

Grooming entails a lot of handling and helps prepare your puppy for handling by the vet and for being touched by children and strangers. Grooming also helps prevent diseases from parasites, skin problems, infections, gum disease, and so on.

You'll need to decide if you are a "do-it-yourself" groomer or want to rely on a professional. This may depend how complex your puppy's grooming needs are. A breed-specific book or Web site may help you decide. If you need a professional, ask your vet and friends for references and take the time to visit groomers in advance of getting your puppy to check out both the groomer and the facility.

Ask your veterinarian or groomer to show you how to brush your puppy's teeth. Some veterinarians recommend tooth brushing on a daily basis. It's not that your puppy really needs so much tooth brushing, but it really helps habituate her to having hands in her mouth—and it's also a great safety exercise.

It is helpful if more than one member of the family learns to groom the family dog. This is a wonderful opportunity for family bonding and it prevents your puppy from limiting her tolerance of handling to just one person (see Chapter 10 on socialization).

Groomer Checklist
- ☞ Is the facility clean? Are the dogs at ease or do they seem distressed?
- ☞ Ask if you can observe the groomer while he's working on a dog. Many groomers allow clients to watch the grooming through a special window.
- ☞ Look for a groomer who uses gentle methods, such as using treats to keep hesitant or distressed dogs calm and still.
- ☞ Talk to a potential groomer about your desire to socialize your puppy well to the grooming experience.

Training

When you bring a puppy into your home, training is not a luxury—it is a necessity. The human world is a bizarre and confusing place for puppies—it is our responsibility to teach them how to navigate it with success and confidence. You may find the training in this book to be sufficient. However, a DVD or video, such as Paul's *The Dog Whisperer: Beginning and Intermediate Dog Training,* will definitely help in the training process. Online resources include downloadable video clips on various aspects of training, such as those available at *www.dogwhispererdvd.com.* Or you may want to pursue one-on-one sessions or group classes with a trainer who uses only nonviolent, positive methods.

If you decide to find a local trainer, take your puppy to a class as soon as possible. You may have to enroll several weeks in advance, so we suggest reserving a spot in a class even before your puppy is home. Puppy "kindergarten" classes are commonplace nowadays for puppies under the age of five months. Some classes will accept puppies as young as seven or eight weeks but most trainers require that your puppy has had at least the first two inoculations in the vaccination series, and some might require the full series.

You can find listings of qualified trainers in your area through organizations such as the Association of Pet Dog Trainers, the National Association of Dog Obedience Instructors, and the International Association of Animal Behavior Consultants. Some trainers have been certified through nationally recognized organizations, which indicates that they have demonstrated a certain degree of knowledge, education, experience, and expertise in their field. The Certification Council for Professional Dog Trainers, which certifies trainers by a designation of "CPDT" (Certified Professional Dog Trainer) is a good place to start. Only trainers who have passed a comprehensive examination and have at least 300 hours of professional experience are allowed to carry the designation CPDT. You can find a listing of CPDTs in your area by going to *www.ccpdt.com*.

Some training experts address complex problem behaviors such as aggressive and fearful behavior, separation anxiety, and so on. These experts may refer to themselves as behavior consultants, behavioral experts, or behaviorists, although this last category is usually associated with someone who has a PhD. However, certification is not a guarantee that a trainer uses only positive, nonviolent techniques.

Trainer Checklist
The following questions for your potential dog trainer appears courtesy of Nicole Wilde, author of many canine-related books including the authoritative *So You Want to Be a Dog Trainer* and *Help for Your Fearful Dog* (Phantom Publishing; *www.phantompub.com*).

1. "How long have you been training?" This one is a little tricky. Sure, you want someone who has at least a few years of experience. However, a trainer with thirty years of experience is not necessarily better than one with ten years of experience, if the more experienced trainer hasn't changed their methods or improved in all that time. Which leads us to . . .

2. "What is your background and do you pursue ongoing education?" The best trainers regularly attend seminars and workshops to further improve their skills and learn the latest techniques. Avoid those who think they already know it all.

3. "What sort of methods do you use?" Another tricky one. I haven't heard of a trainer yet who advertises "rough, punishment-based methods." It just doesn't sell. Although a trainer might call herself "positive," find out exactly what that means. For example, what would she do if a dog did not obey a command? If a trainer uses choke chains, by definition she is using "corrections." (Within every style of training, there is a range of trainers, some much gentler or harsher than others.) If she uses clicker training or lure-reward training properly, she is using positive methods. Some trainers call themselves "balanced," which means they use both corrections and praise/reward. But even among "balanced" trainers there can be a great variation in training methods and amount of force used. The bottom line is, if anything a trainer does to your dog makes you uncomfortable, speak up, and if necessary, stop the session immediately and find another trainer.

4. "Do you train full time?" There are trainers who do other jobs while training on the side. That doesn't mean they're not good. For basic obedience, someone who trains part-time might be fine. But for serious behavior issues, seek out a trainer who has been training full-time for at least a few years and has experience with the particular issue your dog needs help with.

5. For in-home training, can you do one session at a time, or are you required to pre-purchase a package of sessions? Is one better than the other?

6. Does the in-home trainer work only with the dog? Or will they train you to do so? The second option is desirable because after all, you're the one the dog will need to listen to in the long run.

7. For serious behavior issues, how much expertise does the trainer have? Some trainers specialize in specific behavior problems, while others won't handle issues such as aggression.

8. For a group class, will you be allowed to observe a class first? A good trainer will have no qualms about letting you observe a class.

9. How many dogs per class? In a large class you'll get less personal attention. Look for a small class, where the trainer demonstrates with students' dogs hands-on and gives feedback. Dogs and people should look like they're having fun, not stressing out.

A professional trainer should welcome questions and have a pleasant attitude. If you feel a trainer is being rude or unfriendly, move on. There are others who will welcome your business and treat both you and your dog well.

Choosing Caregivers

If you will be leaving your puppy alone for hours at a time, you may elect to hire a dog walker or place your puppy in a doggy daycare. A dog walker will visit your home for a half hour to an hour and take your puppy for a potty break and a walk and share some playtime. This can be especially helpful as the dog walker will provide socialization, exercise, play, and even potty training.

A doggy daycare is a facility where a group of dogs spends the day together in a supervised setting. The benefits of daycare include the opportunity to learn good social skills with other dogs, since the dogs interact all day long in an off-leash situation. Some facilities also have enclosed outdoor areas for exercise and play. You might find a very good daycare facility, but ultimately decide that it's not the right environment for your puppy. Daycare can be overwhelming for a puppy who is not used to being around a large group of dogs or for one who is particularly shy or fearful. Some puppies need a much gentler introduction to group interaction than others and become chronically distressed in a daycare situation. Take some time to observe your puppy in the daycare environment to be sure it's right for him.

When you're going out of town, you have three basic options—have someone stay in your home, have your puppy stay at someone else's home, or have your puppy stay at a boarding facility. The advantage of a dog sitter is that your puppy will remain at home, which lowers her stress about being apart from you and the environment she knows. You can find qualified dog sitters in your area by asking trainers, friends, and vets for their referrals or through professional organizations like Pet Sitters International (*www.petsit.com*).

Dog Walker or Dog Sitter Checklist

- Ask the dog walker or sitter to come to your home for an interview and to meet you and your puppy. Be clear about how you would like your puppy to be handled. Observe how the dog sitter interacts with your puppy and if your puppy seems comfortable or distressed. If the meeting goes well and you hire the sitter, be sure to give her written instructions on feeding and any specific medical needs.
- Ask if she is bonded and insured. This gives you a certain amount of security that the dog walker or sitter will take good care of your puppy (and house), since she takes on a degree of financial liability for your puppy.
- Ask about her training philosophy and make sure she doesn't use any physical punishment. For example, ask how she handles a puppy who pulls on the leash. Before the interview, you may want to review "Walk Without Pulling" in Chapter 18 so you'll be conversant on the topic.

🦴 If your puppy is being potty trained, discuss the regimen so she can maintain your schedule.

Daycare or Boarding Facility Checklist

🦴 Pay a visit without your puppy. Notice if the facility is odor free and looks clean and well cared for. Look for non-skid or rubberized floors, which minimize injuries to dogs who are running around and jumping.

🦴 Ask about the ratio of dogs to daycare workers. Obviously, the more people there are, the more likely it is that your puppy will be safe and happy. If workers are overwhelmed by the number of dogs they must care for, there is more opportunity for problems.

🦴 Observe how the staff treats the dogs. Do they exhibit care and compassion?

🦴 Observe the dogs. Are they having fun? Or is play allowed to get overly rough, frenetic, and chaotic? Are dogs cowering or hiding because the atmosphere is too frightening?

🦴 Ask if there is a section specifically for puppies so they can be separated to rest and calm down from time to time?

🦴 Ask if they have a special procedure for introducing new dogs that will allow your puppy to be eased into the group dynamic.

🦴 Ask the individual or facility manager about their training philosophy and how problem behaviors are handled. Make sure they don't use any physical punishment. If a fight breaks out among the dogs, ask how they handle it.

🦴 If your puppy is being potty trained, discuss the regimen so they can maintain your schedule.

Dog Parks

Increasingly, many communities are providing public, off-leash dog parks as places where dogs can legally and safely run and play in a large enclosed area. Your puppy should be at least six months old before going to a dog park and even then, some parks are very high risk. On the plus side, dog parks provide social contact with other dogs and people, as well as exercise, free of charge. A dog park can give your older puppy an opportunity to learn appropriate dog-to-dog behavior with dogs of all ages, sizes, and temperaments.

> **Note:** Puppies under the age of six months need to be introduced to larger and older dogs in appropriate ways. Because of the risk factor regarding health and physical safety, dog parks are not the answer.

The downside to dog parks is the high volume of dogs passing through them, pooping, peeing, slobbering, and generally spreading bacteria around. Make sure the park is kept relatively clean, and that you supervise your puppy while in the park to make sure he doesn't eat or roll in any poop that might be lying around. Another potential drawback to public dog parks is that an awful lot of rough play can go on, which could be quite frightening and even dangerous to a puppy. In addition, some dogs at these parks do not have the greatest social skills, and can frequently behave downright aggressively. Notice how other dogs are behaving and if play becomes too rowdy, interrupt it before a problem arises. Puppies thrown into play with the "big kids" might end up getting turned off to being around other dogs, and therefore develop fearful or aggressive behavior toward other dogs. So if your puppy seems fearful or displays any aggression, leave the park right away. The good news is that some dog parks have a separate area fenced off for small dogs and puppies to help avoid this problem. Check out your local dog park (or regular park, for that matter) before you decide to take your puppy there.

Dog Park Checklist

- ☞ Read the posted rules to see if puppies are allowed.
- ☞ Observe the people at the park. Do they supervise their dogs to make sure they don't get too rough?
- ☞ How clean is the park? Do people pick up their dogs' poop?
- ☞ Is water available?
- ☞ If a person is not following park guidelines, is there a volunteer park monitor, or does the rest of the group seem to work together to keep things safe?

Safe dog parks all have one thing in common: A good park is one where people will not put up with aggressive dogs and they look out for one another. Dog parks are usually maintained by a volunteer board of directors from the community. Find out if there is a number posted at the park for a board contact that you can call and ask about park safety and monitoring.

If you decide to take your puppy to the park, try to go at a time when the canine traffic is light, perhaps early in the morning or midday. The busiest time tends to be 5:00 to 7:00 P.M., when people get off work and go out with their dogs for some fun. Don't take food or toys as doing so often causes problems. Best and safest of all is if there is a separate small-dog section where your puppy is less likely to get trounced in exuberant play.

Chapter 5

Bringing Your Puppy Home: Kenneling, Potty Training, and Introduction to the Household

Plan to have at least a few days off when you bring your new puppy home, as a good deal of direct supervision is key to giving your puppy the guidance she needs. Direct supervision involves using management tools such as baby gates, exercise pens, and/ or tethers to keep your puppy safe and allow you to keep an eye on her. Obviously, this is also helpful for potty training.

The First Trip Home

Arrange to pick up your puppy at least an hour after she has eaten—or, if possible, before she has been fed. If your puppy is "empty" you are more likely to avoid motion sickness or peeing and pooping in the car. Also, in case she has a sensitive stomach, refrain from giving her treats before the ride home.

The safest way to transport your puppy home in the car is to bring another person along to sit in the back seat and hold the puppy. This will minimize the bumping and jostling of the car ride, yet still give your puppy loving and comforting contact with another living being at this stressful moment. If you are alone, a crate or carrier in the back seat is the next best solution. Under no circumstances should a puppy be allowed to bounce around freely on a car seat—this is dangerous and stressful. If you are taking your puppy home by car over a long distance, make sure that you stop every hour to let your puppy eliminate (unless she is sleeping). If your puppy will be traveling by plane, make sure to follow all breeder recommendations.

Checklist for the First Trip Home
- ☞ Make sure your puppy is "empty": no food for at least an hour before the trip.
- ☞ Bring someone to hold your puppy in the back seat.
- ☞ Keep the trip quiet and calm . . . no rock'n'roll on the radio.
- ☞ If the trip is going to be long, make stops for elimination every hour, but don't wake her to eliminate.

The First Few Hours

Once you arrive home, give your puppy ten minutes or so in the yard so she can eliminate. This is your first step in potty training as the very first location in which your puppy eliminates often creates an association with that location as an elimination "spot." This association can be surprisingly strong and long lasting. Keep her in a contained area or on a leash if she is used to one. (See the following section, "Introducing Your Puppy to the Collar and Leash.")

Take her in the house and let her explore for about a half hour, but closely supervise. Redirect her attention if she starts to chew on anything by making "kissy" sounds or lightly clapping your hands, then call her to you. If you see any signs that she might need to eliminate, like sniffing the ground, circling a spot, or arching her back, take her outside again. In this first half hour, you can introduce her to other family members or friends. Keep it happy, friendly, and a little low key. It is of the utmost importance that her initial experience in meeting new people is positive. No crowding around the newcomer with everyone trying to be the first to pet. Do not rush toward the puppy or make loud noises or sudden movements.

Friends and family members can encourage your puppy to say hello by holding a treat out in an open palm. If the puppy seems to be enjoying this—as almost all puppies do—and continues to approach or climb on to the person, it's okay to progress to gentle petting on the top of the head and down the back. If the puppy does not want to approach, however, or moves away, do not pursue her. Let your puppy take her time in gaining the confidence she needs to approach new people. If she wants to stay away today, let her—you can always offer her another treat later, or tomorrow. If your puppy is enjoying everything thus far—and that means approaching people and asking for attention, not just tolerating attention—you might try playing with a toy.

Introducing Your Puppy to the Collar and Leash

A collar and leash are indispensable management tools. If your puppy struggles and protests when she first feels the collar around her neck, as many do, don't worry. It is quite easy to get your puppy to feel good about these lifelong friends. As you put the collar on, give her several treats to take her attention off the strange new feeling. If she struggles at all, or paws at it, interrupt her with an upbeat, happy tone of voice, give her a treat, and engage in some interesting activity like following you around the house or playing with a toy. You can also try putting it on just before feeding her. Using these methods, you are creating a positive association between the collar and the food.

When you go outside for potty breaks, put a leash on your puppy. If she shows any reluctance to walk while on the leash, use a happy tone of voice and throw treats in front of her to encourage her to follow you. Soon enough, she will be associating the leash with the fun of going outdoors for walks and play. She will learn to love the leash. In the meantime, if there is any lingering struggle with either the collar or leash, continue to distract your puppy from it and engage her in something pleasurable.

Introducing Your Puppy to Children in the Household

Children and puppies are what life is all about, but it sometimes takes a little time to get them used to one another. Many puppy behaviors, such as nipping and jumping, which are simply annoying to adults, can be downright dangerous for children. A twenty-pound puppy can easily knock over a two-year-old child.

A nip at the height of an adult's calf can nail a crawling baby squarely in the face. All initial introductions should occur with one child at a time, while the puppy is on leash or being held by an adult. The child should be standing or seated in a chair or held by the parent (see Figure 5-1).

Figure 5-1

Terry's daughter, Viola, is held by his wife, Debora, as she is introduced to a new puppy.

Note: Children and puppies should never be left alone. Either one could easily get hurt. Always supervise and manage the puppy's access to the children by kenneling, baby-gating, or use of an indoor exercise pen.

Impress on your children, now and in the future, that puppies are their friends. They aren't toys and should not be pushed, pulled, ridden like a horse, or hit. The child should be taught to pet gently. If at any point your puppy jumps on you or your child, cross your arms against your chest and turn away (see Figure 5-2). When your puppy has his paws on the ground again, you can face him and praise, pet, and treat him if he sits (see Figure 5-3). If the puppy continues to jump or the person or child is afraid, carry or gently pull your puppy back away with the leash.

Figure 5-2   **Figure 5-3**

If a puppy jumps, cross your arms against your chest and turn away.

When your puppy has his paws on the ground again, you can face him and praise, pet, and treat him if he sits.

Note: Since your puppy is looking for attention and play, the goal is to teach him that jumping means a person or child will disengage and withdraw attention. If the child pushes the puppy away, the puppy gets the wrong message because in puppy-speak, being pushed away reinforces the notion that jumping is a fun game. This actually perpetuates the behavior you are trying to eliminate.

Children five years old and older can help train the puppy to do basic behaviors like sit and lie down, stay, and go-to-your-bed. Children age seven and older can also be given the job of feeding. However, care must be taken if a child is feeding a puppy or a dog of any age. When the child places the food bowl on the floor, the child's face is close to the dog's mouth. The puppy, in his excitement to eat, might jump up and play-fully nip the child's face. To keep everyone safe, follow these rules:

1. Put the puppy on a leash and tether him to the wall or piece of furniture or have an adult hold the leash.
2. Have the child ask the puppy sit and say "stay."
3. Then have the child put the food bowl on the floor and slide it to the puppy with his foot.
4. As the child says "okay," the puppy is released to get the food. (Also see feeding suggestions in the socialization exercises in Chapter 10.)

Rules for Children
- Be gentle and kind. Don't hit or pull the tail, pinch the ears, and so on. Never tease a puppy.
- Never chase a puppy.
- Don't lift your puppy off the ground.
- Let your puppy sleep without waking him up.
- Never bother a puppy while he is eating.
- Have fun and train your puppy using positive methods.

Introducing Your Puppy to Other Dogs in the Household

Have another person help you introduce your puppy to your other dog(s) by asking him to bring the older dog on leash to an outside meeting place. If your puppy is under four months old, meet outside your house, in the front or backyard. If your puppy is more than four months, the meeting place can be a quiet spot at a public park or in your friend's yard. With both dogs on leash, let them sniff and greet while you keep the leashes nice and loose. Then take a short walk together around the yard.

Try this: Have your helper hold the puppy's leash while you hold your older dog's leash. While your helper pets and plays gently with your puppy, you will pet and play with your older dog. For the moment, continue to hold the leashes, in case your older dog becomes resentful of the puppy for any reason. If everything goes well and your older dog accepts the puppy and wants to play, drop the leashes and let them. Do this only in a fenced-in area.

Play Aggression

Generally, well-adjusted adult dogs will tolerate a puppy's attempts to play with great patience and will join in the play when the puppy is "playing by the rules." Sometimes, however, a puppy will bite too hard or persist too long without a break, and the adult dog will growl, bark, or even lay his mouth on the puppy to warn him. Do not be alarmed; this is a natural part of learning how to safely interact. If your older dog cannot tolerate any level of play, immediately separate the dogs and call a qualified trainer.

After ten or fifteen minutes of off-leash interaction, feed your dogs. Separate your puppy from your older dog with a baby gate, but lay out their food dishes so that they can see each other while eating. As with the walking, petting, and playing, you are associating a positive event for your older dog with the puppy's presence. You are also putting appropriate management measures in place to assure that both dogs are safe. As the months go by and your dogs get more and more used to each other, you can gradually remove management equipment, like gates that separate them at mealtimes, but continue to supervise closely.

Home Alone Training

After a few hours of dealing with people who are consumed with "new-puppy-itis," your puppy will be worn out. This is a good time to start teaching her that it's safe to be alone and separated. Home alone training consists of short-term and long-term periods of being away from you, whether you are out of the house or in another room. This training is important because in real life people have to work for a living and can't stay home all the time to keep the puppy company. You will also be hedging your bets that the puppy doesn't develop separation anxiety.

Before confining your puppy, give her a bit of exercise and a chance to eliminate. When your schedule permits, such as on weekends, use short-term home alone training for one or two hours to start with. Put her in a kennel (if she's used to one), in a small room with a baby gate, or in an exercise pen with her chew toys and leave the room. Play soft music and ignore any whining. Most puppies settle down within twenty minutes and go to sleep. If your puppy is between eight and twelve weeks old, ideally you can leave her alone for periods of up to an hour or two during the day and then, of course, you have to take her out to eliminate. Older puppies can go longer; more on this in the potty training section below.

If you are going to be gone for more than a couple of hours, obviously you will need to do home alone training for longer periods of time. This means that you can't confine her in a kennel or any other small, closed area. It's likely your puppy will need to eliminate before you return so she will need ample space away from her sleeping area. You don't want her to mess her sleeping area. You can put her in an exercise pen that surrounds an opened kennel or baby-gate her in the room. Another choice would be a room with a tile or linoleum floor such as a bathroom or laundry room, if it isn't too small, and baby gate the doorway. Whether you leave her in an exercise pen or other room, you'll want to cover the floor with newspapers or pee pads.

When Should a Puppy Be Given Free Range in the House?

Your puppy has to earn the right to be free in the house while you're away. Although there are some exceptions to the rule, virtually every puppy can eventually be given this freedom. Once you are sure that your puppy is housetrained and he won't chew things while you're gone, he can be given freedom one room at a time. This normally happens between the ages of nine and twelve months.

Resist the temptation to spend every moment of your day with your puppy during her first few days at home—when it's time to go back to work, the puppy will be thrown into a completely different routine. Your goal is to convince your puppy that you will always return and that being left alone and separated from you is no big deal.

Home Alone Tips

Stay relaxed. Dogs have an anticipatory response. The first thing you'll want to do is to stay relaxed whenever you put your puppy in her confined area, and whenever you leave or return home. If you have a high level of energy when you depart and return, your puppy will pick up on that and begin anticipating and feeding on your excitement. It's a vicious circle. So stay calm, matter-of-fact, and relaxed. Say nothing or give her a simple "see ya" when you leave. Then, on your return home, ignore her totally until she relaxes even a little bit (within ninety seconds), then reward her with petting and affection and release her. As time goes by, she'll learn that the more she remains calm, the more attention she receives.

Exercise. A tired puppy has less energy to complain. Give your puppy ten to twenty minutes of exercise before confining her.

Make chew toys available. Puppies can relieve stress by chewing. Give her a treat-filled Kong or a chewie like a bully stick or chicken strip.

Play music. Many puppies learn to relax if they hear soft music. In addition, music provides a continuity to their day. If they hear music while you're home, they associate the sounds with your company and hearing it in your absence will be comforting.

Provide comforting scents. Leave a T-shirt or other soft item of clothing with your smell in your puppy's confined area.

Provide an area for her to eliminate. If you cannot return in time to let your puppy eliminate, provide ample space outside her sleeping area. Do not confine your puppy in a kennel if you cannot return in time. Use an exercise pen or a baby-gated room instead.

Kennel Training

By kennel training we mean getting your puppy accustomed to resting, sleeping, and chewing on toys while being confined. We'll address this next, since being comfortable in the kennel can be a tremendous help in potty training.

Even if you don't plan to kennel your dog very often as he gets older, the kennel is a tremendously helpful management tool that keeps your dog from getting into trouble and it's also a big help in potty training. Additionally, it prepares your puppy for trips to the vet or groomer, where he is occasionally housed in a kennel until you pick him up. Some puppies come "kennel-ready," having been acclimated to a kennel before being adopted. If your puppy is happy and confident about being in the kennel, you can skip the rest of this section. That being said, never leave a young puppy in a kennel during the day for long stretches. The rule of thumb is up to two hours for eight to ten weeks of age; up to four hours for ten weeks and older.

Allow your puppy to acclimate to the kennel slowly, gradually increasing the time she spends in it by very small increments. It is much better to go too slowly than to go too quickly and risk making confinement in the kennel a distressing experience. You might end up with a puppy who thinks the kennel is San Quentin. Always look for signs of distress, like barking, drooling, pacing, or trying to chew through the bars. If she shows any of these signs, do less—that is, go back as many steps in the process as you need to in order to make her comfortable again. Any individual step could take five minutes, five days, or five months to accomplish. Don't be in a rush—let your puppy decide the pace of the training. No matter how quickly or slowly your puppy progresses, learning will "stick" best if you break up your training into five- or ten-minute sessions, separated by at least half-hour intervals in between.

Kennel Training Tips

- 🦴 Throughout the day, when your puppy isn't looking, place a bunch of treats in the kennel. He will quickly learn to go to the kennel to see if any treasure awaits him there.
- 🦴 Feed your puppy's meals in the kennel, with the door open. As soon as he isn't showing any hesitation about going in his kennel for his meal, close the door until the meal is finished.
- 🦴 If you ever see your puppy enter the kennel on his own, immediately praise him and throw him highly valued food treats. (See "The Magnet Game" in Chapter 16.)

Caution: If your puppy chews on the bars of his kennel, tries to bend open the door to escape, or cries and whines for longer than twenty minutes, do not kennel him! Being confined can be very stressful for some dogs. His anxiety is likely the result of separation anxiety and needs the attention of a qualified trainer or behaviorist. Continued kenneling will likely result in serious injury to your puppy.

Teaching Your Puppy to Get in the Kennel

Once your puppy likes the kennel, you can put the kennel "on cue," as professional trainers call it, and teach him to go there when you ask him. Training your puppy to go to the kennel is the same basic protocol as teaching Go To Your Spot (on page 241), with only a few subtle differences. Since the kennel is a closed space, you will be sensitive to your puppy's acceptance of the space and when the door is open or closed.

Step One

Place the puppy's bed or mat inside the kennel and prop the door open. Put your hands in a starting position, closed and resting against your chest. With the hand closest to the kennel, toss a highly valued food treat, such as a small piece of roast turkey breast, into the kennel. If your puppy goes in to get it, praise him lavishly, but do not close the door to the kennel. Let him come right back out if he wishes. Repeat this five to ten times.

If your puppy hesitates or backs away from the kennel, try the "Hansel and Gretel routine" by placing a trail of small treats, spaced closely together, leading to the kennel door. Give lots of praise as he takes each step, eats a treat, and advances ever closer to the kennel door. If your puppy approaches the kennel and then backs up again, that's okay—just place another row of treats leading to the kennel door. If you don't push or force him in any way, in subsequent sessions he will gain confidence and start to approach more closely. When he comes right up to the threshold of the kennel door without any hesitation, extend the trail of treats into the kennel but do not close the kennel door yet. Let your puppy come out of the kennel whenever he wishes.

Step Two

Now label the behavior by saying "go to your kennel," or "go to your crate," just before you toss the treat into the kennel. Other options include "kennel up," "go to your bed," "go to your den," or "park it." The exact words you use are not important, as long as you are consistent. After you have done this five or ten times, with your puppy going into the kennel each time, try saying your phrase again, but this time don't toss a treat in the kennel. If your puppy goes in the kennel, praise lavishly and give him a jackpot (several treats, one after the other) after he is in there. Repeat this step five to ten times, rewarding with a treat each time. If your puppy doesn't go in the kennel within forty-five seconds, return to the previous step of saying the word and throwing the treat. Repeat this five times and then try "word only" again. Don't worry if your puppy doesn't get it in one session.

Tip: If you say the word and simultaneously turn your head toward the kennel, your puppy may follow your gaze to see what you are looking at. Give your puppy forty-five seconds to respond. You can encourage your puppy with praise if he moves toward the kennel, but do not treat.

Step Three

Ask your puppy to "get in the kennel"; after he enters, close the door, praise, and give him a highly valued food treat. Immediately open the door and release him. Repeat this five to ten times. You are teaching your puppy that there is a positive association between the closed door and food. If he seems comfortable with this game, keep the door closed for two seconds and once again, treat through the door and release him. Keep these sessions short and positive.

Tip: Prepare a stuffed Kong toy in advance, as described in Chapter 3. Ask your puppy to go to his kennel. When he enters, reward him with the Kong, then close the door for thirty seconds to one minute while he works away at his yummy reward. Then let your puppy out of the kennel and take the Kong away. Some time later, ask him to go to his kennel again, give him his stuffed Kong again, and this time close the door while you walk about the house for a minute. If at any point he becomes distressed and loses interest in the treat-filled Kong, take note of how long he has been in the kennel, let him out, and a little later, let him out sooner. Your goal is to confine your puppy for only as long as he feels comfortable, not any longer.

Assuming that everything has gone smoothly thus far, wait a while and then put him in the kennel again. This time leave him in there with his Kong a little longer, perhaps for up to two minutes. Take the Kong away each time you let your puppy out of the kennel so that he clearly associates the Kong with being inside the kennel.

Potty Training

We choose the phrase "potty training" because "housebreaking" suggests that your puppy has established a bad habit which needs to be "broken." Nothing could be further from the truth. A puppy does not need breaking, which connotes punishment. He needs education.

Most puppies are reliably potty trained by the time they are seven months old. In the interim, accidents will happen. You are bound to get a puddle or pile, or two, in your house over the course of a few weeks. The process outlined here should minimize accidents and the amount of clean-up you'll have to do on the carpet and kitchen floor. Be patient, be consistent, be compassionate, and if you follow the rules, your puppy will be potty trained before you know it.

Note: Always watch for the signals that your puppy may have to eliminate. Signals include panting, circling, sniffing the ground, or glancing at you, if for only a split second. These are all potential indicators you puppy "has to go." As much as your puppy may want to "hold it," it takes time for the muscle control to develop.

Element One—Keep a Regular Schedule

Set up regularly scheduled feeding and potty times, and be consistent. Your puppy's digestion and elimination will become regular and this will make potty training more reliable. If your puppy can reliably predict when she will have the opportunity to visit her outdoor potty spot, she will become more and more likely to wait for that opportunity. In the beginning, plan about eight regular trips outside per day.

These times are:

1. first thing in the morning;
2. within twenty minutes after eating;
3. after mid-morning play sessions;
4. after being confined (sleep/nap);
5. within twenty minutes after eating;
6. after afternoon play or rest sessions;
7. within twenty minutes after eating;
8. last thing before going to bed.

You can use the above scheduling guidelines as a starting point, but every puppy is an individual. If, for instance, you notice that your puppy consistently fails to potty outside within twenty minutes after eating, but always starts to potty indoors forty-five minutes after eating, adjust her schedule accordingly.

Once you have established a schedule that seems to be working, keep it consistent, even on weekends. As she gets older, your puppy will learn to adjust to a more flexible schedule. But right now, for her sake, keep it boringly predictable.

Notes:

- 🦴 If your potty spot is in a public place such as a tree or lawn, always pick up after your puppy. Most towns and cities have pooper scooper laws that require you to do so.
- 🦴 Pick up the water bowl an hour or two before bedtime to minimize the possibility of nighttime urination.
- 🦴 Avoid scheduling too many trips outside. If your puppy has too many opportunities to potty, it will be harder for her to distinguish between appropriate potty times and inappropriate times.

Element Two—Pick a Spot

The emphasis of potty training is teaching your puppy to eliminate in a particular place or places—which happen to be outdoors. Dogs like to establish stable peeing and pooping spots. Once a puppy urinates in a particular spot, she is prone to urinate in that same spot again. Successful potty training therefore capitalizes on a puppy's own natural tendencies.

When you take your puppy out to potty, take her on a leash to the spot you have chosen and stand there. If your puppy eliminates in "the spot," throw a party. Praise enthusiastically as soon as she finishes and, most importantly, give an extra special food treat. You want to make a lasting impression on your puppy so she has a strong desire to return to this spot for elimination in the future. After she has eliminated, you can play in the yard or go for a walk as part of the reward.

Note: Whenever you take your puppy outside to eliminate, go the spot immediately, without walking or playing beforehand. You want the puppy to associate the trip outdoors with elimination and nothing else.

If you stand at the spot for more than five minutes and your puppy has still not eliminated, go back inside. In about twenty minutes, go outside and try again. But what should you do in the meantime, you ask? That unrelieved bladder and bowel has you concerned about your new Persian rug? Well, that brings us to . . .

Element Three–Inside Management

During the weeks of the initial potty training process, when your puppy is inside, he should always be managed. If you want to be successful, this rule is non-negotiable. This is accomplished by kenneling or penning your puppy, baby-gating him in the room with you, or by putting a leash on him and tethering the leash to you or something in the room. (See "Tethering" on page 78.) When you move to another room, move the puppy and the baby gates or tether with you. Every time. One convenient solution might be to have a tether in each room of your home, already tied to something, which you can clip and unclip from your puppy's collar. Another solution can be to tie your puppy's leash to your belt or belt loop. In this way, wherever you go, your puppy goes.

This inside management of your puppy, first and foremost, allows you to keep him in sight. Supervision of your puppy is important because you want to be able to interrupt him if he starts to eliminate inside. Notice that we use the word *interrupt*, which means you need to witness your puppy in the act of eliminating. Look for signs like sniffing the floor or the walls, circling a spot, arching the back, or lining up the body parallel to vertical surfaces. When you see your puppy starting to pee or poop inside the house, urgently say "uh-uh-uh-uh-uh-uh-uh-uh" and immediately take him outside to his spot. Reward him lavishly if he continues eliminating outside. If, after five minutes, your puppy doesn't eliminate, calmly go back inside, clean up any mess, and continue to supervise. No hard feelings. Try outside again a little later.

Dogs live in the moment, making associations between their behavior and its consequences within a second or so. After your puppy is finished eliminating, it is too late to teach him anything of significance about where he chooses to potty. Giving feedback of any kind after the act is accomplished is notoriously ineffective in potty training.

Note: Hitting a puppy for eliminating in the wrong place, rubbing his nose in it, or yelling with a scary voice will cause emotional distress and will have the opposite effect of that which is intended. Do not punish any unsupervised indoor pottying after the fact.

The only way you can give effective guidance in potty training is by rewarding outside and interrupting inside. For this reason, another common mistake in potty training is leaving the puppy outside for long periods of time on a tie out, unsupervised. If the puppy is pottying when he is alone outside, there is nobody there to let him know he is doing the right thing.

There are, of course, times when you need to go out and must leave your puppy confined. A three-month-old puppy should be capable of holding his need to eliminate for up to four hours during the day, but every puppy is different. If a puppy absolutely has to eliminate, he will do so no matter where he is. If your puppy eliminates in his kennel, even once, you run the risk of him establishing the kennel as a potty spot and the kennel will lose its usefulness as a potty training aid. So, again, do not confine your puppy for longer than he is physically capable of holding his bladder and bowel.

Another Option—Paper Training

You may have an irregular schedule, which might make it difficult to keep a consistent potty schedule. Or you may frequently have to leave your puppy confined for longer periods of time. In either of these cases it is likely that you will need to confine your puppy to an exercise pen or a room with newspapers or puppy pee pads (available at pet stores) rather than a kennel. If you establish a legal indoor potty spot and your puppy gets in the habit of using the paper more often than the outside, don't worry—it is simple to transfer the potty spot outside. When you are able to make timely trips outside, simply take a sheet of newspaper with you and place it down right outside your door. Put your puppy on the paper and wait there with him on leash for five minutes. If he eliminates on the paper, reward him with a treat and spend time outside. If he doesn't eliminate within five minutes, take him back into his confined space and try again twenty minutes later. As he catches on to eliminating on the paper, move the paper a little further from the door every day, until you have gotten your puppy to pee and poop on a sheet of newspaper lain over the spot you would like him to use regularly.

While your puppy is confined inside, you will still lay down a sheet of newspaper for him, but each day you will move it a foot closer to the exit (ideally an outside door). In this way, you are prompting your puppy to move toward the door when he feels the urge to eliminate. Once the outdoor spot has been firmly established, you can stop putting papers down inside. The result should be that your puppy will refrain from eliminating inside since the cue for it—the newspaper—is no longer there. Please note that you will still need to consider your puppy's physical ability to "hold it," so you will have to establish a timely potty schedule once the indoor papers have been eliminated.

Once your puppy is consistently eliminating outdoors, go out without the paper and wait at your puppy's spot for five minutes. If he eliminates outside without seeing or feeling the paper, throw a party with treats, toys, and much hoopla. If he doesn't, go back inside and try again twenty minutes later. Repeat until successful. Paper training takes longer, but can be a viable option for those who are just unable to make the eight trips a day outside needed for a very young puppy.

Other Potty Training Aids

"Puppy pads," which serve the same purpose as newspapers in paper training are available for use in penned or gated areas (not kennels). The difference is that they are absorbent and they are usually scented with a chemical that allegedly attracts dogs to eliminate on them, allowing you to establish a legal indoor spot more quickly and easily. You can use a puppy pad in the same way you used the single sheet of newspaper in paper training— by taking the pad outside and transferring the potty spot there.

Some people don't want to establish an outdoor potty spot at all. Either for convenience or reasons of physical disability, regular trips outside are not an option. For these people the best option is a "pet-a-potty," which is similar to a kitty litter box. They are plastic rectangular boxes that are filled with grass sod or absorbent pellets that can be emptied in the garbage after use. The process of training your puppy to potty in the indoor potty is exactly the same as that for outdoor potty training. You simply lead your puppy on leash to the litter box at scheduled times, reward successes, then supervise, confine, and interrupt at other times.

The First Night

When you bring your puppy into your home, it may be difficult for him to suddenly adapt to sleeping without being surrounded by the warm fur and beating hearts of his mother and littermates. Your puppy is a social animal and he is healthiest when he is with his family. Family means safety; family means security. So, to make the transition easiest, the ideal location for your puppy's kennel at night is next to your bed. Provide a comfortable blanket or bed inside the kennel or exercise pen. Many people prefer to have their dogs sleep on their own bed, but you may want to hold off on this until your puppy is six months old to avoid the problem of the puppy peeing in the bed. Also, you won't have to be concerned about rolling over on the puppy or kicking him off the bed. Puppies can not only get injured, they can develop hypersensitivity if they find themselves being unexpectedly knocked to the floor. When your puppy reaches the age of six months and potty training is on track, you can teach him to earn the right to be on your bed (see Chapter 14, "Rest").

In preparation for the first night at home, don't give any food or water to your puppy after 8:00 P.M. About a half an hour before going to bed, play with her a little bit to tire her out. Then take her outside for her final elimination. When you are back inside, matter-of-factly put your puppy in her kennel and close the door. For most puppies, it will take up to twenty minutes to settle down. Sometimes a ticking clock helps to calm nighttime anxieties, but don't put it in the kennel with the puppy. Ignore any whining as, in most cases, it will end of its own accord within twenty minutes. By the third or fourth night, the puppy should settle within minutes.

Set your alarm for four hours of sleep so that you can get up to take your puppy outside for elimination and avoid any peeing or pooping in the kennel. When you come back in, put her back in the kennel matter-of-factly and ignore any whining. After a few nights, start to increase the length of sleeping time by setting your alarm for an additional fifteen minutes. By gradually extending the sleeping time, your puppy will gain more control of her bladder. Then continue to set the alarm fifteen minutes later every few days, until around the age of four or five months, when your puppy should be able to sleep the whole night through without having to pee or poop. If at any point your puppy eliminates before you get up, shorten the timeframe and work forward a little more slowly.

Never keep a puppy in a kennel if he is distressed. If the puppy whines, paces, paws, or drools for more than twenty minutes and will not settle down, it is necessary to call a professional trainer. In the meantime, put your puppy behind a baby gate in the bathroom or kitchen. Or better yet, put the puppy in your bedroom in an exercise pen with an open kennel inside it. The extra room provided by the exercise pen often reduces the puppy's stress.

The First Few Days

The first few days of your puppy's life at home are centered around socializing (which is covered in Chapter 10), kenneling, and potty training. You will also continue easing your puppy into your absences with "home alone training," so she will adapt to your work schedule much more quickly. You're ready to add tethering.

Tethering

The term *tether* is used for a leash or cable that holds a dog in place. Tethering is a prevention and management method that helps keep your puppy out of trouble, especially if he is prone to jumping, bolting out the door, or chewing illegal objects. It is also useful for potty training, so he can't slip off and eliminate in the house. You can use a leash or a wire, chew-proof cable as a tether. There are a number of ways to tether:

Tethering to You (The "Umbilical Cord" Method)

If you hook one end of a leash to your belt, your puppy is tethered to you. The late trainer Job Michael Evans called this an "umbilical cord," which is a nice metaphor.

Tethering to Furniture or Eye-Hook

You can also tether your puppy by clipping a tether to an eye-hook that's secured in a baseboard or attach the tether to a piece of furniture (see Figure 5-4).

Figure 5-4

You can tether your puppy to a piece of furniture while you are reading a book, eating dinner, watching TV, or working on the computer.

Tethering to a Door

There are two ways to tether to a door: (1) You can wedge one end of the tether under a door to secure it. (2) Open the door and hook one end of a tether to the doorknob on the other side. Then slip the tether under the door and close the door. The idea with both of these methods is to keep the leash flat along the floor so your puppy won't choke herself or get tangled up in the leash. (See Figure 5-5 for the doorknob method.)

Figure 5-5

When tethering your puppy to a door, slip the leash handle over the doorknob on the other side of the door, drop the leash to the floor, and slip it under the door. Then close the door.

Tethering on a Walk

Whenever you are on a walk and stop to talk to someone, step on the leash so your puppy cannot jump. Keep some slack in the leash. If there's too much slack, the puppy will jerk himself if he jumps. If there's not enough slack, the puppy's head will be forced down and he'll be very uncomfortable. Your puppy is now by your side and in position to be rewarded whenever he sits or lies down. This tethering method teaches him to sit or lie down whenever you stop while on a walk (see Figure 5-6).

Figure 5-6

Tethering on a walk: When you're on a walk and stop to talk with someone, step on your puppy's leash. Reward him whenever he sits or lies down.

The First Few Weeks—Your Puppy's Daily Schedule

The following chart should give you a basic idea of what a typical day with your puppy will look like for the first few weeks. It is a broad outline that you can use as a reminder. Aside from kennel and potty training, you will find details for the individual elements in the following chapters.

Here's a sample schedule for your puppy's day. Vary it as necessary depending on your circumstances. Obviously if you are at work all day, you'll have to fit the activities into your day as best you can. (Also refer to "Home Alone Training" on page 78.) The Magnet Game is not included in this list because it's something you'll want to practice throughout the day, such as whenever you see your puppy lie down or pick up appropriate toys.

Puppy's Suggested Daily Routine

8 A.M. to 10 A.M.
Potty on arising
Meal
Potty again whenever necessary after
    meals, rest, or activities
Play, training, and exercise
Socialization activities (see page 118)
Supervised free time for exploration
Rest and alone time

10 A.M. to Noon
Potty again whenever necessary after
    meals, rest, or activities
Socialization activities (see page 118)
Play, training, and exercise
Supervised free time for exploration
Practice tethering: for example, while you
    are on the computer
Rest and alone time

Noon to 2 P.M.
Potty again whenever necessary after
    meals, rest, or activities
Play, training, and exercise
Supervised free time for exploration
Meal
Socialization activities (see page 118)
Practice tethering: for example, while
    you are eating

2 P.M. to 4 P.M.
Rest and alone time

4 P.M. to 7 P.M.
Potty again whenever necessary after
    meals, rest, or activities
Meal
Play, training, and exercise
Socialization activities (see page 118)
Supervised free time for exploration
Rest and alone time

7 P.M. to 8 P.M.
Potty again whenever necessary after
    meals, rest, or activities
Play, training, and exercise
Socialization activities (see page 118)
Practice tethering (such as when watching TV)
Rest and alone time

8 P.M. to 8 A.M.
Potty as necessary overnight

Chapter 6

Breath: Your Most Important Training Tool

Most people are surprised when they come to Paul's class for the first time and, before they even begin to work with their dog, he teaches them a breathing exercise. But, to this day, no one has ever questioned it. Perhaps that's because the benefits are so obvious when you do it for the first time.

So what does your own breathing have to do with training your puppy? Raising a puppy can sometimes be stressful. It's important to remain clam and nurturing, so here's how to help the human part of the dog-raising experience stay steady and cool. By beginning each training session with a breathing exercise, you will stay steady and cool by developing and maintaining focus and control. The flood of oxygen in your body sharpens your awareness and improves your reaction time, enhancing learning for both you and your puppy.

The fact is that your puppy responds to your emotional state. When you're upset, your puppy gets upset. When you're happy, your puppy tends to be happy. When you're frightened, your puppy may feel threatened. Puppies learn to associate their person's behavior with certain consequences, and the cycle starts with our emotions. From feelings of joy and happiness to frustration, despair, anger, and rage, our emotions are translated into physical expressions. Dogs are able to "read" even the most subtle of these human behaviors through our body language, smells, and breathing patterns.

When you are stressed, your breathing becomes shallow. The muscles in your body tighten, especially the muscles in the face, and there is a chemical reaction from the adrenal glands. Because a dog's senses are much more highly sensitive than ours, they pick up on these changes in your body and emotions. Depending on the degree of your stress and emotional response, a dog's fight-freeze-or-flight syndrome can be triggered.

If you relax and focus your energy through breathing exercises, your puppy is more likely to mirror your attitude. Paul has demonstrated this phenomenon numerous times in shelters full of barking dogs by simply quieting his mind and doing the breathing exercise. Spectators are always surprised when the cacophony of barking stops and the dogs start to relax. Therefore, by making a breathing exercise the first step of every training session, you will tap into the powerful emotion-behavior connection between yourself and your puppy.

When you breathe more deeply and fully, a greater amount of oxygen is released in the blood and more toxins are released from the body. More oxygen is also sent to the brain, which helps keep us alert and focused on the tasks we perform. Also, in order to breathe deeply and fully, we must of necessity relax some of the tension that we normally hold in the muscles in order to allow for full expansion of the diaphragm, abdomen, rib cage, and lower back. This release of muscle tension also promotes calmness because it allows our bodies to have a greater range of movement and expression. At the same time, the breathing exercise focuses our concentration so our attention is not as distracted by physical discomforts, aches, and pains. Dogs learn to recognize the minute physical changes we display and they learn to associate these displays with what happens next. So if we begin to breathe deeply, the dog sees and feels the rhythmic motion, smells the chemical change happening in our body, and links these observations with consequences. In this case, he is petted, thrown treats, and spoken to with a friendly, calm voice. As a result, the dog relaxes because we are relaxed.

Breathing is partially an automatic process, like the heart beating. Our autonomic nervous system makes sure we breathe night and day, because otherwise, of course we would die. The way that we breathe, however, is directly controlled by our will. We can decide to breathe deeply, shallowly, with different parts of our breathing apparatus, and even stop breathing for limited periods of time.

Most people tend to breathe shallowly, using a fraction of their lung capacity, and mainly use only one part of their breathing apparatus—the upper rib cage, for example, or the mid-abdomen. When asked to breathe deeply, many people will puff up their chests, or push out their bellies, holding everything else tightly, in a huge effort to draw in more air. The result is generally the opposite of what is intended in that not much more oxygen is taken in, yet a huge amount of energy is expended.

How We Breathe Can Help Puppies Relax

Terry's experience with breathing exercises is typical of those who incorporate this quick, easy, and valuable tool in their lives. When he first enrolled in Paul's dog training class about ten years ago, Terry learned the Complete Breath Exercise. As instructed, he did it before every training session with his puppy, Magoo, as well as in moments of high stress. These high stress moments were common as every time Terry returned home Magoo had destroyed more and more of the house. At the time, Terry admits that he held old prejudices about the use of a kennel as a safe management tool, because he thought it was somehow cruel. So, instead of using a kennel, whenever Terry left the house, he puppyproofed the kitchen and baby-gated Magoo there, leaving chew toys for him to play with. Inevitably, Terry would come home to discover the kitchen's vinyl flooring strewn on the floor in long strips or ascertain that the cabinets were quite tasty to the canine palate.

Terry knew enough not to punish Magoo for the destruction after the fact, but he would throw a panicked fit as he imagined his landlord's reaction. Terry's wildly emotional reaction was received by Magoo as a confusing type of punishment—his favorite person had just come home and proceeded to fly into a rage. What Magoo expected to be a joyful and stress-relieving moment—after all, his person had finally returned home—turned out to be a torturous nightmare, as he went cowering while Terry surveyed the damage and ranted. At the time, Terry didn't realize that his stress-induced reaction only served, unintentionally, to heighten Magoo's stress, increasing his dependence on Terry. This led to even more stress the next time Terry left, which led to more destruction, leading to more fits of rage, which led to higher stress, and on and on.

After Terry incorporated the breathing exercise in his daily routine, he took three complete breaths whenever he arrived home, just before he placed his key in the lock of his apartment door. The effect was magical. Magoo's destruction seemed less and less each day. Weird as it might sound, Terry began to think that Magoo was psychically receiving his calming thoughts as he stood outside the door. On reflection, Terry realized that when he first started practicing the Complete Breath Exercise, Magoo was not any less destructive. However, Terry was accepting the destruction more calmly. Terry says when he discovered some new bit of Magoo's mayhem, he now had a greater peace that allowed him to first accept his own responsibility for not having foreseen and prevented what Magoo did through good management; and further, feel more compassion for the anxiety Magoo must have been feeling about his absence.

From that point on, whenever Terry arrived home, he greeted Magoo happily at the door, before anything else, regardless of what bits of kitchen may have been lying around. Gradually, of course, Magoo started gaining confidence as their relationship strengthened—and the destruction truly did decrease. Then Terry started thinking more clearly and rationally about positive ways to prevent and change Magoo's destructive behavior and finally got him a kennel and a Kong toy (see Chapter 3). This entire chain of positive events would not have happened, however, if Terry had not taken those first three breaths.

Calmness does not mean absence of sound and activity. It refers to an inner calm, a sense of well-being and freedom from anxiety, which allows one to respond to people and situations with purposefulness, rather than with counter-productive chaos.

Your emotional state affects your behavior, whether you are calm, fearful, angry, or whatever, which in turn affects your puppy's emotions and behavior. So, if you can influence your own inner state, you can provide a quiet, calm, secure teaching environment in which your puppy can learn. The calmer and quieter you are, the clearer you can be in your training and the more discerning you can be in judging your puppy's reactions. Your puppy will repay you with calm responsiveness and faster learning.

The Complete Breath Exercise

The complete breath consists of smoothly inhaling and exhaling through the nose, without any stops, for equal lengths of time. This exercise can be done sitting, standing, walking, or doing anything, with eyes open or closed. (If you're driving or walking across a street, keep your eyes open!) Before starting, do a mental scan of your entire body, including your head, face, shoulders, chest, arms, back, abdomen, pelvis, hips, legs, and feet. Notice where you are carrying muscle tension and release that tension by just by "letting it go." Now that you have relaxed a little, begin the exercise.

Note: If at any point you feel dizzy, stop the exercise and rest. When you try it again, do only one breath, rather than three.

1. Imagine that your lungs are two water glasses and that you are slowly going to fill them with water. As you first start to breathe in, imagine you are pouring water into the bottom of the glass. Without pushing or straining, allow your abdomen to expand outward along with your lower ribs. As you continue, imagine the water filling the middle of the glass as you allow your mid-chest to expand all around, including the back. As the water reaches the top of the glass, allow the top of your chest to expand into the shoulders. It is important not to strain.

2. Without taking a pause at the top of the breath, allow the water to drain out of the glasses from the top to the bottom. Again, breathe only through your nose. Near the end of the

exhalation, gently push your stomach muscles inward and upward toward your spine, in order to expel any remaining breath.

3. As soon as you have finished exhaling, gently begin taking in your next breath. Although it has taken you almost a minute to read this exercise, the whole process takes about six seconds—three seconds in, three seconds out. Do a series of three complete breaths, timing the inhalations and exhalations to be equal in length. You can start out by counting inwardly to three for each inhale and each exhale. Keep the transition from inhale to exhale smooth, without a stop or "catch" in the breath.

Note: If you are a singer or play a wind instrument, your lung capacity will be larger. Hence, you can breathe in and out for longer periods of time. The key is to keep the inhalations and exhalations smooth and equal. For example, if you are breathing in for six seconds, breathe out for six seconds.

Over the course of a few weeks, gradually lengthen the amount of time for each inhale and exhale. You can do the exercise just after waking up and before going to bed. Other good moments are before taking on any stressful or challenging task, such as before a training session with your puppy, before going to work, or while cleaning up the poop from the living room floor.

After three months, make an assessment of your progress. If you are calmer and less stressed, healthier and more energetic, and have improved concentration and greater efficiency, you will be encouraged to continue practicing. After all, the proof is in the pudding. Your puppy will thank you for it!

Chapter 7

The Nine Ingredients for Optimum Health and Growth

In recent years, the concept of holistic health has become more and more mainstream as people begin to view health and behavioral problems as more than just symptoms and realize problems are more likely influenced by more than one simple factor. "Holistic" means looking at health from a whole being perspective—body, mind, and spirit. This approach tends to be more detailed, suggesting that all aspects of life affect health, including a dog's (or person's) environment, diet, and even his thoughts. Greater awareness of how one arena affects all the others—and then adjusting for imbalances—helps us restore as well as maintain good health.

Paul has developed model of holistic health for puppies and dogs called the Nine Ingredients. Incorporating these nine ingredients into everyday life promotes optimum health, safety, and growth for your puppy. They are:

1. High-quality diet
2. Play
3. Socialization
4. Quiet time
5. Exercise
6. Employment
7. Rest
8. Training
9. Health care

You'll notice that these same ingredients are needed by humans for happy, well-adjusted lives.

Terry remembers many years back, when he was a student in Paul's dog training class and everyone was asked to memorize a poem that he wrote to help students remember the nine ingredients. To this day, after many years of professional studies and his own successful career as a trainer and behavior consultant, he says he still refers back to and teaches others this simple children's rhyme as an organizing principle:

Food and play and socialize,
Quiet time and exercise,
Give your dog a job to do,
And lots of rest when day is through.
Train with love, respect, and care,
And see your vet throughout the year.

When combined appropriately there is a synergy in these nine ingredients, with each ingredient affecting the whole. Mental, physical, and emotional health manifest when these nine ingredients are working together in harmony. To do this, each of the ingredients must be "fed," so to speak, with the highest quality and the proper quantity. In this analogy, "food" is not only stuff we put in our mouths, but everything we take in through our senses. Whatever we taste, hear, see, feel, and touch affects our mental, physical, and emotional health.

What we see is visual food: Beautiful flowers, a smiling baby, a person we love affect how we feel in a wonderful way.

What we hear is auditory food: Harmonious music, the sweet song of a bird, a friend's laugh trigger feelings of joy and contentment.

What we smell is olfactory food: A home-cooked meal, a fragrant rose, salty ocean air inspire a sense of comfort and well-being.

What we feel is tactile food: A loving hug, an appreciative pat on the back, a friendly handshake feed our sense of connectedness and community.

Our puppies are fed through their senses too, but they can't make choices like we can. They eat what we feed them. Sometimes it's pinches and pokes from small children; heavy perfumes; loud music and yelling; startling noises and motion from airplanes, garbage trucks, motorcyclists, joggers, and skaters. These "foods" ultimately affect dogs' safety, health, emotions, and behavior. Positive training is rooted in awareness so that the choices we make, which means the environment we put our puppies in and the "foods" they eat as a result, help them grow, thrive, and enjoy life.

The Wolves Within—*Author Unknown*
A Native American Tale

An old Grandfather, whose grandson came to him with anger at a friend who had done him an injustice, said, "Let me tell you a story. I too, at times, have felt a great hate for those that have taken so much, with no sorrow for what they do. But hate wears you down, and does not hurt your enemy. It is like taking poison and wishing your enemy would die. I have struggled with these feelings many times."

He continued, "It is as if there are two wolves inside me; one is good and does no harm. He lives in harmony with all around him and does not take offense when no offense was intended. He will only fight when it is right to do so, and in the right way.

"But the other wolf, ah! He is full of anger. The littlest thing will set him into a fit of temper. He fights everyone, all the time, for no reason. He cannot think because his anger and hate are so great. It is hard to live with these two wolves inside me, for both of them try to dominate my spirit."

The boy looked intently into his Grandfather's eyes and asked, "Which one wins, Grandfather?"

The Grandfather replied, "The one who wins is the one I choose to feed."

If any one of the nine ingredients is not "fed" or provided in the proper amount or quantity (not too much or too little) or is of insufficient quality, your puppy's health and behavior are affected. So if you want to change your puppy's behavior, think first about providing and keeping these ingredients in her life balanced.

So how and what will you feed your puppy? If your puppy is constantly barking, jumping, peeing, and so on . . . you know, puppy stuff . . . take a "mental snapshot" of her daily life. Ask yourself if all of the nine ingredients are being sufficiently fulfilled, or if one or more of the ingredients is out of balance— either too much or too little. Very frequently, if you adjust one or more of the ingredients increase your puppy's exercise, for example, or give her more stimulating things to do at home— problem behaviors will resolve of their own accord, without the need to incorporate any additional training or to request help from a professional trainer.

Think about your own experience. When you don't eat or sleep well, or work too much, or don't have anything interesting to do, or don't see enough of your friends, or don't keep your mind stimulated, your anxiety and frustration build. And when you feel bad, you behave differently. You act crabby toward others, don't work as efficiently, make more mistakes and are prone to having accidents. So once again, the trick is to catch yourself, take a breath, and relax. Then look at the Nine Ingredients and do your best to provide whatever is missing.

This whole philosophy is based on common sense. It requires your commitment and daily practice. And, just like any other commitment you make in life, meeting all of your puppy's physical, mental, and emotional needs will become part of your daily lifestyle and routine.

Combining the Ingredients for Easy Use

The Nine Ingredients are to be thought of holistically, in relation to one another, rather than separately. Memorize the poem, then you can run through the mental checklist and it will become a snap to creatively combine different ingredients during the day. For example, you can take your puppy to a park for an hour, let her play with the other dogs and meet the other people, throw a ball to her for awhile, and practice your recall ("come when called") while you're there. In this way, you have provided for four daily ingredients—exercise, socialization, play, and training—all in one fell swoop. The possible combinations are limited only by your imagination.

Each of the following eight chapters is devoted to one of the nine ingredients, except for training, which is covered in an expanded section in Part II, "Behavior and Training."

Chapter 8

A High-Quality Diet

"Your puppy is what he eats." Health and behavior are affected by what goes in your puppy's mouth. Food is fuel. It's a compact and distilled form of "life" energy that, when eaten, transforms into growing bones and muscle, brain matter, and nerve pathways, which motor your puppy's running, jumping, playing, and the thousands of other behavioral forays into a world of positive and negative consequences. The quality and quantity of the food that your puppy eats can therefore naturally affect how he behaves and how successful he will be in surviving the challenges of life. Too much feeding, especially if the food is low quality, can cause obesity, leading to stress, pain, and inability to participate fully in play and social activities. These factors can then lead to boredom and anxiety, causing excessive barking and chewing. Too little food can lead to a lack of stamina and insufficient growth, resulting in nervous behaviors such as excessive licking and grooming.

Why Not "Regular" Puppy Chow?

Some of us are old enough (ahem) to remember when a good deal, if not all, of a dog's meal was provided by the family's leftovers. Four or five decades ago, commercially prepared pet foods became popular out of concerns that human leftovers don't always contain all or enough of the nutrients that dogs need for good health; and leftovers may also contain ingredients that dogs are unable to digest properly. Pretty good thinking, actually. So

95

does that mean the puppy chow that you find on the grocery store or pet store shelf is the best choice?

An increasing number of veterinarians recognize the nutritive pitfalls of the majority of commercially prepared dog foods, including some of the so-called premium or prescription brands. Alfred J. Plechner, DVM, for example, has found links between the use of commercially prepared dog foods and skin allergies, kidney disease, liver disease, seizure disorders, and pancreatitis, among other health problems.

As of this writing, widespread pet food recalls in the U.S. have affected numerous brands, including some that are considered top of the line, due to ingredients that contained poisonous substances. The fact is that most commercially available foods are of very low quality even when the ingredients are all considered "safe" and "acceptable." Andi Brown, author of *The Whole Pet Diet: Eight Weeks to Great Health for Dogs and Cats*, and the Director of Halo, Purely for Pets, which makes pet foods from only human-grade ingredients, explains it this way: "Many pet foods, even the so-called natural ones, may include byproducts, which are foodstuffs rejected for human consumption but permitted in pet foods. This includes beaks, feet, feathers, hooves, hair . . . and bones. . . . Saddest of all, and as truly awful as it sounds, over the years several pet food manufacturers have been caught processing the remains of dog and cat carcasses that had been euthanized, obviously with highly toxic substances, including their pet tags and collars."

We have no idea how widespread the practice of selling euthanized animals as an ingredient for pet food is, but years ago a professional working in an animal shelter told Paul this was happening at his shelter. According to Ann N. Martin, in her highly researched and acclaimed book *Food Pets Die For*, some veterinarians and rendering plants say it is common, while pet food manufacturers vehemently deny it.

Another problem with most commercial pet foods is that the extreme heat used to mass produce both dry and canned food destroys much of the nutritional value of the ingredients, including beneficial bacteria and enzymes that are crucial for digesting the food properly. Even when high-quality ingredients are used, processing destroys some of the nutritional value.

The Best Food Options

There are three basic options for providing your puppy a natural, high-quality diet—"human grade" canned or dry pet food with nutritional extras added, home-cooked food, or an all-raw diet. A good rule of thumb is that the more a food is processed, the less nutritious it is. So fresh is best and canned is better than dry kibble.

"Human Grade" Canned and/or Dry Food with Nutritional Extras Added

There are a number of pet food manufacturers that offer high-quality foods made of human-grade ingredients; these foods are available in pet stores, health food stores, and on the Internet through companies like NaturesPet.com and Puplife.com. It will be more expensive, but well worth it in terms of the health-giving benefits your puppy will derive from it. To make up for the loss of nutrients due to processing, you can add one or more of the nutritional extras listed below.

Stay away from Foods Containing:

Meat byproducts, meat meal, wheat, corn, artificial preservatives, sugars, additives, and colors. Other foods to avoid include: chocolate, onions, too much garlic, greasy foods, and cooked bones.

There are dozens of human-grade foods on the market today, including PetGuard; Halo, Purely for Pets; Merrick (the brand Paul feeds his dogs); Canidae; Wellness; Asmira; Eaglepack; Innova (makers of California Natural, which Terry feeds his dog); Solid Gold; and Newman's Own Organics. Even though these companies have high-quality products as of this writing, product quality can change as companies change management or policies or standards. We urge you to keep this in mind, to be continuously alert, and to *read labels* and product brochures carefully, even for products you have been using for a long time. There may be other fine suppliers or new companies not listed here.

Nutritional Extras

Most of the nutritionally rich foods and supplements listed below can be mixed into your puppy's food. Some, like carrots, apples, and pieces of meat and cheese, can be given as treats as part of the training process.

Raw vegetables: Add ⅛ to ¼ cup of raw vegetables for every 10 pounds of your puppy's weight. Choose one of the following that your puppy likes best: grated carrot, zucchini, chopped lettuce, or green beans. Or give a small whole raw carrot as a treat from time to time.

Raw fruits: Give a small amount of raw fruit such as apples or watermelon a couple times a week. (**Note:** raisins and grapes can be toxic to dogs so just avoid them to be safe.)

Organic meat: Add ⅛ to ¼ cup of raw, broiled, or baked organic meat to the meal for every 10 pounds of your puppy's weight. Choose from chicken, turkey, beef, or lamb; free range is the best.

Raw egg: Eggs are a great source of antibodies. Mix a raw egg into the food once a week or so. To minimize the possibility of salmonella poisoning, use fresh organic eggs from range-fed chickens. How do you know if an egg is fresh? It will sink to the bottom of a bowl of cold water. If it floats, it's a bad egg.

Acidophilus: To help balance the beneficial bacteria in the body, add ¼ to ½ teaspoon acidophilus liquid or powder or the contents of one capsule once a week or use High Potency

Digestive Enzymes from PetGuard. Acidophilus is found in the refrigerator section of natural foods stores.

Yogurt: Give 2 to 3 tablespoons for a small puppy or 4 to 6 tablespoons for a large puppy. Use a plain, natural culture yogurt from the health food store. Add to the food or serve as a treat occasionally, up to several times a week.

Cottage cheese and other dairy products: Cottage cheese is an excellent source of protein that is easy to digest. Add a small amount to the food up to three times a week. If your puppy is ill, cottage cheese can be fed daily. Goat's milk is naturally homogenized and therefore easy to digest. It also has a more complete nutrient balance than cow's milk. If your puppy gets diarrhea from cow's milk in the form of cream, half-and-half, or whole milk, discontinue it.

Note: We use cheese for treats and almost all of our clients do also. However, some puppies don't have the enzymes needed to digest any milk products. To determine if your puppy can eat cheese, give him three or four small pieces in his meals for a few days. If he becomes constipated or has loose stools, discontinue the cheese and use other food treats instead. Choose from meat such as roasted turkey and high-quality dry treats that are made by reputable pet food companies.

Vitamin and mineral supplements: Choose a vitamin and mineral supplement for puppies made from high-quality natural ingredients by a natural pet products company. These products come in powders that are added to the food, such as Anitra's Vita-Mineral Mix, Body Guard (from ProTec), or Good Gravy (from Pet Nutrition). Other products come in the form of tasty chewable supplements, such as Yeast and Garlic Wafers (high in trace minerals and B vitamins) and Multi-Vitamin and Minerals (both from PetGuard) or Vita-Dreams (from Halo, Purely for Pets).

Home-Cooked Food

Homemade diets are time-consuming to prepare but well worth the effort for those who want to maximize the nutritional content. There are a number of books and Web site sources of homemade diets for dogs, including Andi Brown's *The Whole Pet Diet: Eight Weeks to Great Health for Dogs and Cats*, which gives more than twenty-five recipes. You can add any of the nutritional extras listed above to your puppy's home-cooked food.

A Raw Food Diet

Puppies and dogs thrive on enzyme-rich foods that more closely approximate their ancestors' diets in the wild; therefore, a growing trend is to feed an all-raw diet or mostly raw diet. All-raw diets include raw meat, such as beef, fish, poultry, venison, lamb, and rabbit, combined with veggies, fruit, high-quality oils, and other ingredients such as parsley, ginger, and garlic. Some raw-food diets also include grains.

Many people have two concerns when they consider switching to a diet that includes raw meat:

1. Can the uncooked bones cause breaks or punctures to the stomach and intestines? When he first pursued the raw-food option, Paul had this concern and was assured that bones are not a health hazard unless they are cooked or frozen. Even chicken and turkey bones are okay. Many people have been feeding raw meat bones like chicken necks and backs to their dogs for years and they've never had a problem. All that being said, Paul still errs on the side of caution and grinds raw bones before feeding.
2. Will the bacteria in raw meat cause illness? A dog's digestive system is ideal for dealing with bacteria because it is short and acidic. Even the bacteria found in old buried bones don't prove problematic for most dogs.

Note: Your own digestive system is not as tolerant of bacteria as a dog's, so always be sure to wash your hands after touching uncooked meat.

If you want to feed your puppy a raw food diet, we suggest reading up on the subject in books such as *The Barf Diet: Raw Feeding for Dogs and Cats Using Evolutionary Principles* by Ian Billinghurst; *Raw Dog Food: Make It Easy for You and Your Dog* by Carina Beth Macdonald; and two books by Monica Segal, *K9 Kitchen, Your Dogs' Diet: The Truth Behind the Hype* and *Optimal Nutrition, Raw and Cooked Canine Diets: The Next Level.*

Feeding Schedule

When you adopt your puppy, ask the breeder or shelter how many meals he is currently getting and keep as close to that schedule as possible. Most puppies under four months old need to eat three or four times a day. As they get older, only two feedings will be necessary. Talk with your holistic vet about your puppy's specific needs.

Note: As you train your puppy, you will be providing lots of highly valued, high-quality treats throughout the day, so you'll need to adjust the amount you feed at mealtimes accordingly.

Switching to a New Diet

Always switch to any new diet gradually, allowing your puppy's digestive tract time to adjust, and monitor how he responds to it. At first, mix one part of the new food with ten parts of the old food, then gradually increase the amount of the new food over a period of ten days to two weeks until he is eating only the new diet.

Need for Fresh Water

Dogs require a source of fresh water at all times. If water is not available, dehydration can occur faster than most people realize, particularly in hot weather. Water is not only a vital source of fluids but it also contains essential minerals needed by the body. So keep your puppy's water bowl full of water and available at all times. Wash it daily so bacteria and mineral deposits don't build up. Also keep a bottle of water in your car when you're traveling and with you when you are out for a walk or a hike, especially if the weather is hot.

Chapter 9

Play

Play is one of the greatest elemental necessities for both dogs and humans. Our health, happiness, and evolution are linked to how much fun we have. Think of it: We, as human beings, love to play sports and games, tell jokes and laugh, and run around and act foolish. Dogs run, jump, roll in the grass, wrestle, and chase. Play provides the opportunity for human-canine communication. Play is a huge stress reducer for both you and your puppy. When your puppy is less stressed, he is less likely to develop health and behavioral problems. When you are less stressed, you are also healthier and happier. We all feel better, more relaxed, and more in harmony. Play rules!

What Is Play?

One of the definitions for the noun "play" in the *Random House College Dictionary* is: "fun, jest, or trifling, as opposed to earnest." The verb "to play" is defined as: "to do something in sport which is not to be taken seriously." These definitions offer a great insight into an aspect of your puppy's temperament. When dogs and puppies play with each other, they wrestle, chase, pounce on each other, and so on, yet they do not hurt each other. They are fighting "in jest," by going through many of the motions of fighting, but with a lower intensity and with what we could call a "lighter" quality. When your puppy chases a ball, or chews on a chew toy, he is hunting, chasing, and "eating prey." Playing is a great release that channels these impulses. But much of play also seems to serve no good purpose at all, aside from giving pleasure.

Figure 9-1

Doggy "tunnels" and other fun activities such as climbing on boxes help stimulate your puppy and keep him happy and healthy.

By providing structure in playing games with your puppy, you teach him appropriate ways to use his mouth, cooperative give and take, and self-control of his aggressive impulses. It is vital that he have playful interaction with you. Playing with other dogs and with chew toys, although important for your puppy, are not enough. Regular puppy-human interaction can make the difference between a wild, rambunctious dog who doesn't know his limits with humans, and a happy, well mannered, cooperative friend.

Play includes tricks and fun things to do like fetch ("take it" and "drop it"), hide-and-seek, jumping up to chase bubbles (nontoxic), and tug. Even the rare puppy who seems disinterested in play can be taught to love toys and playing games. One way to do this is to catch your puppy playing with something and encourage that behavior by joining in. If you see your puppy doing something that looks like a game, it is a game. Play whatever games your puppy offers.

The Rules of Play

The very first play session of the very first day is the time to start teaching her the rules of play:

- **Rule Number One:** No teeth on skin.
- **Rule Number Two:** Drop the toys or food when asked.
- **Rule Number Three:** Wait patiently for permission to take a toy or food in your mouth.
- **Rule Number Four:** Stop playing when asked.

We will give you easy, step-by-step instructions to teach these rules in the "take it" and "drop it" behaviors in Chapter 18. Through these four simple rules, your puppy will learn to refrain from grabbing things, including your hands, feet, and clothing, and to let go of things when asked.

Playing Tug

The question of playing tug of war with rope toys and other objects is a bit controversial among trainers. Some trainers think that playing tug with a dog teaches them the power of their mouth and, hence, increases the tendency to bite. However, there is no scientific evidence to suggest that playing tug with your puppy will turn him into Cujo or cause him to act more aggressively. In fact, if you teach your puppy to play tug within certain structured guidelines, the opposite is actually true. Puppies can learn to share objects with you rather than compete over them. They can learn that it is inappropriate to put their mouths on humans and that puppy teeth are only to be used on specific objects. (See "Mouthing and Nipping" in Chapter 20.)

Any toy your dog likes can be used as a tug toy. In addition to the classic tug rope, alternative tug toys are soft Frisbees, squeaky toys, and plush stuffed toys. However, be aware that these toys can present dangers. An eager puppy can chew and swallow the strings on a rope toy or choke on the "squeakies" or stuffing torn out of other toys. Therefore, we suggest that rope, plush, or squeaky toys be available only when you are supervising your puppy. When you want to play tug, bring the tug toy out; then put it away when you are not around.

As with any other game, in order for "tug" to be beneficial to your relationship with your puppy, you will follow the rules of play stated earlier. In other words, your puppy must drop the toy (i.e., stop tugging) when you ask him to, and he must wait for your permission to take the toy in his mouth (i.e., to start tugging). If tug is played incorrectly, that is, without a "take it and drop it" structure, your puppy soon realizes that he's faster than you and decides that keeping toys away from you can be very rewarding. This easily becomes the "chase the puppy around the house" game. Incorrect tugging can also inadvertently teach a puppy to be "grabby" with his mouth. This is not the same as aggression, but it is annoying at best and painful and dangerous at worst. The bottom line is that tug of war can be a blessing or a curse depending on how it is used.

When you are playing tug, your puppy's arousal level will be elevated. He might even growl during tug games. A "play growl" is higher pitched and less intense than a truly aggressive growl. You can judge the non-serious intent of this growl by seeing that, if you stop playing, your puppy will immediately stop growling and happily come to you with the toy, asking you to continue to "take the toy away." Your puppy will learn to control his excitement if you frequently interrupt the tugging and ask for the toy. So whenever your puppy gets too excited for your liking, stop playing, ask for the toy back, and wait for your puppy to settle down before playing again. Because he wants the game to continue, your puppy will soon learn to calm himself when he gets too excited. In this way, tug of war actually teaches your puppy how to more effectively control aggressive impulses.

Of course, every puppy is different in terms of how much a game of tug or fetch gets him "hyped up," and how long it takes him to calm down. In rare cases, an arousing play session, even if interrupted frequently, can lead to even more grabby, jumpy, and mouthy behavior. If you are having trouble with such a puppy, call a professional trainer.

A final warning about playing tug is to not jerk the toy harshly, which can injure your puppy. Steady pulling on both sides, like a family picnic tug of war, is the safest way to play. Don't allow yourself or your puppy to behave in any way that might cause either one of you to be injured.

How to Safely Play Tug
Tug is a great game as long as it is done correctly. Here are a few rules:

- Teach the puppy to "drop it." (See page 233 for the "drop it" rules.)
- Before releasing the tug object, always say "okay."
- When your puppy is holding an object in his mouth, do not lift him off the ground by holding onto the other end of that object.
- Avoid jerking the object back and forth.

Chapter 10

Socialization: Providing a Map to the Human World!

Life happens. Puppies bump their heads, step on bees, and get sick. People accidentally step on tails and drop loud, clattering pans on the kitchen floor. You can't protect your puppy from everything in life. He needs to learn to roll with the punches. Socialization is interaction with life and all it has to offer, and being able to adapt to its challenges. "It's all about surviving errors," as Dr. Karen Overall puts it.

When accidents happen, be a good actor. Help your puppy get through them using the same principles you've been using so far by staying in control. In an excited, upbeat voice, say, "Yay! I dropped the pot! Here's a piece of cheese!" Or, "Oh, hooray, I stepped on your tail—here's a piece of chicken!" Of course, you'll be dying inside for being such a klutz and you'll want to apologize and cuddle the poor guy. But do your best to suck it up and teach your puppy that life ain't no big deal. With repeated positive exposures to the same situation, he'll learn how to cope in a balanced way. (Obviously, if you really hurt your puppy, get aid immediately!)

Puppies need to explore. They need to meet people. The whole purpose of this chapter is to help your puppy become acclimated to the sights, sounds, and smells of the world in a safe way. But the trick is not to baby your puppy. You want to let your puppy say hello to people of all shapes, sizes, and mannerisms—as long as they don't overwhelm her. It's up to you to decide your puppy's

109

sensitivity level. What you don't want to do is introduce an emotionally vulnerable puppy to good ol' Uncle Bob. He's the guy in the family who thinks he knows everything about dogs and, as soon as he sees your puppy, roughly grabs her while yelling in a booming voice, "I've had dogs all my life. They love rasslin'. Come here, Fido."

Of the many goals you have for your puppy, put socialization at the top of your list. By "socialization" we mean doing your absolute best to get your puppy used to, tolerant of, and positively enjoying all of the people, animals, places, and situations that he will be experiencing in his life. We expect our puppies to easily accept being lifted on to the vet's table and poked with a needle. We expect them to be patient while groomers douse them with water and shampoo, buzz them with frightening electric clippers, and clip the nails on their sensitive paws. We expect them to greet new, strange dogs of all sizes and appearances as if they were long-time family members and not as intruders competing for food, space, and affection. We ask our puppies to be friendly to outsiders coming onto their turf—hairy bearded men with loud booming voices as well as running, jumping, shrieking children; people in strange uniforms carrying large threatening packages as well as strange wheeled creatures such as crying babies in strollers, kids on roller blades, cyclists, cars, and lawn mowers. The list goes on.

> Taking the time and effort to socialize your puppy early on will pay off in huge dividends as he gets older. Socialization increases the probability that your dog will be friendly, safe, and well tempered.

If you would like your puppy to be able to handle all of these experiences calmly and with aplomb, then it takes schooling. School starts as soon as you get your puppy and the first subject is socialization. Socializing your puppy is actually more important than teaching him behaviors like sit, down, stay, come when called, or walk nicely on the leash. Think of socialization as providing a map to a world that is alien to your puppy—the human world. This "map" will lead her to everything she wants in life—safety, food, affection, play, and security. Socialization can be easy and fun.

A Puppy's Developmental Stages

To better understand the importance of socialization, it helps to look at the developmental stages of a puppy's life. In the 1940s and 1950s, psychologists John Scott and John Fuller studied the physical and behavioral development of hundreds of puppies and dogs over a thirteen-year period. They identified three specific periods in a puppy's development. Please note that the ages during which each developmental stage occurs vary somewhat from puppy to puppy and that some of the stages overlap a bit.

The Neonatal Period—Birth to Twelve Days

The Neonatal Period starts at birth and lasts until the puppy is approximately twelve days old. In this first period of physical and behavioral development, the eyes and ears are shut and the sense of smell is still poorly developed, although the sense of taste is present. The effective inability to hear or see shuts newborn puppies off from the world outside the nest, and therefore keeps them relatively immune from psychological influence by environmental factors. Because of this early sensory isolation, the need for socialization is limited during the neonatal period. At this stage, touch is the most significant sense in terms of influencing future behavior so responsible breeders gently handle puppies in the litter for several minutes a day. Gentle lifting and handling tends to produce a puppy who is less emotionally reactive and more stable in later life, and who will better tolerate being held by humans (see Figure 10-1). If you are choosing a puppy from a breeder, it is important to ask the breeder if she has done this early handling.

Figure 10-1

During the first few weeks of life puppies should be gently handled for several minutes each day.

Most social behavior is centered around the mother during the neonatal period. The newborn puppy does not have the ability to crawl far from the mother or the nest and his most purposeful activity is directed toward nursing. At this age puppies respond particularly to cold and react immediately if they lose physical contact with their mother or littermates by emitting a high-pitched distress yelp. This alerts the mother that one of her puppies has moved away from her, allowing her to quickly retrieve him. In addition to nursing, the mother's nurturing also includes licking the puppy's anogenital region in order to stimulate the defecation process.

The Transition Period—Two to Three Weeks
Sometime between two and three weeks of age, a puppy transitions from a life centered solely around his mother and gradually

ventures into the big world outside the litter. The beginning of this period is marked by the opening of the eyes, which increases the puppy's ability to orient to the environment. The puppy starts clumsily walking, as opposed to crawling, but still doesn't venture very far from his mother. Although puppies still nurse at this stage, the first puppy teeth start poking through the gums by the end of the third week and they are able to start eating semisolid food. Some mothers will feed their puppies regurgitated food as part of the weaning process. During this stage, puppies are able to eliminate without being stimulated by the mother and start urinating and defecating outside the nest. This is a crucial pattern that can be exploited for potty training later on.

A puppy will also begin to play with his littermates during the transition period, marking an interest in social contact with others, in addition to the already-established relationship with his mother. This period ends with the opening of the puppy's ears, evidenced by the appearance of a "startle response" to loud sounds, such as a whistle or a hand clap. When he hears a loud sound, his ears will perk up and he will turn to the sound, perhaps with a flinch. A puppy will also start wagging his tail during this period, specifically in response to greeting people who solicit his attention. This is evidence of a willingness and eagerness to make positive emotional connections with us humans and marks an increase in the puppy's need for "contact comfort." An experiment that underscored this desire for contact gave puppies a choice between a wire dummy that dispensed milk or a cloth dummy that did not. Interestingly, the puppies consistently preferred the softer, more comforting cloth dummy to the milk-dispensing dummy.

Whereas the puppy was virtually oblivious to the world outside the mother and the nest in the neonatal period, by the end of the transition period she is equipped with brand new senses and is extremely sensitive to the environment. In general, at the beginning of the transition period, a puppy has difficulty learning that a particular sight (for example, a flashing light), a sound, or odor will predict the arrival of food. However, by the end of this stage the puppy's ability to make this kind of connection is essentially the same as an adult dog's. If, during this period, you flash a light just before you give the puppy food, the puppy will soon learn that the light predicts the arrival of food, and will wag his tail and hurry over to his bowl. If the mother is regurgitating food, puppies will learn that when the mother leaves the nest and returns, she might have something yummy for them. In anticipation, puppies will jump up to lick the mother's mouth. This jumping up to lick, incidentally, is likely the basis for the jumping up behavior that puppies exhibit toward humans later on, when we have taken the place of the mother in the puppy's new family. They are falling back on a behavior they learned during this transitional period which basically means, "take care of me."

The Socialization Period—Three to Sixteen Weeks

From the age of about three weeks to sixteen weeks, a puppy is like a sponge, absorbing all the experiences the world offers. This is the "critical socialization period" when your puppy gets her first impressions of which situations are "good," that is, safe and rewarding, and which are "bad," threatening, or painful. The information she gathers and processes during this period affects how she will react to certain sights, sounds, and sensations as an adult dog.

Let's say a puppy has repeated positive experiences with people coming over to his house on a daily basis. Guests give him tasty treats, play fun games with him, and refrain from doing anything frightening or too overwhelming. A puppy in this situation will be more likely to have lifelong positive associations with guests coming over and, as an adolescent and adult dog, will therefore be more likely to greet guests happily and in a friendly manner. But what if a puppy has a single bad experience with guests coming over to the house? Maybe they made loud noises and sudden movements toward him that frightened him. That puppy might greet future guests with fearful or aggressive behavior.

But by far the most common mistake in raising a puppy is that the puppy is given no experiences with guests coming over to the house. When leading busy lives, most people don't give much, if any, attention to inviting guests over for the sake of their puppy.

After all, he does great with the family. He's friendly, playful, and happy. Why would there be any problem with other people? To you, people are people, whether at home or away, whether family or guest. But your puppy experiences something else—your guests are not you. Your guests are different. If your puppy never, or only rarely, experiences unknown people entering his house, he will not have enough information about whether the situation is "good" or "bad." As an adult dog, he will not know how to react. And all too often when a dog doesn't know how to react to something, he depends on reactions that nature has preprogrammed for him—run away from it or bite it (or variations in between).

Socialization Beyond Sixteen Weeks

If your puppy is older than sixteen weeks and hasn't been properly socialized, don't give up. It is never too late! The socialization schedule below will help no matter how old your puppy is.

Note: Social skills need maintenance, just like any other skills. Imagine making friends in nursery school, playing and learning how to get along, and then having no contact with anyone outside your family for another fifteen years or so. You wouldn't be able to function very well. The same is true of your puppy. Socialization is an ongoing process.

The Socialization Process

There are five simple rules to socialization:

1. **Don't coddle your puppy.** Socialization is all about creating an environment where a puppy can gain confidence in himself and his abilities. Do not pamper your puppy as that can easily lead to neediness. The idea is to provide him with opportunities to do it things for himself, not to do something for him. Some puppies socialize to their new environment very quickly, while others need extra time and experiences to adjust. The socialization exercises listed below are to be used as a template. Always be ready to offer more challenging situations but keep in mind your puppy's sensitivity level.

2. **Make it positive**. Link socialization exercises with a happy, friendly attitude and, as much as possible, with food! Feed her treats at the vet; have the vet feed her treats; feed her treats when guests come over; have guests feed her treats; feed her treats when the mail carrier arrives. . . . You get the idea. Some people are concerned that constantly giving food treats means they are raising a dog who will always require treats or they won't listen. Don't worry about that. As you'll learn, it's easy to wean your puppy off food treats later on.

3. **Keep it short.** Shorter sessions keep things fresh, interesting, and exciting. They also lessen the possibility that your puppy will feel overwhelmed by the situation.

4. **Make it frequent.** Just as shorter sessions keep things fresh, frequent sessions build coping skills and go a long way toward strengthening the trust between you and your puppy. A good rule of thumb is to give your puppy three to five different socialization experiences every day.

5. **Keep it safe.** As you go through the week, you'll be exposing your puppy to more and more situations. Here are some safety considerations:

- Outdoor play sessions are held in fenced-in areas.
- Shade and water are always available.
- Indoor play areas don't have slippery floors.
- No electrical cords, lamps, vases, or other objects that could be knocked over.

Below is a sample plan of how you might organize a week's worth of socialization activities with your young puppy. You can, of course, substitute the suggested times with times that better fit your schedule. No matter what your schedule, put in the extra time and effort for you and your puppy's sake!

The Puppy's Daily Suggested Routine at the end of Chapter 5 shows you how you can fit socialization exercises into your schedule. As weeks go by, use the Additional Socialization Exercises on page 129 to continue to build your puppy's confidence in new situations.

Note: If at any point during these exercises your puppy shows signs of fearful or aggressive behavior, do less or stop the exercise entirely. By "do less" we mean lower the intensity of the experience by creating more distance between your puppy and the person, animal, or place, and by making sounds softer, movements slower, and touches lighter. If the fearful or aggressive behavior continues, end the session. This is especially important if your puppy is between eight and ten weeks old—the "fear imprint period"—when negative experiences tend to have a bigger impact on your puppy's development. If fearful or aggressive behavior continues to be a problem, consult a professional trainer or behaviorist as soon as possible.

Many of these exercises require that you take your puppy to a public place. If other dogs frequent the area, it's important that your puppy be protected by immunization. (See "Infectious Disease and Immunizations" in Chapter 15.) If your puppy is not yet fully immunized, take walks only in places that are reasonably safe and hygienic. In other words, don't walk your puppy in areas where you know there is a lot of dog poop. Even if you are uncertain about the infectious disease risk in a particular area, like a public park, you can still do the greeting exercises, but do so while holding the puppy in your arms.

Do not let fear of disease prevent you from doing this extremely important socialization work. Robert K. Anderson, DVM, has written an open letter to all veterinarians that is posted on the Association of Pet Dog Trainers Web site. He points out: "The risk of a dog dying because of infection with distemper or parvo disease is far less than the much higher risk of a dog dying (euthanasia) because of a behavior problem. . . ." Because it is deemed so important to start socialization early to take advantage of this special window of time in a puppy's life, Dr. Anderson suggests beginning at eight or nine weeks of age.

Note: In Chapter 15 we'll give more details on infectious disease and vaccinations.

Socialization Schedule for the First Week

Here's a basic outline or template of how various suggested socialization activities can fit into your puppy's daily routine, such as when you're feeding him, when friends come over, when you go for a walk, and so on. Choose the socialization activities that will realistically fit into your lifestyle. These are all things you will be doing anyway. Keep in mind that you want to vary the intensity of the experiences to fit your puppy's sensitivity level.

Day One

Meals: Begin with Hand Feeding: Each time you feed today, put your puppy's food in his dish and sit on the floor with the dish in your lap. Hand feed your puppy one bit of food at a time. If you are feeding your puppy wet food or a raw diet, the feeding process may become a little gooey, so you can use a spoon. Some people grind the wet food or raw food; if you do so, let it slightly harden in the freezer, and then cut it up and follow this same routine. Have other household members participate in the hand feeding. This will help your puppy acclimate to people being around the food bowl. As you go through the week, you'll see that this is a step-by-step process that promotes safety so your puppy will be less likely to try to protect his food by growling or biting if a child or another animal approaches. As with all the other experiences in this schedule, you will slowly progress, step by step, one day at a time, to different procedures. Eventually, he will learn that people aren't a threat to take food away; they are the source of all good things!

Introduce Your Friends: Have your friend toss your puppy a treat as soon as she comes in the door. Let your puppy decide for himself if he wants to approach your friend or not. If your puppy approaches your friend and seems happy and comfortable about it, as most puppies will, ask your friend to gently pet him while you give him treats. Then have your friend give him treats. If your puppy is thoroughly enjoying this, have your friend throw a ball or squeaky toy. When play is finished, give another treat. End the session on a high note.

Introducing the Mail Carrier: With your puppy on a leash by your side, go out to her potty spot. After eliminating, take her to the mailbox and stand about six feet away. When the mail carrier begins walking toward you, start giving your puppy a steady stream of treats. Continue doing this until the mail carrier leaves. It's much more likely that tomorrow your puppy will be pretty happy about the mail coming! However, if at any time your puppy seems apprehensive about the mail carrier with his strange uniform and big bulky bag, increase your distance from him. Postal workers are officially advised by the Postal Service to not pet or give treats to dogs on their routes, so please don't ask your carrier to do either of those things.

Go for a Walk: When other people approach, stop and give treats to your puppy until the person passes by. If someone stops and asks to pet your puppy, ask if he would be willing to give your puppy a treat first. After the petting, give another treat. Better yet, arrange for a friend to meet you somewhere on your walk and do this petting and treating routine with your friend.

Gentle Handling: Collar Hold: Sit on the floor with your puppy during relaxation time, before going to bed. You can watch television, or talk with family while doing these exercises. Gently slip your fingers under your puppy's collar and hold it, simultaneously giving a treat and then releasing the collar. Repeat this many times. You want your puppy to associate being held by the collar as a good thing, so that you can easily manage her in situations where you need control. Be gentle with the collar: no rough grabbing, jerking, or twisting. After each collar hold, let your puppy roam around for a minute in the room, then gently take hold of her collar again, simultaneously giving a treat, and then again releasing the collar. You are getting your puppy to look forward to your approach and hold: Not only does she get a treat for being held by the collar, she also gets her freedom again immediately after. It's a no-lose situation!

Day Two

Meals: Continue Hand Feeding: Today you will continue to hand feed your puppy from the bowl as you did yesterday.

Meeting Children: Go to a park where children are playing. Stand some distance away from the kids with your puppy on a leash. The children will be yelling and running. As your puppy watches, give him a steady stream of treats. If he seems comfortable, move a little closer to the children and continue the treats. You can continue to move closer and give treats, little by little, as long as your puppy does not cower, try to run away, hide behind you, tuck his tail, growl, and so on. If any of the children express an interest in petting your puppy, make sure you explain the rules: one at a time, without crowding around; pet under the chin, gently; and give a treat to the puppy immediately afterward. If at any time during these encounters with children your puppy shows any apprehension, move farther away with the puppy while talking happily and treating him. If he continues to show any fearful or aggressive behavior, end the session immediately. If your puppy is biting or showing extreme anxiety, contact a professional dog trainer who uses only positive methods and, in the meantime, keep everybody safe, including the puppy, by keeping your puppy away from kids.

If all goes well with the kids, keep it short and finish on a high note by going to another part of the park where you can play a quick, fun game with a toy. Be sure to keep your puppy on leash unless the area is fenced and dogs are allowed off leash. If you have children living in your home, do the same kinds of exercises with them and your friends, but do exercises with unfamiliar children as well, so that your puppy doesn't discriminate between your children and all other children. Kids and dogs together should always be supervised, no matter how confident you might feel about your puppy's and/or your child's behavior. Dogs and children can behave erratically and one bad incident can result in a hurt child or puppy, and perhaps a lifetime of continuing fearful or aggressive behavior toward children.

Introducing the Mail Carrier: How are things going? Is your puppy showing signs of friendliness and staying in position or is your puppy acting fearful? Depending on the answer to this question, continue to give the puppy treats. Once again, if your puppy is acting fearful, increase the distance from the mail carrier, as you continue to give treats.

Introducing More Strangers and Other Dogs: Walk to a park or area where you know other people walk their dogs. If you see someone else walking a dog, politely ask if his dog is friendly and if it's okay if your puppy says hello. Keep the leash loose as the two dogs interact—this might mean having to move around quite a bit as your squirmy puppy jumps and plays around the other dog. Many people feel apprehensive about having their dogs meet unfamiliar dogs, not knowing if they're safe. The problem is, if you restrain your puppy and he starts pulling to get to the other dog, he can get frustrated and even more excited. To him, it makes no sense being held back. Being restrained often communicates to your puppy that the other dog must be a threat. This can lead to what's known as leash aggression . . . your dog is fine off leash but aggressive on leash. So keep it loose! If you feel apprehensive at all about your dog meeting another dog, it's better to avoid saying hello. After a minute or two of greeting, give your puppy lots of praise and a treat and continue your walk. You will probably find that getting to meet another dog is a huge reward for your puppy in and of itself, so that you don't have to give him treats. Besides, you don't know if the other dog has any food aggression problems, so it's best to avoid involving treats anyway. If your puppy shows any fearful or aggressive behavior while meeting another dog, move away.

Many cities have off-leash dog parks, but they involve large risks for puppies under six months old. Some dog parks, in fact, have policies against allowing young puppies in (see the section on "Dog Parks" in Chapter 4). For off-leash play in a more controlled environment, make a play date and sign up for a puppy class! (See Day 4 and Additional Socialization Exercises.)

Gentle Handling: Lifting and Holding: Warm up with some collar holds, as you practiced last night. Now put your hand under your puppy's chest and lift him off the ground. Hold him to your chest for a split second (see Figure 10-2). If your puppy squirms, wait until he stops squirming before releasing, and immediately praise him and give him a treat. Normally we do not use physical force to hold a dog in position because positive training does not force a dog to submit. Rather, our goal is to teach a dog to willingly cooperate. Therefore, it is critical that you do this handling exercise correctly. Hold your puppy firmly but not tightly and release him the instant he is still. To make this even easier for your puppy, give him a treat when you release him. He will quickly learn to relax and actually enjoy being restrained. By teaching the puppy to relax when being held, he will better "roll with the punches" later in life. Take it slowly and don't push. This lifting exercise prepares your puppy for being lifted by others—such as children, the vet, or the groomer—who may or may not have good handling skills.

Figure 10-2

To get your puppy used to being held and restrained practice holding her firmly but gently until she relaxes. When you feel her muscles relax, say "okay" and give her a treat.

Day Three

Meals: Begin Feeding in the Bowl: Today, place your puppy's food dish on the floor in front of her and put one bit of food into the bowl. Wait for her to eat it before dropping another. Do this until the entire measured amount is finished.

Introducing More Friends: This time, ask your friend to knock or ring the doorbell. At the sound of the knock or bell, give your puppy a treat. Once your friend enters, repeat the routine from Day One.

Go for a Walk: Go to a place where a number of people are congregated. Keep your distance from the crowd and give your puppy a steady stream of treats. As your puppy gets more comfortable, gradually move closer and continue to give treats, until your puppy can be in the midst of a crowd without any discomfort. At any sign of apprehension from your puppy, however, move farther away again. Continue your walk and continue to treat when other people approach. Continue to look for friendly dogs to greet on leash.

Gentle Handling: Add Holding Paws: Warm up with a few collar holds, then give your puppy a treat. Gently hold and lift your puppy a few times, as you did yesterday, then give a treat. Now, lift a paw and gently squeeze it in your palm, simultaneously giving your puppy a treat. Repeat this with the other three paws, then start again with the first paw, until you have lifted and squeezed each paw several times. Always give a treat after handling each paw. If your puppy is struggling to pull free, or nipping at your hands while you do these paw exercises, try just touching the paws with your finger for an instant while the paw remains on the ground, then treating. Your goal is to start at a point where your puppy is comfortable enough to remain still. As your puppy grows relaxed about having her paws touched by a finger, without flinching or nipping, gently hold the paw in the tips of your fingers and give a treat. Gradually progress to lifting the paw, then to lifting the paw and squeezing it. Paws tend to be very sensitive, so don't worry if it takes you many days, or even weeks, of exercises to gradually get your puppy used to having her paws lifted and touched. In the meantime, you will have to refrain from actually clipping your puppy's nails. You may get to start clipping by the end of the week (see Day Seven, below) or you may have to wait a few weeks, depending on how quickly your puppy adjusts. But the lifetime payoff for your patience will be enormous—a dog who accepts nail clipping without struggling, hollering, or biting.

Remember, Don't Coddle Your Puppy

All socialization exercises should be introduced at an intensity that challenges but doesn't scare your puppy. You want a confident puppy; not a needy puppy. If your puppy is already frolicking through the adventures that are before him, skip the easy stuff and just have fun.

Day Four

Meals: Add Food to Bowl While Puppy Eats: Today, for each meal, put the bowl on the floor and drop a handful or spoonful of food into it. While he's eating, drop more food into the bowl. Do this five to ten times until he has finished eating his measured amount for this meal. Include all members of the household in this feeding process. On day three, you were putting food into an empty bowl and now you are putting food into the bowl while the puppy is eating. This helps your puppy acclimate to hands coming toward the bowl while he is eating.

More Socializing with Other Dogs: Have a play date. Invite a friend over who also has a puppy for an off-leash play session. (If you don't know anyone with a puppy, invite a friend who has a friendly adult dog who likes to play with other dogs.) You accomplish two socialization tasks at once here: creating positive associations and social skills with houseguests and other dogs. Once the puppies are off-leash and playing, don't be alarmed at the wrestling and mouthing—that's how puppies play. There will be a lot of back-and-forth interaction, with the puppies taking turns chasing each other, being on top when wrestling, making soft contact with their mouths, and so on. Take breaks every few minutes to allow the puppies to rest and to avoid getting them overly aroused. If one of the puppies bullies the other without letting the other "win," or if one of the puppies is constantly hiding and squealing without any attempt to initiate play, interrupt the play session. After a few minutes of cool down time, allow the puppies to play again. If the lopsided situation continues, then one of the puppies clearly is not having fun and the session should end.

Go for a Walk: Repeat the exercises you have been practicing all week meeting people, dogs, children, and so on.

Gentle Handling: Continue Lifts, Holds, and Paw Touches. Yesterday you gave him treats *while* he was being touched; now you will give him a treat *after* every exercise.

Day Five

Meals: Teaching Your Puppy to Leave His Food While Eating: Today, put one-half of your puppy's usual morning meal in her bowl and place it on the floor. While your puppy is eating, place an extra special treat like a piece of cheese or boiled or roasted chicken next to the puppy's bowl and say "leave it" or "drop it" as you do so. Wait for your puppy to take the treat and then repeat this process five to ten times until the she has finished all the food in her bowl.

More Socializing with People: To get your puppy used to strange appearances, put a hat and sunglasses on and give your puppy treats and play with her. After a few days of doing this, invite a friend over and ask him to wear a hat or sunglasses or invite a friend who has a beard. Unusual "additions" to a person's face can be frightening to a puppy who has never seen them before. Repeat the same process you did with other friends earlier in the week.

Go for a Walk: Meet lots of people, dogs, and kids. Give treats.

Gentle Handling: Adding Nail Clippers: Continue lifts, collar holds, and paw touches, following each exercise with a treat. Now lift your puppy's paw and touch it with her nail clippers, then give a treat. Repeat three to five times; make sure to touch all four paws.

Day Six

Meals: Taking Your Puppy's Food Away: Fill your puppy's bowl with a food that is of lesser value to him than his normal meal. An example would be to use a handful of kibble. Put the bowl down and let him eat. As he eats, pick his bowl up from the floor and drop an extra-tasty treat inside, such as chicken, turkey, hamburger, or cheese. Then put the bowl down again. Repeat this five to ten times. Congratulations! You have taught your puppy that being approached while he is eating and having his bowl taken away is one of the best things that could happen to him. No food guarding problems here—the puppy learns that when someone takes his food away, it is replaced by something even better.

Go to the Vet's For Fun!: Who says a visit to the vet's office needs to be all poking, prodding, and sticking with needles? Drive to the vet's, sit down in the waiting room, feed your puppy treats, and pet and play with him. Ask the receptionist if she would be willing to give your puppy a treat. You want a visit to the vet's office to be viewed as a positive, fun experience so that your puppy won't fear the place as so many do.

Go for a Walk: Meet lots of people, dogs, and kids. Give treats.

Gentle Handling: More Touches with Nail Clippers: Gently lift your puppy a few times, hold his collar lightly, give his paws a few light squeezes, then give a treat. Touch a nail with the nail clippers but do not clip the nail yet. Repeat this for each one of his nails on each of his paws.

Day Seven

Meals: Continue to Take Your Puppy's Food Away: Now you will progress to an intermittent schedule by occasionally picking up your puppy's bowl while she is eating, dropping in an extra-valuable treat, such as chicken, turkey, hamburger, or cheese. Then place her bowl back on the floor. Incorporate this routine of occasionally picking up the food bowl and putting a special treat into it once or twice a week for the rest of your dog's life.

Introduce More People: Invite several guests over your house, say for Sunday brunch. Have everyone give treats and play with the new puppy.

Gentle Handling: Adding Clipping of the Nails: Warm up by lifting each of your puppy's paws and touching each nail with the nail clipper, but don't clip yet. Give your puppy a treat after touching each nail with the clipper. If your puppy is completely relaxed about this procedure and does not pull her paw away, struggle, or chew on your hands or the clippers, you can try actually doing some clipping. Are you ready? A dog's nails (like ours) are very sensitive. If you clip the nail too short you can cut the vein or nerve and cause bleeding, as well as a lot of pain. One bad experience can turn your dog off to nail clipping for a long time. Add to this the fact that puppy nails are smaller and therefore the vein and nerve are even closer to the nail tip than in an adult dog. So play it safe! When you clip tonight, clip only the tiniest, most miniscule piece of nail off the tip. Every time you clip a little piece off one of your puppy's nails, make a very big deal by praising super-enthusiastically as you give a treat.

As the weeks go by and you feel more comfortable about nail clipping, you will be able to take a little more off the tip of the nail. Always exercise caution. For dogs with clear nails the task is easier, since you can see where the pink vein begins. Puppies with black nails present more of a challenge. Clip just enough so that the tips of the nails do not scrape along the floor when your puppy walks. If you have any doubts as to how short to clip, you might ask a professional groomer to demonstrate it to you. Groomers are very confident and quick when they clip nails. The puppy picks up on the confidence level and this helps to relax him. If you are hesitant and unsure, your puppy will pick up on that too. But before going to the groomer, be sure that your puppy is ready by doing all the preparation work to relax her.

You did it! You did the best thing you could have ever done for your puppy by completing a week's worth of socialization exercises. You helped her start to assimilate to the world she is going to live in for many years to come. You took a huge step in the direction of preventing debilitating fearful and aggressive behavior. Your work is not over yet, though. As the weeks and months go by, continue to practice the exercises you practiced this week. In addition, introduce new people, places, and situations to your puppy by replacing some of the items in the table above with items from the list below. The principles remain the same: keep it positive (friendly voice and highly valued food treat), keep it short, make it frequent, and keep it safe. Progress slowly, in small steps. If your puppy ever balks at where you're going, change the way she feels about it by playing "find it" (see Chapter 19). If this doesn't work, it's okay to gently pull but never jerk your puppy. If necessary, you can pick your puppy up.

Additional Socialization Exercises

We are going to get you started with each of the additional socialization exercises below and then you can progress at your own rate. Just keep in mind that it is not necessary or advisable to try to get your puppy used to a new situation in one session, especially if it is something she is nervous about. On the other hand, some puppies are so fearless that they have no problems with any of these situations.

Introducing the car: If your puppy already likes riding in the car, as most puppies do, you can eliminate this exercise. If your puppy has never been in a car or is uncomfortable with it, start by gently lifting her and placing her on the seat and giving her a treat. Don't close the car door or start the engine. Play a short game with a favorite toy and give her treats as you play. Then lift her out of the car and start over. Repeat this routine three times and do two or three sessions a day as it fits your schedule. After several sessions, if your puppy seems relaxed, you're ready to start the engine. Place her in the car, give her some treats, play with her, but don't go anywhere. Just keep the engine going for a few minutes while you happily talk to your puppy while feeding her treats inside the stationary car. Again, when your puppy is relaxed while the engine is running, it's time to start moving. At this point, most puppies will be ready to go for a ride. If your puppy is uncomfortable when the car starts moving, make the trip short—like down the driveway and back (really!) or to the corner and back. Gradually add more and more distance to your trips. Note: For extremely sensitive puppies, there are some wonderful herbal products on the market that will settle your puppy's stomach. If your puppy is extremely sensitive and won't tolerate any car riding, call a professional trainer to assist you in this process.

Go to puppy class: One of the best preparations you can make for your puppy's smooth social adjustment is to enroll him in a puppy kindergarten class. A puppy class provides unique socialization opportunities with novel people and dogs, since everyone is there for the same purpose. Since your puppy loves riding in the car now, the ride to class is a great first opportunity to take a little bit of a longer trip. The reward to your puppy for riding in the car today is that he gets out and has an hour of fun, learning, treats, and playing with other puppies. With all the treats he got in class, your puppy can probably skip the midday meal, but don't forget to visit the potty spot when you arrive home.

Walking on slippery surfaces: Lay down a trail of treats across the floor, à la Hansel and Gretel, by placing a trail of small treats, spaced closely together, leading to the slippery surface. Give lots of praise as he takes each step, eats a treat, and advances ever closer to the scary surface. If your puppy approaches the slippery area and then backs up again, that's okay—just place another row of treats leading to it. If you don't push or force him in any way, in subsequent sessions, he will gain confidence and start to approach more closely. When he comes right up to the threshold of the slippery area without any hesitation, extend the trail of treats onto the slippery area itself. Another suggestion is to put small rubber-backed or non-skid rugs close enough together across the slippery floor so that your puppy doesn't have to have four paws on the slippery surface at once. Use the same Hansel and Gretel treat placement from one rug to another. Over time, gradually extend the space between the rugs until your puppy gains confidence and is eventually able to walk across the entire surface.

Going up and down stairs: Start with one step from the top (going up stairs) and one step from the bottom (going down stairs). Treat reward each step your puppy takes. Note: Only practice on carpeted or non-skid surfaces!

Visiting the groomer's (see "Go to the Vet's," above): Visit the groomer's shop without actually leaving your puppy there for grooming. Talk happily, treat, pet, and play in the waiting area. Ask the groomer if she would be willing to give your puppy a treat. Then leave. On a return trip, see if the groomer would be willing to put your puppy on the table without actually grooming her. Ask the groomer to give her treats, show her some of the grooming tools, and perhaps touch her with some of them, give her more treats, and then end the session.

Having ears cleaned (see also "Gentle Handling"): Start by touching the ears lightly and treating on each touch. Progress to holding the ears for longer periods of time, flapping them back, and so on.

Progress from gently handling the ears to doing it while a cotton ball is in your other hand and a bottle of ear cleaner is open on the floor in front of you. Give a treat, as always, and repeat many times. Now put some cleaning liquid on the cotton ball itself, while you handle an ear with the other hand. Treat and repeat.

Once your puppy is comfortable having his ears handled, as well as with the sights and smells of ear cleaning, touch his ears with a wet cotton ball and then give him a treat. Gradually progress to longer periods of ear cleaning, always giving a treat when you finish.

Having lips lifted and teeth inspected (see also "Gentle Handling"): Start by touching your puppy's muzzle lightly with the fingertips and treating. Progress to placing two, then three, then four fingers on the muzzle, treating every time. Finally, progress to laying your palm on the top of your puppy's nose, and draping your fingers on one side of the muzzle while your thumb is on the other side. Jackpot by giving several treats, one after the other. Progress to lifting your puppy's lips with your fingertips for one second, then treat. Lift the lips for two seconds, then five, then ten, and so on.

The rustling of a plastic bag: Put bag on the floor with treats on it. Pick up the bag and give a treat. Next, rustle the bag a little and then give another treat, and so on.

Passing cars: Start as far back from the street as you can, with your puppy on leash at your side. As soon as you spot an approaching car, 100 feet away or more, start giving your puppy a steady stream of treats until the car has passed. Progress gradually to moving on to the sidewalk, but never closer than three feet away from the curb. Then progress to delaying the treats until the approaching car is fifty feet away, then twenty-five feet away, then ten feet away. Eventually you will be able to reduce the reward down to a single treat, just as the car is passing you. If your puppy looks at you when the car passes, jackpot!

Larger crowds of people: Follow the same procedure as with small crowds (see "Go for a Walk" on Day Three of the socialization schedule), gradually increasing the number of people to whom you expose your puppy at one time.

Elderly people and people walking with canes: Some dogs react fearfully to people who do not walk in the same way as the majority of people with whom they come in contact. If you encounter someone walking slowly, irregularly, or with the aid of a cane or walker, try to keep your distance at first while happy talking and treating. If your puppy seems comfortable, gradually decrease the distance while you continue to happy talk and treat.

Vacuum Cleaners and Other Moving, Noisy Objects

The following, more in-depth protocol should be used with vacuum cleaners, lawn mowers, baby strollers, wheelchairs, people on crutches, and any other strange objects that make noise or move strangely. Some puppies don't have any problems with these distractions, in which case you can ignore this entire process. Always check for your puppy's comfort level and reactions.

Level One

Step One: When the puppy is not in the room, lay out treats in Hansel and Gretel fashion leading up to the vacuum, which is turned off. Bring the puppy in and let her explore. If the puppy goes right up to the vacuum, eating all the treats as she goes, progress to the next step. If your puppy seems hesitant, continue laying out the treats for a few days. Hesitant puppies normally stay outside the critical distance of six feet from the object they are afraid of.

Step Two: Touch the vacuum and simultaneously treat your puppy. Repeat five to ten times. Repeat several sessions as necessary until your puppy seems relaxed.

Step Three: Move the vacuum perpendicular to your puppy, simultaneously throwing her a treat. You can also have a friend stick treats in your puppy's mouth as you move the vacuum. If your puppy seems okay, ask her to sit (or lie down). Say stay and continue with the previous step of moving the vacuum and simultaneously treating. Repeat five to ten times, then add more movement, and so on.

Step Four: "Look for the Look." Ask your puppy to sit (or lie down) and stay. Move the vacuum but do not treat your puppy. Wait. Your puppy will look away from the vacuum and look at you. Click, praise, and jackpot. Your puppy has now made the association that the vacuum is associated with treats.

Level Two

At this level, you will be adding a second challenge by turning the vacuum on. Stand ten feet from the vacuum with the puppy by your side. Ask your puppy to sit (or lie down) and stay. Have a friend quickly turn the vacuum on and off. Treat your puppy as the noise occurs. Repeat five to ten times. Over several sessions, gradually increase the time the vacuum is on to one minute.

Level Three

Step One: At this level, you will be adding a third challenge by combining the movement of the vacuum with the sound of the vacuum. Stand ten feet from the vacuum with the puppy by your side. Ask your puppy to sit (or lie down) and stay. Have your friend turn the vacuum on and move it perpendicular to your puppy. Treat your puppy *as the vacuum is moved.* Repeat five to ten times.

Step Two: "Look for the Look." Ask your puppy to sit (or lie down) and stay.

Turn the vacuum on and have your friend move it perpendicular from your puppy but do not treat her. Wait. Your puppy will look away from the vacuum and look at you. Praise and jackpot her. Your puppy has now made the association that the moving vacuum in an "on" position is associated with treats.

Level Four

Decrease the distance from the vacuum to your puppy a foot at a time, always returning to Level One each time.

To review, always begin at a distance your puppy is comfortable with (six to ten feet):

1. Form a positive association with the object standing still.
2. Form a positive association with the object moving.
3. Ask your puppy to sit (or lie down) and treat while the object is moving.
4. Ask puppy to sit (or lie down), move the object, and wait for puppy to turn away from the object and look at you.
5. Repeat entire process while the object is turned on.
6. Combine movement with sound.
7. Gradually decrease distance between the object and the puppy.

Chapter 11

Quiet Time

Light, breath, water, and food are necessities for a healthy life . . . for most of us mortals anyway. Quiet time, in the form of relaxation, is equal in importance to these necessities because without it, there can be no health, no creativity, no love. Without proper rest and relaxation, the mind cannot concentrate, the body cannot function, and all higher forms of creativity and thought are cauterized. All that is left is an instinct to survive. Rest comprises two components: sleep—which we'll cover in another chapter—and relaxation.

A puppy's reactions to stress are, in part, determined by the sensitivity of his sympathetic nervous system. Physiological responses to stress include increased respiration, muscle tension, and pulse rate, as well as interference with glandular functioning. As a result, without the opportunity to get away from it all every once in a while, the puppy begins to shut down. When that happens, her willingness to cooperate with us is replaced with a cranky rebelliousness, often leading to aggressive and destructive behavior.

Relaxation is rooted in the ability to remove oneself from an environment that sometimes assaults the senses. From a metaphysical point of view, it is vital to reconnect with the source from which all energy arises—a state of physical, mental, and emotional well-being and quiet. Everything an animal does with any degree of efficiency is rooted in the replenishment that relaxation provides.

Puppies need a place where they can go to be out of the spotlight. Sometimes they let us know when they need some alone time. Terry shares the following story about his dog Magoo. When Terry adopted him, Magoo was extremely needy, following Terry from room to room, suffering whenever separated from him, and sleeping beside Terry's bed every night. These are classic symptoms of separation anxiety. Then something strange happened. A few months into Magoo's life at home, he decided one night to sleep in another room. At first Terry was worried by this uncharacteristic behavior, but Magoo showed no signs of physical illness and there were no changes in the environment or the daily routine. So what accounted for Magoo's newfound independence? He had settled in and become familiar with his environment. Magoo gradually learned that he no longer had to remain in survival mode, constantly on the lookout for threats to his life. And this allowed something else to manifest. For the first time in who knows how long, Magoo was learning to relax.

When called into the bedroom at night, Magoo would promptly respond. He'd stay a while as Terry petted him, but he then soon wandered back to the living room to sleep. Terry let go of trying to interpret Magoo's behavior as somehow pathological and realized what was going on. Just like humans, a dog sometimes just needs some quiet time on his own.

Magoo still loves the company of his human family, as do the vast majority of dogs but, again, just like other dogs, he also needs occasional time off. This is especially true during the holiday season when relatives visit and dogs are showered with extra attention, including overenthusiastic petting by children. The constant attention and activity of kids can be an overload for any puppy or dog.

If you have prepared your puppy for his kennel, you have already established a place where he can be away from others and feel happy and secure. You can also use a blanket, rug, or doggy bed as a safe haven. Simply teach your puppy to "go to his spot" (see page 241) and then place it in an out-of-the-way location when guests arrive. This could be under a table, in the corner of a room, or on a stair landing.

As we said before, quiet time allows a puppy to physically, mentally, and emotionally relax. In addition to providing the space and time for your puppy to go off on his own, you can also facilitate a relaxation response in a number of ways, including the following:

Your Energy Level

If you are stressed out, your puppy will pick up on that stress. In Chapter 6, you learned a simple breathing exercise that will help you relax. This, in turn, will enhance your puppy's ability to relax.

Calming Music

Just as music can calm and relax us humans, there is evidence that certain types of music can relax a puppy or dog's nervous system. If your puppy is overly sensitive, you might want to leave music playing while you are away. Select classical music that is calming rather than overly dramatic. Other choices include any of the albums by Dr. Steven Halpern, a pioneer in music that nurtures body, mind, and spirit (*www.innerpeacemusic.com*).

Tellington TTouch

Developed by internationally recognized animal expert, Linda Tellington-Jones, TTouch is a method of gentle, hands-on body work done with the intent of activating cellular intelligence to help your puppy "be all she can be." With five minutes a day of TTouch, you can help shape your puppy's personality and behavior, deepen the understanding and bond between you and other family members and your puppy, and enhance her health and well-being. Perhaps one of the greatest benefits is the enhancement of a puppy's willingness and ability to learn, making training easier, more fun, and faster.

TTouch is comprised of a collection of circular movements of the fingers, as well as lifts on the skin that release tension, promote relaxation, and teach a puppy to learn how to learn. You can begin with the "Lying Leopard TTouch." With slightly curved fingers, place your hand on your puppy's shoulder. Using the pads of your fingers, lightly make contact with the skin and gently push it in a circular direction, going around in a circle one and a quarter times. Then slide your fingers an inch away, and make another circle. Be sure to move your puppy's skin rather than simply sliding your fingers over her fur. Make the lightest possible circles and connected slides, covering every inch of the body from head to toe.

TTouch can also assist with the discomfort of teething and help prevent unwanted chewing. This is done by making gentle TTouches around the puppy's lips and gums. The effects of TTouch are cumulative, so practice five minutes of Lying Leopard TTouch before you teach a basic lesson, at the beginning of a puppy class to enhance attention, or at bedtime. You can do TTouch yourself or learn from a certified TTouch practitioner. To see a video clip of the Lying Leopard TTouch, or for more information, go to *www.TTouch.com*.

Massage Therapy

Massage has many therapeutic benefits and most dogs and puppies enjoy the experience, becoming relaxed and quiet. A puppy is used to the gentle licks of his mother's tongue. You can help him relax by giving him tender, loving strokes. Over time, your puppy will teach you just where he most loves being stroked. Massage therapy has the added benefit of helping to socialize your puppy to handling. You don't have to be trained in massage—just be fairly gentle and avoid any deep muscle massage. If you want to read more on massage for companion animals, we recommend Dr. Michael W. Fox's excellent books, *The Healing Touch for Dogs: The Proven Massage Program for Dogs,* and *The Healing Touch: The Proven Massage Program for Cats and Dogs.*

The Powers of Flowers

In the 1930s, British bacteriologist and homeopathic physician Dr. Edward Bach believed that a healthy state of mind is the key to maintaining good health. He held that illness was caused by emotional imbalance and sought a new, natural healing method. To deal with the causes, he turned to nature, specifically flowers.

Dr. Bach identified thirty-eight "essences," called Bach Flower remedies, which are used for emotional and, hence, physical healing.

Rescue Remedy, a combination of five flower essences—impatiens, clematis, rock rose, cherry plum, and Star of Bethlehem—is the product most commonly used for dogs (and people!). This combination is said to ease stress and anxiety, allowing the body to relax. You can also select from the thirty-eight individual remedies for specific issues, such as agrimony for restlessness, clematis for inattention, or rock rose for panic. Bach Flower remedies are available in most health food stores and homeopathic pharmacies. For more information, go to *www.bachflower.com*.

Aromatherapy—Feeling Well with Smell

Aromatic oils have been used for therapeutic purposes dating back to ancient Egypt and the Far East. Until recently, scents from flowers, fruits, and other plants were used mainly in perfumes and bath oils; however, the popularity of essential oils for healing is once again expanding. Aromatherapy incorporates the use of essential oils through either inhalation or absorption through the skin.

Essential oils work with the body to promote healing by stimulating and supporting the body's own healing abilities. They have many properties; some are antiseptic or bactericidal and others act like antibiotics and antivirals. When the essential oil is inhaled through the lungs, the fumes cross over into the bloodstream and are carried throughout the body. They are used for myriad health problems, including inflammation, dermatitis, and cuts and burns, and also to improve appetite and relieve pain.

A number of essential oils are also used therapeutically for relaxation, including:

- Chamomile for depression, especially related to separation anxiety
- Geranium or patchouli to quiet and calm the nervous system

- ⊶ Hops to calm nervous tension
- ⊶ Jasmine or rosemary for depression or exhaustion
- ⊶ Lavender for relaxation
- ⊶ Sandalwood for depression, tension, and stress
- ⊶ Ylang-Ylang for nervous tension, stress, or anger and frustration

Essential oils can be purchased at most health food stores. They come in dropper bottles and can be inhaled or used with direct application such as a compress or a poultice. They are extremely potent so handle carefully. The quality of essential oils varies considerably so be sure to use the highest quality to decrease the possibility of contaminates and increase the medicinal results. Because essential oils evaporate when exposed to air, you can be sure that the oil you are using is of good quality by putting a drop on a piece of paper. If it is a high-quality oil, it should evaporate, leaving no oily residue.

How to Use Essential Oils

Essential oils are highly concentrated and should be used sparingly. When your dog is resting or sleeping, put ten drops of the oil in a cup of hot water and place it near his head. If you have a way to keep the cup warm, such as a coffee warmer, do so for about a half hour. Another option is to purchase an aroma pot that is warmed by the heat of a candle.

Chapter 12

Exercise

A balanced exercise program keeps your puppy healthy. Too much exercise can cause pain or injury. Too little exercise weakens the immune system and often leads to obesity. Your puppy needs exercise daily for his physical, emotional, and behavioral health. Incidentally, when you exercise your puppy, you will most likely be obliged to improve your own exercise regimen. So you and Sparky can start feeling better, learning better, and communicating better!

Scientific studies have shown that exercise can help puppies cope with stress. It increases stress-reducing neurochemicals like endorphins and serotonin, which make your puppy feel good. Some evidence even suggests that regular vigorous exercise can exert the same degree of influence on a dog's behavior as some tricyclic antidepressants, a type of medication commonly used by veterinarians and behaviorists to combat fearful and aggressive behavior.

The Right Amount of Exercise
A bare minimum of exercise for any puppy should be two sessions of twenty to thirty minutes per day, although many puppies will require more than that. Below you will see some suggestions and guidelines for adapting physical exercise to your puppy's individual needs.

Exercise should always be enjoyable. If your puppy seems exhausted, hurt, or unwilling to exercise more, don't push him. If you are exercising in warm weather, or live in a generally warm climate, be particularly careful about overexerting your puppy. Dogs are much more sensitive to heat than humans and are more susceptible to heat stroke any time the temperature rises above seventy degrees. It is best to exercise in early morning or in the evening, when the sun is low in the sky and the temperature is cooler. Always have lots of fresh, cool water on hand. On hot days, carry a portable sports bottle of water with you, even if you are only going for a walk. A cloth Frisbee can double as a water dish, giving you a convenient way to cool your puppy off after a play session. Finally, avoid walking on hot pavement, particularly blacktop, in the middle of a hot day. A puppy's sensitive paws can easily burn and blister. We'll give you a more detailed list of cautions relating to sunburn, blistered paws, and heatstroke in Chapter 15.

Energy Levels

To a certain extent, breed differences will determine how much exercise your puppy will need. Field dogs, such as retrievers and spaniels; herding dogs, such as Border collies; and terriers are high-energy breeds and tend to need more exercise to keep them healthy. Guard dogs, such as German Shepherds; hounds, such as beagles; fighting breeds, such as boxers and bull terriers; and working dogs, such as huskies, tend to need a moderate amount of exercise. Toy breeds, giant breeds, and other non-sporting breeds tend to need less exercise than the others. But every dog is an individual and your puppy may very well differ from the breed "type." A restless and hyperactive puppy probably needs more exercise, while a fatigued or lethargic one probably needs less. Ask your veterinarian about any specific exercise limitations or needs your puppy may have.

Age Appropriate Exercise Programs

There are four basic types of exercise: aerobic, strength building, stretching, and balancing. A good exercise regimen combines all of these types in a balanced way.

Age Two to Three Months

Start your puppy's exercise program when he is about two months old. Do the majority of your exercise on soft earth and grassy surfaces. Short, five-minute walks on hard pavement surface are okay, but no long jogs or mile-long treks yet. Yards and parks are best at this stage—but not off-leash dog parks. Carry your puppy in any area where you know a lot of dogs walk, congregate, or poop and pee to protect him from diseases like parvovirus.

Note: Many puppies are hesitant to leave their immediate or familiar surroundings until they reach four to five months of age. There are certainly exceptions, however. If you are walking your puppy on a leash and she balks, you can pick her up, walk a few paces outside her comfort zone, and then put her back down. She will then race back to your yard.

Exercise Suggestions

- Start your exercise with a warm-up walk. If you are in an enclosed yard, this can consist of encouraging your puppy to follow you, off leash, as you move around. This will also help lay the foundation for training exercises like come when called and heel. If you are not in an enclosed space, use a leash.

- Gently coax your puppy up a short flight of stairs, like an outdoor stoop, using treats and gentle encouragement. Hold a treat above the first step, or actually place the treat on the step, so that your puppy has to step up on the step with her front paws in order to get the treat. Then see if you can coax her to put her front paws on the next step up while her back paws come up on the first step. In this way, lure your puppy up one step at a time, rewarding each step she takes. Try going up and down the flight of steps a couple of times, but don't overwhelm her, since steps can be pretty scary for a puppy at this age.

- Play a five-minute game of ball, tossing the ball only so far as she is interested in chasing it. Encourage her to run back with the ball each time by patting the ground in front of you, making kissy sounds, using a high-pitched voice, and running in the opposite direction to get her to follow you. If she is still not bringing the ball back, throw the ball a shorter distance, even if it is as little as a foot away. You can also try holding an identical ball in front of you, so that she runs back to you to get the new ball.

For stretching work, give your puppy a five-minute massage. Here are just a few suggestions:

- Using your fingers and the flat of your hand, give long, deep strokes with steady, light-to-moderate pressure beginning at the neck and going all the way down your puppy's back, following the line of the spine.
- Using a gentle circular motion with fingers, apply light to moderate pressure along the back of the neck, between the shoulder blades, along the front and sides of the rib cage, in the "armpits," in the abdomen, and at the top of the hip joints.
- Take one of your puppy's paws in the palm of your hand with your thumb on top. Use your thumb to gently massage in small circles, working all the way up the leg. Repeat this for each leg.
- Gently take the base of one of your puppy's ears with your thumb on the outside of the ear and your forefinger on the inside and, with a little pressure, but no pain, slowly slide your fingers to the top of the ear. You can repeat this a few times for each ear—it frequently has a very calming effect.

For more massage techniques, we recommend *The Tellington TTouch* by Linda Tellington-Jones, *The Healing Touch for Dogs: The Proven Massage Program for Dogs*, or *The Healing Touch: The Proven Massage Program for Cats and Dogs* by Michael W. Fox; and *Four Paws Five Directions* by Cheryl Schwartz, DVM.

Massage is also excellent for acclimating your puppy to being handled by humans and can be done in conjunction with the socialization exercises outlined in Chapter 10. If, at any time, your puppy shows resentment about this handling by biting at your hands and snarling, do less and systematically pair your touch with food treats.

> When massaging your puppy, be gentle. If your puppy is showing discomfort or trying to move away, you may be massaging too deeply.

Age Three Months to Four Months

When your puppy is between three and four months of age, you can take longer walks (including on pavement), and your puppy's immunity should be strong enough that you don't need to carry him anywhere. You might also try some light jogging for short distances. Massage your puppy after vigorous exercise.

Age Four Months and Up

By four months of age your puppy should be ready for longer walks, light running for short distances, and an introduction to swimming and the Frisbee. Build his stamina and strength by increasing the distance and duration of these exercises in small steps.

Exercise Suggestions

❧ "Obstacle courses" provide wonderful opportunities so your puppy can run and jump and learn good balance. Start by asking for jumps over or onto low barriers (six inches high) like a retaining wall. Coax your puppy with lots of enthusiastic talk and holding a treat above the wall. Reward with the treat when your puppy jumps. Soon the fun of jumping will be rewarding in itself. Caution: A puppy's joints and muscles are still developing. Avoid jumps from any height that would cause his bones to jar when he lands. A good rule of thumb is that jumps should be no higher than six inches for small puppies and twelve to eighteen inches for larger puppies.

☞ Create a "hurdle course," using a wooden stepladder, laid on its side. Your puppy will have to step over each rung of the ladder as he walks from one end to the other. Encourage and reward your puppy with enthusiastic praise and treats.

☞ Use outdoor football bleachers for balance work. Terry's dog, Magoo, jumps on to the lowest bench in the bleachers and walks along the narrow length of it while Terry walks beside. Then Terry and Magoo gradually work their way up the bleachers, going to progressively higher benches. Start out by coaxing your puppy up with treats and praise. If your puppy is unable to climb the bleachers, you can pick him up and place him on them so he still gets the balance work. Always hold the puppy's leash for safety. (Note: Some smaller breeds with short legs, such as pugs, may never be able to climb bleachers.)

Swimming

Swimming is a particularly good exercise, since it combines aerobics with strength building. Never force a puppy into water. Even the so-called water breeds, whose ancestors were bred to work in the water, such as Portuguese water dogs, Newfoundlands, poodles, and spaniels, sometimes need a little time to adjust to the water. Paul's first dog, Tara, was a golden retriever who refused to go in the water until she was nine months old. Then you couldn't keep her out. To introduce your puppy to the water you can set up a small plastic kiddy pool to practice in your backyard. Fill the pool with two inches of water and place a large rock in the center with some treats on the top. If your puppy refuses to go into it, start with a dry pool. Every week, add another inch of water until the water is up to the puppy's body. For backyard pools, it's essential to never leave your puppy unsupervised.

Emergency Pool Training

Many puppies have been known to drown when they fall into a pool, unable to escape. You can avoid such an emergency by teaching your puppy the location of the steps to the pool. To do this, put a highly visible and attention-grabbing object by the steps. It might be a large colorful flowering plant, a twelve- to eighteen-inch-high American flag, or a blinking safety light. This visual clue will help orient the puppy to the location of the steps so that if she happens to fall in, she will easily find her way to safety.

To teach your puppy to find the steps, have one person pick up the puppy and walk into the pool, supporting the puppy under his chest. Turn and face the steps and have another person outside of the pool, at the top of the stairs, with treats in hand. Gently lower the puppy into the water as the person who is outside the pool encourages her to come. When the puppy reaches the stairs and climbs out, enthusiastically praise and jackpot the puppy with many treats. Repeat three to five times. If your puppy shows signs of distress or hysteria, do not, under any circumstances, carry her back into the water. Call a professional trainer.

Many puppies will not go in backyard pools but will play at lakes or in the ocean. The reason for this is that there is a gradual slope leading into the water, whereas with swimming pools, the puppy is forced to step off into the unknown. One suggestion is to get a swimming pool ramp that mimics the slope of the beach. To encourage your puppy to go into the lake or the ocean, you can throw one of her favorite toys into the water so she'll chase it. Many puppies are also encouraged to go into the water when they see other dogs already in it. Finally, you can stand in the water and have your puppy take treats from your hand while she is standing on the beach or in shallow waves.

Cautions Around the Pool
- 🦴 Never leave a puppy unsupervised around the pool. For safety, put the puppy in an exercise pen in the shade with plenty of water in case you fall asleep on your lounge.
- 🦴 Practice the Emergency Pool Training protocol.
- 🦴 Never force a puppy who is afraid of water into the pool.

Chapter 13

Employment: Giving Your Puppy a Job to Do

"The dog ate my homework." That may be a top excuse students give to teachers but sometimes it's actually true. If you don't provide your puppy with her own "work," in the form of interesting and rewarding tasks that she can do on her own, she will find her own tasks to do. And those tasks may include destroying your work. In other words, if you don't give your dog a job to do, she will become self-employed. In the wild, a puppy has to spend the first year and a half learning how to hunt for food, protect herself from predators and the elements, find mating partners, and provide for offspring. These tasks are challenging, time consuming, and ultimately rewarding—the very definition of "employment."

But when a puppy is brought into a human home, there is no food to hunt, no mate to find, and no predators to stave off. So, to fill the vacuum, a puppy may herd the children or retrieve your slippers. She may guard her food and toys or protect the home from the mail carrier and even nice Aunt Minnie. In essence, the dog becomes "self-employed," and this is one of the main reasons that people have problems with their dogs.

Here are some of the top occupations that puppies and dogs take on:

1. They become gardeners. At the end of the day you come home and find your sprinkler heads and flowers torn up.

2. They become official greeters, jumping all over your visitors and knocking them over when they walk in the door.
3. They become home decorators. You come home and find all of your cushions and designer shoes chewed to perfection.
4. They become alarm systems. They announce the arrival of "intruders," including guests, the mail carrier, the neighborhood kid who is selling cookies, the squirrels and birds in the trees, and so on. The only problem is that you can't turn them off except when they are sleeping. So the neighbors hear your dog barking all day and all night long. And if the dog is aggressive, poor old Uncle Bob might soon be referred to as "Lefty."
5. They become hunters. Paul's dog Molly used to "capture" dead fish from around Lake Erie and proudly lay them at his feet as she walked in the door.
6. They become firefighters. They put out all the imaginary fires on your furniture.

The solution is simple. Become your puppy's employer. Employment is important because it not only provides the stimulation that your puppy needs but also because it promotes and develops a sense of self, purpose, and pride. When you become your puppy's employer, you tell him when and where he should do things like chew, dig, and bark. You control everything your puppy wants and give him what he wants when he does something for you first. Then, the gardener puppy learns to dig in a sandbox. The official greeter learns to lie down on his spot when the doorbell rings. The home decorator chews on appropriate objects, such as bully sticks, chicken strips, and smart toys such as food-dispensing Kongs. The alarm system puppy learns to bark three times when the mail carrier or a visitor arrives and then lay down. The hunter learns to chase, track, hunt, and kill Frisbees, pieces of cheese, and Buster Cubes. And the firefighter learns the proper places and times to eliminate.

To help illustrate the importance of puppies and dogs "working" for their living, Paul developed the term *canine currency*.

When you institute the concept of canine currency, you pay your dog in response to appropriate behavior, which is looked at as his work or his job. A dog then works for the currency, which is represented by food, affection, play, and special privileges.

Here are some canine "work-for-pay" examples:

- ☙ "Want to go outside? Sit first."
- ☙ "Want to chase the ball? Lay down first."
- ☙ "Want to go for a walk? Open the fridge and get me a soda first." (Don't laugh; virtually every dog can be taught to do this.)

The idea is, you promise that you will give your dog everything she wants—petting, praise, food, exercise, and meeting other dogs and people—as long as she does something for you first. In Chapter 16 we will introduce the Nothing in Life Is Free regimen, in which your puppy will work for almost everything in her life, and enjoy doing so. Jobs can include retrieving toys, doing tricks, and playing games. Paul's dog Grady teaches children how to interact with dogs safely as part of Paul's Paws for Peace children's program. Children learn how to safely approach and pet a dog and how to treat a dog with kindness and respect. Grady also demonstrates twenty different tricks. Not a bad job!

Smart Toys as Employment

In Chapter 3, we discussed the concept of smart toys. These toys present a problem that your puppy will be motivated to solve, usually because they involve dislodging food from within the toy. They are designed to keep your puppy occupied, by himself, and concentrated on a task for an extended period of time. Smart toys are probably the principal method of employment you will give to your puppy for the first few months. Provide them whenever you leave your puppy alone or other times when it is clear that he needs an activity that you cannot provide with your presence. By giving your puppy a job to do, you will go a long way toward preventing destructive chewing, ceaseless barking, nipping for attention, and other problems. (Also see Chapter 20 on problem behaviors.)

Hint: You can give your puppy all her meals in food dispensing toys, foregoing the food dish all together. This includes stuffing the toy with homemade food, canned food, kibble, cottage cheese, or any combination.

Using Employment to Add Challenges

As your puppy grows to five months and beyond, training can increasingly provide employment as you teach her to find and retrieve objects, bark once to let you know that company has arrived, then be quiet when you ask, and do tricks for friends and family. Anything that presents a challenge to your puppy and focuses her on a time-consuming yet rewarding task will increase her self-confidence and teach her appropriate ways of using her natural abilities in the human world.

Keep challenge and reward in good balance. Too much challenge and not enough reward will discourage your puppy and cause her to lose interest in the task at hand. Challenging her beyond her physical and emotional abilities will stress her and could even frighten and traumatize her. So, when asking your puppy to solve a challenging problem, whether getting the food out of a toy or climbing a flight of stairs, start at a level that you can realistically expect her to be successful and for which she shows sustained interest.

Chapter 14

Rest

Uninterrupted, restful sleep is just as important for animals as it is for us humans.

Where Should Your Puppy Sleep?

As we previously mentioned, having your puppy sleep in the bedroom really strengthens the human-animal bond. We can't say enough about the benefits this provides. However, for those who don't want a puppy sleeping in the bedroom, you can set up the puppy's kennel or exercise pen in the hall, bathroom, or kitchen. It will take extra time for your puppy to get used to this arrangement but most puppies settle in within about a month once they learn that they're always safe.

How Much Sleep Does Your Puppy Need?

Puppies can sleep for up to sixteen hours a day, and they should be allowed to do so. Keeping your puppy constantly active with no downtime allowed for rest during the day can exhaust her, leading to irritability, among other things. On the other side of the coin, if a puppy sleeps too much during the day, she may be spending too much time alone and not have enough exercise, socialization, and play. The consequences of either situation can result in puppies who bark constantly, chew slippers and other "illegal" objects, or exhibit any number of other undesirable behaviors.

Several years ago, a couple called Terry and complained about their five-month-old puppy's barking and destructive behavior. Both of them worked long hours, leaving the puppy alone for eight hours at a stretch, five days a week. Miraculously, there was never any destruction nor were there any potty accidents during the day while the couple was gone. When they got home, they would exercise the puppy and play with him for about a half hour, then they would have dinner, relax, and go to bed. As soon as they got in bed, the puppy would start barking, bring them toys, and keep them awake with his attention-seeking behavior. They did not want to kennel the puppy at night, since they kept him kenneled all day long. Eventually, the puppy would seemingly settle down and the couple would get to sleep. In the morning, however, they would invariably find the edges of their blanket shredded, the bedposts chewed, or some other new bit of destruction.

Clearly, the puppy was dealing with his daytime isolation and boredom by sleeping during the day. He had adapted his sleep patterns so he would be awake when his caregivers were home. Unfortunately, since they were asleep the caregivers were obviously unable to provide the attention and stimulation that the puppy needed, so that's when he would unleash the torrent of energy inside him. His destructive behavior was an expression of the activity that he needed during the day.

The couple's problem was solved by adding a half-hour walk before they went to work and another half-hour walk just before bedtime. A dog walker was hired to visit the puppy during the day and the puppy was given smart toys to play with in addition to some extra quality play and training time with the couple each evening. The puppy was also taught to bark on cue. (See "Problem Behaviors," page 279.)

If your puppy gets the right amount of activity during the day and evening, punctuated by periods of rest, he will adjust to your routine.

The Importance of Undisturbed Sleep

Just as with humans, a puppy's sleep consists of alternating cycles of rapid eye movement (REM) and dreamless states. During the REM cycle, some of your puppy's built-up stress is resolved through dreams. However, the dreamless cycles of sleep afford the greatest degree of relaxation. Therefore, a complete, uninterrupted sleep cycle consisting of both REM and dreamless states is essential for your puppy's health. In short, you should let sleeping dogs lie.

If you have to awaken a sleeping puppy, do so gently. You can softly hum or whistle or call your puppy's name. Or tap the ground and the vibration will awaken him. And some puppies have no problem being awakened if they are gently stroked. Every puppy is different. The key is not to startle him. Safety is of utmost importance; if you are having problems such as a puppy who snarls or snaps when awakened, call a professional trainer.

Note: If a child sees a sleeping puppy "running and whining in his sleep," she might want to wake him because "he's having a nightmare." Be safe. Teach children that the puppy is fine and not to awaken him. Let puppies finish their dreams.

Chapter 15

Health Care

If your puppy is getting a healthy diet, adequate exercise, socialization, training, and rest, you are well on the way to keeping her in top physical and emotional condition. In this chapter, we'll address the health issues that are of particular concern to your puppy's well-being, including safety in hot weather, neutering and spaying, preventing infectious diseases, and dealing with parasites. Health care needs vary with your puppy's stage of development, size, breed, and genetic influences, so always check with your veterinarian for specific recommendations. We also suggest that you read more about canine health care in books such as *The Natural Dog: A Complete Guide for Caring Owners,* by Mary L. Brennan, DVM, and Norma Eckroate; *Dr. Pitcairn's Complete Guide to Natural Health for Dogs and Cats,* by Richard H. Pitcairn, DVM, PhD, and Susan Hubble Pitcairn; and *Four Paws Five Directions,* by Cheryl Schwartz, DVM.

Preventing Sunburn, Blistered Paws, and Heatstroke

Even the most caring people sometimes don't think about sunburn on a puppy's nose or burns and blisters to the paws from hot surfaces, such as pavement or sand on the beach. Here are some rules of thumb about taking your puppy out in hot weather:

- Always carry water with you.
- If it's 85 degrees Fahrenheit or warmer, no walking between 11 A.M. and 5 P.M.

- In temperatures above 75 degrees Fahrenheit, walks should be of a short duration and in shade.
- If the pavement is too hot for your bare feet, it's too hot for your puppy's paws.

Special consideration should be given to some breeds that do not tolerate hot weather as well as others. This is true of those who have heavy coats, like the Newfoundland. It is also the case with brachycephalic breeds, like the pug, Boston terrier, boxer, Pekingese, Shih Tzu, and bulldog, which have been bred for the characteristics of "pushed-in" or "snub-nosed" faces, often resulting in respiratory problems that make them more sensitive to higher temperatures and extended exercise.

Dogs are particularly vulnerable to heatstroke due to overexertion or being left in cars or yards in hot weather. Never leave your puppy in a car in warm weather. Every year news reports abound with cases of both infants and dogs that were left in a car in hot weather with disastrous results. The popular idea of cracking a window so she'll get some air is fine if the temperature is below 65 degrees Fahrenheit and you're parked in the shade, but it really doesn't help at all when it's hot outside and the sun bakes down on a parked car. Also, remember that the sun moves—one minute your car might be parked in the shade, but a few minutes later it's in direct sunlight. If the temperature is 85 degrees Fahrenheit outside on a hot summer day, the inside of the car can reach 120 degrees Fahrenheit within half an hour. Your puppy can suffer brain damage or death if her body temperature reaches 107 degrees Fahrenheit, which is only 5 to 7 degrees above normal body temperature. (A dog's normal temperature ranges between 100 and 102.5 degrees Fahrenheit.)

Signs of heatstroke include excessive panting, vomiting, a fast pulse rate, and high body temperature. If you suspect heatstroke, do not delay. Get your puppy to a veterinarian immediately. If that's not possible, soak her in cool water until her temperature goes down. Ice packs around her head will also help.

If you have to leave your puppy in a car in an emergency situation, we suggest leaving the air conditioning running. Carry a spare set of keys and leave one set in the ignition, lock the car, and use the second set to unlock the car when you return. If you do this, put a large sign in a visible place somewhere on the car windows so any Good Samaritans who are concerned about your puppy will know that he's safe. For long trips, you can also make a bed of ice for the puppy to lie on. You can do this by filling a large plastic tray with ice and covering it with a towel. The bottom line is—never stay away from your car for more than a few minutes.

Note: Leaving keys in a running car could lead to car theft. Also, in some states, it's illegal to leave an animal alone in a parked car.

Neutering and Spaying

The surgical sterilization of puppies is referred to as neutering for a male and spaying for a female. If a male dog is intact, he may "mark" his territory by spraying strong-smelling urine in your house. Neutering reduces marking up to 50 percent. An unneutered male will instinctually attempt to reach any female in heat by any means possible . . . think: "escape at all costs." If he does escape, he also risks injury from fights with other males or getting hit by traffic. Neutering reduces male dog-to-dog aggression up to 40 percent.

Likewise, females in heat will also attempt to follow their instinctual urges, accompanied by yowling and more frequent urination, including in the house. Another benefit of altering for both sexes is a decreased risk of some diseases, as well as certain types of aggression. So, unless you are definitely going to breed your dog, we strongly advocate neutering and spaying.

Most vets recommend the best time for neutering and spaying is just as puberty sets in or, for a female, before the first heat. This is around six months of age for small and medium dogs and seven to eight months for larger breeds. However, these days most shelters participate in early sterilization programs, requiring puppies to be neutered or spayed before adoption in order to reduce the huge problem of overpopulation. Therefore, puppies are now being altered as early as six weeks of age. If your puppy has not yet been altered, talk with your vet about the timing. Our veterinary medical sources suggest that it's still a good idea to wait until puberty if you have that option.

Infectious Disease and Immunizations

A puppy is more vulnerable to diseases such as distemper and parvovirus in the first three to four months of life when her immune system is developing; therefore, conflicts arise between socializing her and keeping her safe from disease. If you find yourself in an area that concerns you, err on the side of safety and carry your puppy until her immune system is protected by vaccinations or other protective measures, according to your veterinarian's recommendations. If your puppy exhibits any signs of illness such as vomiting, watery diarrhea, diarrhea streaked with blood, fever, lethargy, refusal to eat, or discharge of pus from the eyes or nose, call your veterinarian immediately.

There is some controversy among veterinarians as to which vaccinations should be given to puppies, at what age they should be given, or even if they should be given at all. Holistic veterinarians sometimes recommend homeopathic remedies called nosodes instead of or, as an adjunct to, conventional vaccines. Homeopathy is a system of medicine developed in 1796 by Samuel Hahnemann, a German physician. It is based on the principle that "like cures like," which is also referred to as the "law of similars." Hahnemann found that a substance that produces a certain set of symptoms in a healthy person can cure a sick person who is manifesting those same symptoms. A homeopathic "remedy" is a very dilute medication (often in parts per million) which is "potentized" by succussion (vigorous shaking). The medication stimulates the body's defense systems, allowing the body to heal itself. A nosode is a specific type of homeopathic remedy that is a more natural form of immunizing the body against a specific disease. It is similar to a regular vaccination in that its active substance is the bacteria or virus of a specific disease. However, as with other homeopathic remedies, the active substance is extremely dilute and has been "potentized."

Increasingly, veterinarians point to evidence that conventional vaccinations can trigger the onset of the disease against which the puppy is being vaccinated, or actually lower resistance to the disease if the vaccination is administered at too early an age. There is also evidence to suggest that too early and/or too frequent vaccination can cause long-term immune system deficiencies, which holistic vets call vaccinosis, that can affect the endocrine system, central nervous system, kidneys, joints, and skin.

Other evidence suggests the immunity afforded by an initial series of puppy vaccinations can sometimes last as long as seven years for distemper and parvovirus, with booster shots giving no advantage of lengthened or strengthened immunity. According to Dr. Jean Dodds (a leading veterinary researcher into canine immunology and blood disease), as reported on *http://itsfortheanimals.com*, "Studies are now showing the duration of immunity from vaccination is now accepted to be at least five or more years for the clinically important diseases of dogs and cats. . . . In the years between or instead of boosters, serum vaccine antibody titers can be measured to determine the adequacy of immune memory." Vaccine antibody titer testing measures antibodies specific to certain diseases, which are present in an animal's blood. Titer testing can determine whether your dog retains immunity from any infectious diseases to which she may be exposed. It is much safer to have the dog's immune titer levels tested than to automatically give booster vaccines.

In recent years, the American Veterinary Medical Association (AVMA), a professional organization for veterinarians who practice conventional Western medicine, has also taken a more conservative approach to vaccinations. The AVMA now endorses the position that routine revaccination every year is not necessarily the best choice for every dog, or against every disease. Vets should take individual needs into consideration, rather than apply a "one size fits all" approach. The AVMA recommends that most dogs should receive initial "core" vaccines against parvovirus, distemper, rabies, and canine hepatitis, and then "non-core" vaccines for other diseases, based on individual need. Booster shots are not necessarily called for every year, since immunity frequently lasts longer.

Dr. Dodds recommends a vaccine protocol for puppies that balances protection against serious disease with minimal use of vaccination. She particularly recommends this protocol for animals known to have a genetic background of susceptibility to immune dysfunction or adverse vaccine reactions, or those who have already experienced adverse vaccine reactions. Dr. Dodds emphasizes not vaccinating before eight weeks of age and separating individual vaccinations by three to four weeks. She also recommends using single vaccines, rather than "combined" vaccines which contain three or more viruses in the same shot.

Additionally, Dr. Dodds specifically recommends against vaccines for leptospirosis and Lyme disease, unless these diseases are endemic to your local area. She also advises against bordetella vaccine unless your puppy is going to be housed anywhere with a lot of other dogs, such as a kennel or groomer's. Corona virus is a disease that puppies can contract, but it is rare and puppies recover from it within three days without treatment. In any case, adult dogs do not contract Corona virus, so there is no need for an annual booster shot, even if you do decide to vaccinate your puppy against Corona. After your puppy's first year, Dr. Dodds recommends titer testing for parvovirus and distemper, rather than routine revaccination every year. For the latest research and recommendations on Dr. Dodds' specific vaccination protocol, check the Web site, *http://itsfortheanimals.com.*

You should also check on any legal obligations regarding immunizations. Most areas, for example, require a rabies vaccination by a certain age. Also, if you enroll in a puppy class, you will almost certainly be required to provide proof of vaccination. All this being said, it is up to every individual, in consultation with a veterinarian, to decide on the best course of action regarding vaccinations.

Parasites—Fleas, Ticks, and Heartworm

There are numerous parasites that can afflict your puppy, resulting in health problems that range from minor irritations to life-threatening conditions. Parasites are divided into two basic categories: internal and external.

Internal parasites include heartworms, roundworms, hookworms, whipworms, and tapeworms. Heartworm, which is spread by mosquitoes, is of particular concern because it can lead to death. An oral heartworm preventative is therefore commonly prescribed by veterinarians. Talk with your veterinarian about his recommendations.

External parasites include fleas and ticks. Fleas can cause skin allergies or infections, carry tapeworm, or cause anemia; ticks can carry Lyme disease, Rocky Mountain spotted fever, and other potentially deadly diseases. Frontline and Advantix are the most commonly used flea and tick control products and, when properly used, most veterinarians consider them to be safe and effective. These products are topically administered. If you'd like a more natural approach to flea and tick control, ask your holistic veterinarian for her recommendations.

Part 2

Behavior and Training

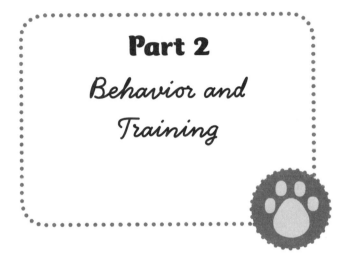

Chapter 16

Training Basics

Training your puppy to sit, lie down, stay, and come, as well as other behaviors, not only helps keep him safe, it also fosters his trust in you. As you progress, a puppy learns that rules establish behavioral boundaries and once a puppy knows what is expected of him, he becomes confident and relaxed.

How Puppies Learn

We can teach puppies to live with us harmoniously and peacefully by taking advantage of two types of learning: classical conditioning (or associative learning) and operant conditioning (or instrumental learning). If you're not interested in the nuts and bolts of training psychology, skip to the section on rewards.

Classical Conditioning

Classical conditioning is a type of learning in which your puppy learns to associate two different things in his environment. Classical conditioning is also referred to as associative learning because it has to do with associating this with that. For example, after a number of repeated experiences, your puppy learns that whenever the leash appears, he's going outside! Hooray! Over and over again, he has experienced: leash, then walk; leash, then walk; leash, then walk; and so on. Whereas the leash was initially a boring old piece of nylon, your puppy eventually does backflips in excitement any time he hears the leash being picked up. In other words, he has learned that the leash predicts something great is going to happen. In classical conditioning, a positive experience is not contingent upon the puppy's behavior. In other words, he doesn't have to sit to go for a walk; the walk always happens no matter what he does.

A simple way to understand classical conditioning is that it affects the way your puppy feels about certain things, which affects his behavior. We take advantage of this in socialization exercises. For example, when guests arrive at the door, treats and play and happiness arrive with them. Classical conditioning is used to prevent fearful or aggressive behavior from developing or to reverse fearful and aggressive behavior if it is already present.

Operant Conditioning

Operant conditioning is a type of learning in which your puppy realizes that her behavior has consequences. For example, if you consistently give your puppy a treat every time she puts her rear end on the ground, she will eventually learn that sitting is likely to result in getting a treat. So she is likely to sit more often. Conversely, if she is ignored when she sits but gets attention every time she barks, she will sit less and bark more. Attention is the reward in this case. In operant conditioning your puppy associates her own behavior with the good or bad things that happen to her.

In practice, there is a good deal of overlap between operant conditioning and classical conditioning. For example, when puppies realize that sitting for guests gets them attention and treats (operant conditioning) they also tend to learn that visitors are fun (classical conditioning). Conversely, if puppies are frightened by loud, boisterous people (classical conditioning), they frequently discover that barking will keep those frightening people away (operant conditioning).

The Hierarchy of Rewards

A reward for your puppy can be many things: petting, praise, attention of any kind, play, going out for a walk, food, and so on. These rewards have a hierarchy of value. In human terms, yummy food treats are generally worth about $10,000 to your puppy. Petting and praise are generally worth about $1. Getting to play with another dog, chase a ball, or ride in the car with you, however, might be worth as much as $20,000, depending on how much value your puppy places on that particular reward in the moment.

Primary ($10,000) Rewards	Secondary Rewards
Special food treats Play (in some instances)	Affection through praise and touching Play, including toys Social interaction, including allowing your dog to go places with you (such as a ride in the car), walking up and down the stairs, going in and out of doors, or being allowed on the bed or other furniture.

Food tends to be highly motivating to dogs over a wide range of situations, which is why we use it so much in training. However, the value of any reward can fluctuate. If the same great reward is given over and over again, it will lose its value. Also, if you give too much of the same reward, it can lose its value. The classic example is the story of the trainer who guaranteed she could get a dog to ignore freshly cooked steak without resorting to any negative training. How did she do this? Shortly before the demonstration, she simply gave the dog more steak than he could possibly eat. Then, when it came time for the demonstration, she offered him yet another piece of steak and he ignored it. The steak had lost its value because the dog couldn't eat another bite. This is a good example of how other rewards, such as praise, can also be misused and lose their power. Of course, you want to praise your puppy consistently. However, your puppy should earn that praise. If you give your puppy praise all the time for doing nothing, he will begin to ignore you. The same goes for your puppy's favorite toys. They, too, should be used as rewards for doing what you've asked rather than something that's always available. Rewards—to be rewards—have to keep their value.

Carrying Food Treats with You

One of the easiest and cleanest methods to keep food treats at the ready is to carry them in a treat pouch (sold at pet stores) or a hip pack (also known as a fanny pack) which are sold in department stores and sporting good stores. Just remember to clean your treat pouch or pack at the end of the day.

Reinforcement Schedules

Successful training is a lot like gambling. You're the dealer who holds the cards as well as the bank that holds the payoff. Your puppy is the player. To keep your puppy interested in the game, you need to dole out the "payoff" (such as food treats, praise, play, and affection) whenever your puppy "wins" (does what you ask). Then, once your puppy is really interested in continuing to play, you will vary the payoff schedule. In this way, you will gradually reduce food rewards for and then eventually wean him off treats altogether. Your puppy learns that the behavior is fun in and of itself and he no longer requires food rewards as a motivation. You will always continue giving the other rewards—praise, play, and affection.

This is done in incremental steps:

Continuous reinforcement: Initially, you will reward your puppy each and every time he responds to your signal; for example, sit, treat, sit, treat, sit, treat, and so on. A few hundred repetitions spread out over several days or weeks may be all that's necessary for your puppy to grasp what's going on.

Variable reinforcement: At the next stage of training, instead of rewarding the puppy after every response, reward after every second, third, or fourth response unpredictably (sit, sit, treat; or, sit, sit, sit, sit, treat), or after two, three, or more different behaviors; for example, sit, down, sit, treat, and so on.

Random reinforcement: In this stage, you progress to rewarding every so often, like the occasional win in Las Vegas. Once the puppy knows that a payoff is coming sooner or later, he will remain motivated.

Learning when to go from one reinforcement schedule to another is what makes a good trainer. Some puppies learn more quickly than others; go too slowly with those puppies and they quickly become bored. Other puppies need to remain on one schedule for a longer period of time; if you go too fast, they become stressed and you end up having to retrace your steps. The key is learning how to use these schedules to keep your puppy motivated.

Weaning Your Puppy off Food Treats
In positive training, you'll use lots of food treats when you start out. But you don't want to have to carry treats around with you for the rest of your life. As your puppy becomes more and more reliable with behaviors, you can start weaning her off food treats. Here are three ways this is done:

1. Consistently use life rewards throughout the day. Anything your puppy likes or wants that isn't food is a life reward. Ask your puppy to sit, lie down, go to her spot, and so on, before allowing her to go outside or chase a ball, petting her, and so on. It is important that your puppy can't get what she wants without doing something for you first, hence the need to keep her on leashes (supervised!), behind baby gates, or in a kennel or dog run.
2. Form behavioral chains. This means adding one behavior after another before rewarding, such as: sit, down, stay, come, and then a food reward. Vary these behavior chains by asking for different behaviors.

3. Use intermittent food reinforcement. Reward every once in a while. Once the puppy knows that a payoff is coming sooner or later, he will remain motivated.

The Six Strategies of Nonviolent Puppy Training
Here are six strategies to guide you in training your puppy:

1. Determine what you want your puppy to do.
2. Practice prevention and management.
3. Play the Magnet Game.
4. Make your puppy earn what she wants, aka, Nothing in Life Is Free (NILIF).
5. Interrupt and redirect your puppy's inappropriate behavior.
6. When all else fails, apply a negative.

Let's examine each of these strategies individually.

Training Strategy One: Determine What You Want Your Puppy to Do.
Quickly—complete the following sentence: "I want my puppy to _____." Chances are you said something like "stop jumping on me," or "not bite my kids' ankles," or "quit chewing on the sofa" or "stop chasing the cat," or "stop digging in the garden," or "stop peeing on the carpet." Stop, no, quit, no, stop, don't! We spend relatively little time thinking about what we would like them to do instead of what we want them to stop doing. Puppies were born to do things.

Puppies were born to chew, bark, nip, jump, dig, and, yes, pee and poop as soon as they feel the need to do so even if it is on your new Persian rug. The trick is not to get them to stop doing these things but to simply teach them to do these things when and where we want. Clarifying what you want your puppy to do sets you up with opportunities to reward him for the behavior you like, whereas focusing on what you want him to stop doing traps you into looking for opportunities to punish your puppy.

The change to a positively stated goal ("I want Sparky to sit") from a negatively stated goal ("I want Sparky to stop jumping") is more than just semantics. Learning to formulate goals positively takes practice. There are three rules:

1. Keep your goals positive. Avoid the words "stop" and "not."
2. Keep your goals active. Use verbs that involve your dog physically doing something, such as sitting, lying down, or coming to you. Avoid non-active or overly general verbs such as, "I want my puppy to be obedient" or "I want my puppy to listen."
3. Keep your goals specific. Include the situation in which you want your dog to do something, like "when guests are over," "when he's out in the yard," or "when I put his leash on."

Here are some examples:

- "I want my dog to sit for greeting when guests come in the front door." (Rather than, "I want my dog to stop jumping.")
- "I want my dog to come to me and lie down when people pass by the house." (Rather than, "I want my dog to stop barking at the neighbors.")

Using these examples, we suggest making a list of ten training goals for your puppy. A good tip for getting started is to think in opposites. If your puppy is chasing the cat, what would the opposite of that action be? Running away from the cat, of course! And if she's running away from the cat, where would the best place be to run to? Why, to you, of course! So now, the alternative for Sparky chasing the cat is for Sparky to come to you when you call her away from the cat. You formulated your goal without using "not" or "stop," yet you found a strategy to eliminate Sparky's cat chasing. You are teaching your puppy to do something for a reward, rather than avoiding something in fear of punishment. Another example would be if your puppy jumps on you or guests, you will think about an opposite behavior that involves staying on the ground. You get the idea.

Once you make this list, you will find that your training time will be reduced by about 50 percent. You don't have to think up dozens of alternate behaviors, either. You'd be surprised how far sit, down, stay, come, and heel will take you in solving problems.

Training Strategy Two: Practice Prevention and Management

Prevention involves setting up the environment so your puppy is safe. We deal with this in detail in the "Safety Issues" section of Chapter 4. Management entails controlling your puppy's access to the environment around him. Use of a leash and collar or head halter, as well as a kennel, baby gates, exercise pens, and fences, will help immensely. These tools prevent unwanted behavior by physically confining or restraining your puppy. If, for example, your puppy is inside his kennel when you leave the house, it is physically impossible for him to chew on your sofa. If he's tethered to your chair while you're eating, he can't steal your food.

Management should be a positive experience for your puppy. We train our puppies to love being in their kennels or exercise pens because of the Kong toy, bully stick, or chicken strip that's inside; go wild with joy when put on a leash because of the positive association with walks; and really enjoy being tethered to furniture because they get so much affection while you're watching TV.

Once the puppy can be trusted to chew only appropriate objects and leave our slippers, the curtains, and the TV remote alone, and we know he's otherwise safe in the house, he no longer needs to be confined. However, in some situations, prevention and management are required for your dog's entire life. For example, you need to be 100 percent certain that your puppy does not run into the street. Therefore, keep him on a leash and let him off leash in fenced in areas only. You will also train him for a reliable come when called and stay. But there's always the possibility that he won't obey, like when he sees a squirrel.

Training Strategy Three: The Magnet Game

The Magnet Game is so named because your puppy's unasked-for behaviors attract you, your affection, and your treats . . . like a magnet. Let's say you're watching TV or washing dishes or working on your computer and you happen to see your puppy sit or lie down on his bed. That behavior becomes a magnet—it attracts your attention and a treat. You didn't ask him to lie down, he just did it. At this point you can: (1) throw him a treat; (2) praise him; (3) get up and pet him; or (4) combine all three as a triple reward. But let's say he sits, which is the behavior you are looking for, and you start to get up to go over and pet him. However, as you're on the way to pet him, he gets up. Since sitting is the behavior you want, not standing, the magnetic attraction has been broken because he got up. At this point, you will immediately turn around and go the other way. If he sits or lies down again, you will immediately begin walking toward him again because the magnet is working again.

The Magnet Game is like the game of "hot and cold," in which the person who is "it" tries to determine which object in the room the other players have selected for her to find. She moves around the room while the other players say "you're getting warm" and "now you're getting colder" until finally the person gets close to the object she's supposed to find and is told, "you're red hot!" It's just the same with a puppy. Each time your puppy gets closer to doing what you want, reward his efforts with praise and treats. When he gets further away from the behavior you want, ignore the behavior—which is the same as saying "You're getting cold." Then, when he finally "gets it," he receives a jackpot—several $10,000 rewards.

The Magnet Game can be played when your puppy is loose or tethered. It's a little bit easier when she's tethered because she's more of a captive audience. So several times during the day, tether her to the bottom of the couch or to a door in a social area where you can supervise her. Never tether a puppy and leave her alone. She should be allowed about four to six feet of leash but not be able to reach you. (Review "Tethering" on page 78.)

Since the Magnet Game requires so much of your active participation, it's also a great way to gain a good understanding of operant conditioning in practice. You reward the behavior you would like your puppy to repeat, and ignore the behavior you don't want. It is always your puppy's behavior that determines the consequences. A puppy stops what he's doing if he doesn't get "paid" in some way, shape, or form. In other words, when there is no longer a reward attached to a certain behavior, the behavior generally ceases. In psychology this is known as extinction. You can think of it as extinguishing a fire; after all, if you don't feed a fire, it goes out.

Think about what your dog gets out of the barking, jumping, chewing, digging, begging, and so on. How is he being rewarded for the behavior? If you stop giving your dog attention for barking, for example, he has no incentive to continue. If you stop giving treats when he begs at the table, there's a good chance he'll eventually stop because there's simply no longer any reason to continue. Another great example of how well ignoring a behavior works is with the problem of jumping. Puppies generally get attention when they jump. Sometimes small cute puppies get petted and larger puppies get yelled at. When you stop petting and stop yelling, the jumping usually stops.

There are cases, however, in which ignoring the undesirable behavior isn't recommended. You don't want to ignore a puppy who is chewing on your shoe, nor do you want to ignore a puppy who barks because it relieves his stress or he just likes to hear himself bark. In these cases, the behavior is self-reinforcing. In other words, he won't give it up because it's serving a purpose. Ignoring a behavior works well when combined with catching and rewarding the behavior you do want.

To review—the four goals of the Magnet Game are:

1. You have clearly formulated what you want from your puppy as an alternate behavior.
2. You managed her so she can't behave inappropriately.
3. You ignored the behaviors you didn't want (unless destructive or self-reinforcing).

4. Finally, you have "caught" and rewarded the alternate behavior when it happens.

We suggest that you use the Magnet Game as 50 percent of your training for several reasons: It's incredibly easy and powerful, and your puppy learns what you want her to do very quickly.

Training Strategy Four: Nothing in Life Is Free (NILIF)

Nothing in Life Is Free is a training strategy that teaches your puppy that she has to work for a living and nothing is given to her without her doing something for you first. This is the same concept as employing your puppy, which we discussed in Chapter 13. Make a list of things your puppy likes, including favorite foods and "life rewards."

"Life rewards" include:

1. Playing with toys.
2. Being petted.
3. Being sweet talked or praised.
4. Getting out of the kennel to greet you.
5. Getting the leash put on for a walk.
6. Going outside.
7. Going for a walk.
8. Going for a ride.
9. Meeting another dog.
10. Swimming (does not apply to all puppies).
11. Coming back inside to be with everyone else.

These are just a few examples of the things that make a puppy's tail wag. In addition, every puppy will have individual, idiosyncratic pleasures. Most of us, when asked what our puppy likes, don't think of all these things. Making a list helps you become aware of the many rewards a puppy can work for and receive throughout the day.

An example of a life reward is being petted when guests come over. For example, Oliver is only to be petted if he is sitting. In addition, you can set a household rule that Oliver is not to be petted "for free" at any time—he must work for his petting. In other words, he must always sit before being petted. After a short time of enforcing this rule, Oliver should get the idea that sitting gets him lots of petting, whereas nothing else seems to do the trick. He will start offering you sits without having to be asked.

This strategy can be very hard to implement at first. We want to pet Oliver because he's so cute. However, if you discipline yourself and integrate the Nothing in Life Is Free regimen, it will be well worth the effort—and it will soon become second nature for both you and Oliver.

Training Strategy Five: Interrupt and Redirect Your Puppy's Inappropriate Behavior

When you're home with your puppy, good management includes setting up an environment where you can see what your puppy is doing at all times. That way, if she starts an unwanted behavior, you can interrupt the behavior as quickly as possible. If, for example, your puppy is tethered or gated in the same room with you, you will see her if she starts to eliminate inside. You can therefore interrupt her with an "ah-ah-ah" and immediately take her outside to continue pottying there (see Chapter 5).

Interrupting unwanted behavior is the next best thing to preventing it. Interruption happens just before or during an unwanted behavior, rather than afterward. It is more effective to interrupt your puppy while she is preparing to urinate, signaled by sniffing the carpet and turning around in circles, than it is to interrupt her once she has already started urinating. And it is more effective to interrupt your puppy while she is thinking about jumping on the table to steal food, rather than after she is already up there. That being said, interruptions can still be effective tools when you catch your puppy "in the act."

Common interrupters include clapping your hands, loud whistles, exclamations of "ah-AH," rapping a desk or table, banging a pot, and so on. The key is to startle, not scare, your puppy. Every puppy has her own sensitivity level and if you scare your dog you will undermine her trust. Choose an intensity that will distract the puppy so she stops what she is doing and redirects her attention to you. The purpose of interruption is to prevent unwanted patterns of behavior from establishing themselves as habits.

Note: Once you interrupt your puppy from doing something, like stealing food from the table, your puppy will hesitate the next time she sees food. She will then look over to you. Jackpot that look with a number of treats! Your puppy has chosen to check with you rather than steal the food, and that is exactly what she is supposed to do.

Training Strategy Six: When All Else Fails, Apply a Negative

Applying a negative isn't as bad as it sounds. Using a negative consequence in a nonviolent way means that your puppy never experiences physical pain or emotional distress but it does modify her behavior. The Nothing in Life Is Free strategy is an example of this because it involves using negative consequences. You are withholding something good from her if she does not behave in a certain way. For example, if she doesn't sit, you do not pet her. To her, that's a negative. Another negative is to walk away from her if she nips, barks incessantly, or jumps.

Then there is the "time out," which can be used as a consequence for nipping, incessantly barking, or continued jumping. The "time out" is a training tool that involves removing your puppy from a situation as a consequence for inappropriate behavior. She is confined behind a gate or in a kennel or she is tethered.

Let's say you're training your sweet Puggle named Atticus and he, being the four-month-old puppy he is, makes a mistake and grabs your hand instead of the toy you're holding. You yell *ow*! (Decide on a phrase, such as "ow," "yipe," or "ahhh," that you will use whenever your puppy exhibits inappropriate behavior.) But instead of backing off, he gets even more excited and really goes for your hand. At this point you can quickly and non-threateningly (in spite of your pain!) say "time out" or "uh oh" or "that's it" or "too bad" and place him in his kennel (if he's acclimated to it), in an exercise pen, or behind a baby gate. There Atticus will remain for two to five minutes. When the time is up, pretend nothing has happened and happily release him. Release him only when he has settled down and relaxed. After a few repetitions, he learns that inappropriate mouthing produces temporary detachment from you. He also learns that when he relaxes it means freedom and socialization. In this example of puppy biting, we would, of course, continue to teach the puppy substitute behaviors such as chewing on appropriate toys, licking instead of biting, taking things gently, "drop it," and so on.

> Never kennel a puppy who is unwilling to go into it or stay in it or is in distress as exhibited by panting, drooling, or whining, or who doesn't settle down within twenty minutes. Instead, use an exercise pen or put her behind a baby gate.

The idea with time outs is that you are addressing the specific behavior—in this case, "inappropriate use of teeth." You correct the behavior, not the puppy. Your attitude is extremely important. Stay upbeat and matter-of-fact. In essence, you're saying to your puppy, "This behavior produces this result; while this other behavior produces this result." If you do this correctly, your puppy will actually put himself in a time out. If Paul's dog Grady doesn't do as he is asked or is acting out-of-control and Paul says "uh oh," Grady puts himself in a "time out" and gets in the van or goes into the kitchen. Time outs are normally used for jumping, mouthing, and barking.

> Correct the behavior, not the puppy.

Time outs should be used judiciously and never in anger. To a puppy suffering from separation anxiety, a short time out may be far too distressing and even cruel.

Chapter 17

Setting Up for Success: How to Prepare Yourself, Your Environment, and Your Puppy

Now that you have set your goals by determining what you would like your puppy to do, rather than stop doing, you'll need to teach her how to do those things. You will be using two methods to teach your puppy and reinforce the behavior you're looking for: the Magnet Game and three-step training.

1. **The Magnet Game:** Rewarding Unasked-For Behaviors.

   The Magnet Game, which you learned in Chapter 16, is incredibly easy because you simply wait for behaviors to occur, then "catch" that behavior by rewarding your puppy with praise, affection, and treats. If you use the Magnet Game as at least 50 percent of your training, the entire process will be faster.

2. **Structured Training Sessions:** Rewarding Asked-For Behaviors.

   This training is a matter of applying some basic scientific principles and asking for specific behaviors in short training sessions throughout the day.

Training success is all about the methods you use and how skillfully you use them. That's what this chapter is about.

Consistency and Repetition

Consistency means that everyone who interacts with the puppy is on the same page and uses the same signals and methods on a regular basis. The more we consistently reinforce a dog's behaviors, the more deeply ingrained those behaviors become and the more we increase the probability that the dog will repeat those behaviors in the future. Puppies learn through repetition, trial and error, and more repetition. How much repetition is required? Training sessions can be anywhere from thirty seconds to five minutes in length. In a really short session, you might do five to ten repetitions of down and that's it. Or do ten downs, ten stays, and ten come when called. A number of short sessions sprinkled throughout the day are much better than one or two sessions that last twenty to forty minutes. Keep it easy, fun, and simple.

Markers—Clickers and Words

When your puppy does what you've asked, you have about one second to "mark" that behavior and let him know it. That's because puppies and dogs only associate what they're doing with a consequence—in this case, the reward—if it comes almost immediately. You can use words to mark a behavior or a training tool called a clicker.

A clicker is a small, hand-held device that makes a cricket-like click when you press it. It gives your dog information very fast, usually much faster than you can say any particular word. Another advantage of the clicker is its distinct sound, which is easily picked up by dog ears. As we mentioned earlier, you only have about a second for your puppy to make the association between a behavior and its consequence—the reward. If you mark the behavior too slowly, it may not have the desired effect. For example, let's say your puppy sits, then gets up and wiggles around before you actually say "good dog." In that case, you have inadvertently rewarded him for getting up and wiggling. However, if you click the instant he sits, he learns to associate or "bridge" the click with the food reward that's coming and he knows that he is being rewarded for what he was doing when he heard the clicker. (Clickers can be ordered at *www.dogwhisperer dvd.com* or by calling 800-955-5440.)

As you work with these lessons, you'll notice that every successful behavior is acknowledged with "click, praise, and treat."

Note: Clickers are very helpful but not necessary. If you don't have a clicker, you can use words to mark a desired behavior instead. For instance, say "good dog" or "yes" or "that'll do" or "hooray" every time your puppy does the behavior you're asking for and he'll get the idea. Be sure to use the same word or phrase consistently. Whenever you see the words "click, praise, and treat" in this book, you can simply praise and treat instead.

Good clicker timing is easy with just a little bit of practice. You must reward your puppy with the food treat right after you click, not before or during the click. Eventually, when your puppy has learned that the clicker reliably predicts a reward, you actually have up to ten seconds to deliver a treat, depending on the situation.

Make sure that you click the instant your puppy responds to your request, and not in order to get a response. For example, click a split second after your puppy sits. Don't click in order to get your puppy's attention, and then ask him to sit. Many beginning clicker training students make this mistake of using the clicker as an attention getter, since it will get your puppy's attention once he realizes it means "treat."

The clicker is used for teaching new behaviors, but is not needed for maintaining those behaviors once your puppy has learned them reliably. In other words, just because you have trained your puppy to sit using a clicker, you won't have to carry around a clicker with you everywhere you go in order to get him to sit. Once your puppy has attained 80 percent reliability at any level of a particular behavior, you can put the clicker away and just use praise. When you go on to the more advanced level of that behavior, your puppy is learning something that is entirely new to him, so go back to using the clicker.

Giving a Clicker Power

Initially a clicker has no value to your puppy. It's neutral. To give it value or empower it, do this: Put it in your hand and immediately after clicking, throw a great food treat to your puppy. Click and treat like this ten to fifteen times. You'll know your puppy has "got it" when she starts looking around for the treat after hearing the click. Most puppies figure this out in one session. For others, do two or three sessions throughout the day. Once the clicker has meaning, you're ready to "mark" the exact behavior you're looking for. For example, when teaching your puppy to sit, click the moment her behind hits the floor and reward her.

In the rare case that your puppy does not acclimate quickly to the sound of the clicker, despite following the procedure above, say "good," "yes," "yay," or "that's it," instead of using the clicker. Your voice will probably not have the same speed or precision as a clicker, but the training principles will still be exactly the same.

Tips for Using a Clicker
- ☞ Make sure your demeanor is happy and fun.
- ☞ Don't startle your puppy by clicking near his ears! Keep your hands on your chest; that way the clicker will be at least two feet away from him.

Some puppies are a bit sound sensitive. If that's the case with your puppy, be cautious and sensitive when introducing the clicker. Here are a few tips:

1. Muffle the clicker by putting it in your pocket or wrapping a towel around it and increase your distance from your puppy.
2. Instead of doing a complete click, which consists of two clicking sounds—one when you press the clicker and another when you release it—press for one click only, and treat. Repeat five to ten times.

3. Once your puppy associates the muffled single click with the treat, you can try a muffled complete click (both pressing and releasing). Then graduate to an unmuffled complete click.

No-Reward Markers

Just as a clicker or the word "good" can mark a correct response, you can help your puppy learn by letting him know when he makes an incorrect response. You do this by using a no-reward marker such as the word "oops," "ah-ah," or "uh-oh." Let's say you ask your puppy to sit but she lies down instead. You can say "oops" and that signals that she lost the chance of getting a reward. Another example is asking her to stay. If she gets up right away, say "oops" and turn away.

Through your use of the no-reward marker, your puppy can learn what behavior will not get a reward in a particular situation. Keep in mind that when your puppy doesn't do what you've asked, you've probably gone too far too fast. Go back to a point in the exercise where she was previously successful, rather than have her repeat mistakes over and over. If you find yourself using the no-reward marker a lot, you're making things too hard. So, whenever you use a no-reward marker, consider it a sign to yourself to make the next training request easier for your puppy.

Unintentional Training

Many problem behaviors are a result of people unintentionally teaching the puppy a behavior they don't want their puppy doing. Pet a jumping puppy when you come home because you are so glad to see him and you end up with a puppy who jumps on anyone who comes in the door. Or let's say you are talking on the phone and your puppy starts barking for attention. A normal response is to interrupt the call and yell at the puppy, "Be quiet!" Once again, you may be rewarding the barking by giving your puppy what he wants—your attention. Giving your dog attention, whether positive or negative, while he is barking may actually reinforce the barking. Telling a dog, "It's okay" while he's shivering because of the fireworks or thunder may actually be reinforcing the nervousness!

The Starting Point—Your Puppy's Learning Baseline

Whenever you ask your puppy to do something, set up the training session so that she can succeed. In other words, begin training in a non-distracting environment and have realistic expectations that she can do what you're asking, both physically and emotionally. If she can't, she'll get frustrated and stop trying and you'll get frustrated and might think your puppy is being stubborn, stupid, or just plain lazy. Just like us, a puppy learns quickly when she builds on her successes. But at what point do you start training a particular behavior and when do you begin to challenge her with distractions? This brings us to the concept of the "learning baseline."

When we talk about a puppy's learning baseline, we are referring to the point at which your puppy will be successful. This is the puppy's starting point. The learning baseline varies for each puppy. It depends on the puppy's stage of development, personality, health, and so on. For example, an eight-week-old puppy without any prior training must be taught to sit beginning with at kindergarten level in Chapter 18. However, if you adopt a six-month-old puppy who already has some training, her learning baseline may begin at the grade school level. You can probably ask this more experienced puppy to sit and begin adding distractions immediately. If you start the younger puppy at the same advanced level, she'll quickly become frustrated. Conversely, the more experienced puppy will become bored if you don't challenge her.

So it's not only important to start at the point where your puppy can succeed, it's also important to keep her interested and mentally stimulated. It's up to you to be on the lookout for those moments when your puppy says, "Got it! This is exciting. What else is there?" That's when you take her to the next level of training for that behavior. Developing an awareness of when to challenge and when to hold back distinguishes a really talented trainer. This awareness keeps the training fresh and motivating—something your puppy eagerly awaits. Sometimes you will be able to go to the next level of a behavior several times in one session; other times you will find that your puppy needs several sessions to figure out what you want.

Sensitivity to Touch, Motion, and Sound

Some puppies are super sensitive and may cower, hide, or freeze up if touched or lifted, if they hear an unusual sound, or if someone moves in front of them. These ultra-sensitive puppies will find even kindergarten training too much to handle. They are too consumed with fear to learn anything you might be trying to teach them. If this is the case with your puppy, call a professional trainer to help you out as this level of behavior modification is beyond the scope of this book. If your puppy exhibits extreme sensitivity or fear, hiring a professional trainer is mandatory. That being said, this book offers some helpful tips for sensitive puppies who are not extremely so.

The socialization exercises in Chapter 10 will help your puppy acclimate to everyday encounters with people, animals, or objects. If your puppy is sensitive (but not ultra-sensitive), here are some steps to get him to feel more comfortable:

1. Recognize and identify the exact environment that triggers the puppy's fearful response.
2. Maintain a distance far enough away from the scary thing or lower the intensity (volume, speed, duration) of the scary thing so as not to trigger the puppy's fearful response.
3. Change the way the puppy feels about the scary thing (classical counter-conditioning) by pairing its presence with treats and happy talk.
4. Repeat the positive encounters in short, frequent sessions.

5. As your puppy gets comfortable with the scary thing at this distance and intensity, gradually decrease the distance while continuing with treats and happy talk.

6. Build your puppy's confidence by teaching him to lie down and relax on cue (operant conditioning). Gradually add the three Ds (see page 193).

In other words, keep it positive, keep it short, make it frequent, and keep it safe.

When you begin any training session, look at your environment from your puppy's point of view and think of the ways in which the sights, sounds, and physical sensations of the world might be distracting him or influencing his behavior. Is there a dog barking in the distance? Are tree branches moving or leaves blowing? Is dirt swirling in the wind? Are airplanes flying overhead? Set up your training environment far away from anything that will compromise your puppy's success.

The Three Steps to Shape Reliable Behavior

Puppies have an oral-eye reflex. When they see something move, their tendency is to follow the movement and then catch whatever's moving with their mouth. This can get pretty frustrating if you're trying to train her but she keeps jumping up trying to grab your hand. That's why most of the behaviors in this book begin with the instructions, "start with your hands on your chest." By holding your hands close to your chest, your puppy is less distracted and more focused on what you are doing. These instructions may sound a bit formal and a little robotic; however, our intent is to simply remind you to move less and focus more. You can put your hands in any position you like . . . just stay relaxed and don't move around so much.

The following example outlines the three steps used at kindergarten level sit:

Prepare: Begin in a non-distracting environment with a good supply of highly valued treats. Put your hands in "starting position," holding them close to your chest.

1. **Get the behavior using a treat (lure) and a hand signal.**
   Facing your puppy, move a food treat (lure) over her head. The hand moving over your puppy's head becomes the hand signal for "sit." As your hand with the lure moves over your puppy's head, she will look up and her behind will automatically lower to the floor. Click, praise, and treat. Repeat ten to fifteen times. Do several sessions per day or over the course of a few days until your puppy reaches the 80 percent success rate—that is, she'll sit eight out of ten times. (Most dogs are successful learning how to sit in one session.) At that point, you are ready to proceed to step two.

2. **Attach a word to the behavior along with the hand signal.**
   Say the word "sit" as your hand with the lure moves over her head. Click, praise, and treat. When your puppy is successful eight out of ten times, put the treat in your other hand and repeat the process, giving the signal with your empty hand. This is to ensure that your puppy is following the signal, rather than being bribed by the food. When your puppy is successful eight out of ten times, go to step three.

3. **Use the word without the hand signal.**
   Put your hands in starting position on your chest and say "sit" without using the hand signal. Then click, praise, and treat.

The Three Steps to Shape Reliable Behavior are detailed in the accompanying chart. These three steps apply to the beginning level of most behaviors, with a few exceptions which will be obvious as you go along.

The Three Steps to Shape Reliable Behavior

Warm Up

- Make sure there is very little distraction in the environment and you're close enough to your puppy so that she will pay attention to you.
- Set your goals.
- Check negative attitudes at the door.
- Breathe!
- Rev up your clicker (if using one).
- Gather $10,000 rewards

1. Get the Behavior

- Encourage your puppy and get her attention by using vocal sounds such as "tch-tch," whistling, or using her name if you know she'll look your way. Or you can get her attention by clapping, patting your leg, waving your hand, and so on.
- Use a food lure in almost all cases when you begin to teach a new behavior.
- Use your hand signal. Start with simple parts of the behavior and continuously reinforce baby steps.
- Do ten to fifteen repetitions of each behavior in each session.
- **Now increase the distance:** If you're 80 percent sure your puppy will do the behavior without using food as the lure, put the treat in your other hand, make the hand signal with the hand that's not holding the treat, click and praise the behavior, and then reward with the treat that you're holding in the other hand.

2. Attach a Word Along with the Hand Signal

- When you're sure your puppy will sit 80 percent of the time you make the hand signal, begin to use the word "sit" immediately before making the hand signal.

3. Use the Word Only

- Use voice only. Then begin adding other criteria: adding duration, distance, and distractions, introducing them one at a time. Go back to the point your puppy was successful (including using a lure if necessary) each time you add something new. Reward each behavior every time. Then, when your puppy is successful 80 percent of the time, ask for more by having your puppy do the behavior two or three times in a row and then giving a treat. Finally, progress to a "Las Vegas–style," intermittent reward schedule—reward your puppy every once in a while so she never knows when the treat is coming.

Increase Reliability by Adding Challenges of Duration, Distance, and Distractions

Once you've taught your puppy how to do a behavior at the kindergarten level, you will proceed to more advanced training for that behavior by gradually add the "Three Ds": duration, distance, and distractions:

- Duration means that you will add more time, having your puppy hold any specific behavior for longer and longer periods of time.
- Distance means that you will add distance between you and your puppy when you ask for behaviors.
- Distractions means that you will add sound (auditory), touch (tactile), and movement (visual) challenges to the behavior.

In the grade school level, you will gradually add a little more time to your puppy's stay, a little more distance to your puppy's come when called, a new distraction when your puppy is lying down, and so on. It's similar to the process you went through in learning to read. First you learned the alphabet, then how to read words, then short sentences, then whole books. Imagine how discouraging and senseless it would have been if your kindergarten teacher had asked you to begin by reading *War and Peace*!

Don't go to the advanced stages until you are confident that your puppy will be successful at least 80 percent of the time at the previous level.

Putting It All Together

Once your puppy has mastered the kindergarten level of a behavior, you're ready to add challenges and lead your puppy through grade school. Later, after your puppy has physically and emotionally matured into an adult dog, you may want to advance to high school and college. At these levels your dog will do what you ask at least 90 percent of the time, anywhere, anytime. (More advanced levels are taught in Paul and Norma's book, *The Dog Whisperer.*)

There are two golden rules:

1. If your puppy won't do what you want him to do, just go back to the last step that he did successfully.
2. Whenever you change the training situation by adding or increasing one of the three Ds, start teaching the behavior from scratch. That is, return to step one for each and every behavior, each time you add a new challenge.

Puppies learn on a curve. They have good days and bad days, just like us. They need time to integrate what they've learned. Each day, begin each exercise at your puppy's learning baseline, that is, his starting point. Build on success.

Chapter 18

The Basic Behaviors: Skills that Will Last a Lifetime

Now that you have prepared yourself, your puppy, and her environment, you are ready to begin the lessons. If you're a visual learner, you might also benefit from Paul's DVD, The Dog Whisperer: Beginning and Intermediate Dog Training, which will enhance the process (*www.dogwhispererdvd.com*). These behaviors may be taught in any sequence; however, the order in which they're taught below is as good as any. Up until full adult maturity, between eighteen months and three years of age, virtually all puppies are able to reach a grade school level of behavioral reliability. This means they will do what you ask in most non-distracting situations. Some can even reach more advanced levels. This book is designed to show you how to start your puppy at kindergarten level and get her through grade school level.

Pay Attention

"Pay attention" is the foundation for all other behaviors. It means: "Look at me. We're about to do something." If you don't have your puppy's attention, she won't do what you ask. For example, if she's running through the house with her squeaky toy or playing with your other dog or cat, she won't sit when you ask. Saying the word "sit" in situations like these is meaningless.

195

Before teaching any other behavior, first teach your puppy to look at you whenever you say her name. This is easy. Within a week your puppy will make the association between the sound (her name) and the treat and start looking at you whenever she hears her name.

Prepare: Begin in an environment that has few distractions or no distractions at all.

Training Without a Clicker?

Each behavior includes the instructions "click, praise, and treat." If you're not using a clicker, simply use your selected word or phrase instead to let your puppy know he did what you wanted before giving him a treat. For instance, say "good dog" or "yes" or "that'll do" or "hooray," and so on every time your dog does the behavior you're asking for and he'll get the idea. In the beginning try to use the same word or phrase consistently. (See "Markers—Clickers and Words" on page 184.)

Step One: Get the Behavior Using a Treat (Lure) and a Hand Signal

Put a treat between your thumb and index finger. Hold the clicker in your other hand. Place your hands in the starting position on your chest, as described on page 186. Put your hand with the food treat in front of your puppy's nose (see Figure 18-1). Then, move the treat from the puppy's nose to your eyes (see Figure 18-2). You are using the treat as a lure. As your puppy's eyes follow your hand moving up to your face, click, praise, and treat. Repeat five to ten times. Most puppies figure this out in one session. When your puppy follows your hand up to your eyes eight out of ten times, you are ready to proceed to the next step.

Figure 18-1

In step one of the pay attention behavior, put a food treat in your hand and hold that hand in front of your puppy's nose.

Figure 18-2

Then move the treat from the puppy's nose to your eyes.

Note: If cannot get your puppy's attention because she's more interested in whatever else she's doing, pick up the tether and lead her away from the distraction.

Step Two: Attach a Word to the Behavior Along with the Hand Signal

Repeat step one, but before you move the hand holding the treat, say your puppy's name or whatever other words you prefer like "pay attention" or "look at me," making a kissy sound, and so on. Immediately give the hand signal (that is, move your lure hand to your eyes).

As your puppy's eyes follow your hand going up to your face, click, praise, and treat.

Repeat five to ten times. Repeat the process in subsequent sessions until she is successful 80 percent of the time or eight out of ten times.

Start Your Training Sessions with "Pay Attention"

Before teaching any behavior, get your puppy's attention by saying his name or making a kissy sound. If your puppy ignores you, redirect his attention by waving a treat in front of his nose and lure him to you. If he is still more interested in whatever else he's doing, pick up the tether and lead him away from the distraction. Then practice the pay attention exercise three to five times. When he is paying attention to you again, you can practice whatever behavior you're working on.

Once you've reached the 80 percent mark, repeat the process except this time hold the treat in your other hand, so that you are giving the hand signal with an empty hand. (This is to ensure that your puppy is following the signal, rather than being bribed by the food. The food should only be a reward, not a bribe.) When your puppy follows your empty hand from her nose to your eyes, click, praise, and treat from other hand.

Repeat five to ten times. Repeat the process until you reach the 80 percent mark, then move on to step three.

Step Three: Use the Word Without the Hand Signal

Keep your hands on your chest. Say your puppy's name (or make a kissy sound or say "pay attention") without using the hand signal. If your puppy looks to your face, click, praise, and treat.

If your puppy does not look to your face, try the following:

Having Problems?

🦴 Drop the treat from your mouth, rather than your hand. Give the vocal signal, and as your puppy looks at your face, let the treat drop from your mouth. This will help her focus on your face because that's where the $10,000 treat is coming from.

🦴 Face your puppy. Put a treat in your hand and stretch your arm straight out from your side, parallel to the floor. Your puppy will look at your hand. Now wait. Within forty-five seconds, your puppy will turn her attention away from your treat-filled hand and glance at your eyes. When she does, immediately click and praise her and give her the treat. Repeat this five to ten times. When your puppy figures this out, she will look at you as soon as you extend your hand. You can now add the vocal signal.

Sit

Sit is a control position. If your puppy is sitting, he's not jumping. If he's sitting, he's not pulling the pot roast off the kitchen counter.

Sit—Kindergarten Level

Prepare: Begin in an environment that has few or no distractions. Put a treat between your thumb and index finger. Hold the clicker in your other hand. Place your hands in the starting position on your chest.

Step One: Get the Behavior Using a Treat (Lure) and a Hand Signal

Holding a treat between your thumb and forefinger, starting with your hand at your puppy's nose level, move your hand with the treat up and over the top of your puppy's nose about two inches from his head. The hand moving over your puppy's head becomes the hand signal for "sit." Go no farther back than the crown of his head. The idea is to get your puppy to tilt his head and look up at your hand. As he looks up, his back end will tend to go down (see Figure 18-3). If you move your hand too fast, he'll back up. If you move your hand too high, he might jump to get the treat. If you move your hand too low, he won't do anything except nibble your hand. You can encourage him all the while with "goooooood dog," "you're the best," "way to go," or the phrase of your choosing in a friendly but not too exuberant voice. As soon as his behind hits the floor, click, praise, and treat (see Figure 18-4). Repeat this sequence ten to fifteen times in each training session. Most puppies are able to learn sit in one session. If necessary, do several sessions per day or over the course of a few days until he reaches the 80 percent success rate—that is, he'll do it eight out of ten times. At that point, you are ready to proceed to step two.

Figure 18-3

Step one of kindergarten sit: With a treat in one hand and a clicker in the other, bring your hand with the treat over the top of his nose.

Figure 18-4

When the puppy's behind hits the floor, click, praise, and treat.

Step Two: Attach a Word to the Behavior
Along with the Hand Signal

Put a treat between your thumb and index finger. Hold the clicker in your other hand. Place your hands in the starting position on your chest. Say "sit" immediately preceding the hand signal of moving your hand over your puppy's head. When your puppy sits, click, praise, and treat. Repeat ten to fifteen times. When you are 80 percent sure your puppy will follow your hand motion, you are ready to move on. **Note:** To get your puppy up from the sit position so you can practice again, simply throw a treat off to the side and say "find it."

Now you're going to increase the distance of the reward by putting the treat in your other hand, the one not making the hand signal. This is to ensure that your puppy is following the signal, rather than being bribed by the food. Place your hands in the starting position on your chest. Say "sit" just before you move your empty hand over your puppy's nose. Click, praise, and treat from the other hand. Repeat five to ten times. When your puppy sits eight out of ten times, you are ready for step three.

Keep Challenging Your Puppy

Sometimes you will be able to go to the next level of a behavior several times in one session; other times you will find that your puppy needs several sessions to figure out what you want. Developing an awareness of when to challenge and when to hold back distinguishes a really talented trainer. This awareness keeps the training fresh and motivating—something your puppy eagerly awaits.

Step Three: Use the Word Without the Hand Signal

Keep your hands on your chest, say "sit," and wait. Give your puppy up to forty-five seconds to respond. If your puppy doesn't sit within forty-five seconds, go back and do three repetitions of step two, then try step three again. As you progress, the time it takes for your puppy to sit after hearing the signal will decrease.

When your puppy sits within three seconds of hearing your voice (without the hand signal), he now knows the sit behavior in that particular context or situation.

Having Problems?

- Watch your hand position. If you move your hand too far over his head, he'll back up. If you move your hand too high, he might jump to get the treat. If you move your hand too low under his jaw, he won't do anything except nibble your hand. You can encourage him all the while with "gooooood dog," "you're the best," "way to go," or another phrase of your choosing.

- If your puppy jumps instead of sitting, say "oops" or "uh-oh" and very quickly pull the treat away. As soon as he is on all fours again, immediately begin the process over, moving your hand over his head and continuing to encourage him. This "oops" or "uh-oh" is your "no reward marker." It tells your puppy that he didn't get it right, therefore he is not going to get the treat. Never do more than two no-reward markers in a row.

- If your puppy simply refuses to lower her behind, use "approximations," or simpler forms of the sit behavior. For instance, you can click, praise, and treat the first "approximation," represented by her behind lowering 1/8 of an inch. Then you can click, praise, and treat her when she lowers her behind another ⅛-inch lower, and so on. Then you can click, praise, and jackpot the final behavior which is her behind actually touching the floor.

- Use the Magnet Game as part of the training process. Throughout the day, whenever you happen to see your puppy sit, "catch" the behavior by praising and throwing your puppy a treat.

- Check with your veterinarian. Make sure that there are no physical problems that keep your puppy from being able to sit.

Sit—Grade School Level

Once your puppy is 80 percent reliable with a "word only" sit at the kindergarten level, begin weaning your puppy off the treats. Start by cutting the treats in half—no, we do not mean make the treats smaller. We mean reward your puppy with a treat 50 percent of the time that he responds to the word "sit." Make it unpredictable as to when he will get the treat, rather than following a pattern like "every other sit gets a treat"—if the pattern is predictable, your puppy will start predicting it! In that case, you will soon have a puppy who responds to "sit" in some way like this: "Hmm, this is the fifth time she's asked me, so I won't get a treat, therefore I don't really need to sit, do I?" So, mix it up, but have the treat count come out to more or less half the time. If you haven't lost any reliability, you can then reduce the treats to 25 percent of the time, and then to every once in awhile. If at any point you notice that your puppy is responding less reliably, go back to a higher percentage of treats for awhile, then cut back a little more gradually and imperceptibly.

You can also incorporate the sit behavior into your puppy's daily routine by implementing the Nothing in Life Is Free strategy using life rewards in the following ways:

- Have her sit before going outdoors, rewarding her by opening the door and letting her have access to the fun and good smells of the yard or a walk.
- Have her sit before you throw her ball, rewarding her by throwing it.
- Have her sit before taking her leash off inside, rewarding her with the freedom to move around the house with you.
- Have her sit before going up and down the stairs, rewarding her with the privilege of staying with you.
- Have her sit before being let out of her kennel, and so on. Use the list of things that your puppy likes that are not food that you made in Chapter 16.

Lie Down

Lie down is another control position, only better. It is more relaxed than sit, harder to get up from than sit, and more difficult to bark from than sit. When you ask your puppy to lie down, it is a way of saying "I really want you to relax."

Lie Down—Kindergarten Level

Begin in an environment that has few distractions or no distractions at all. Put a treat in one hand and hold the clicker in your other hand. Place your hands in the starting position on your chest.

Step One: Get the Behavior Using a Treat (Lure) and a Hand Signal

Start with your puppy in a sit position. Hold a treat between your thumb and forefinger, place it just under your puppy's nose, and move it slowly down to the ground ("nose to toes"). The hand moving to the ground becomes the hand signal for "lie down." Imagine there's an invisible string attached to your hand and your puppy's nose, as though you're pulling her nose to the ground. At the moment she lies down, click, praise, and treat. Repeat. When she is successful eight out of ten times, proceed to step two.

Figure 18-5

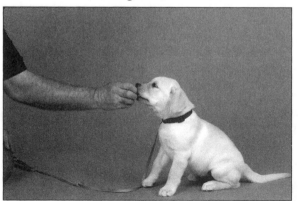

In teaching your puppy to lie down, start with your puppy in a sit position. Move the treat from her "nose to toes."

Figure 18-6

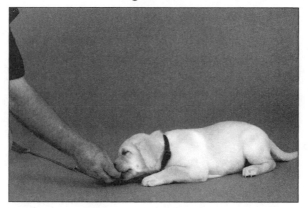

When your puppy lies down, click, praise, and treat.

Step Two: Attach a Word to the Behavior Along with the Hand Signal

Present your hand with a treat just under her nose, say the word "down," and move your hand straight to the ground. Say the word "down" immediately before the hand signal. When your puppy lies down, click, praise, and treat. Repeat five to ten times. When you are sure your puppy will follow your hand motion 80 percent of the time, you are ready to move on. **Note:** To get your puppy up from the down position, simply throw a treat off to the side and say "find it."

Now you're going to increase the distance of the reward by putting the treat in your other hand. This is to ensure that your puppy is following the signal, rather than being bribed by the food. You are still going to use the food as a reward, but not as a bribe. Place your hands in the starting position on your chest. Say "down" just before you place your empty hand under her nose and then move it straight to the ground. Click, praise, and treat from the other hand. Repeat five to ten times. When your puppy lies down eight out of ten times, you are ready for step three.

Step Three: Use the Word Without the Hand Signal

With your puppy in a sit position, say "down" without using the hand signal. (Keep your hands on your chest.) Wait up to forty-five seconds. Even if your puppy gets up, wait the forty-five seconds. If your puppy doesn't get it, repeat step two three to five times. Then try step three again. When your puppy does lie down, click, lavishly praise, and "jackpot" her with several treats.

Having Problems?

- 🦴 Use "approximations," or simpler forms of the down behavior. For instance, you can click, praise, and treat the first "approximation" represented by her head lowering a few inches. Then you can click, praise, and treat her when she lowers her head lower and moves a paw forward. Then you can click, praise, and treat the final behavior when she goes all the way down. If your puppy gets up from the down position, quickly withdraw the treat, say "oops," and start again.

- 🦴 Try curling your hand around to your puppy's side instead of moving it straight down. The puppy has to turn her head and body to reach the treat. This sometimes helps to facilitate the process.

- 🦴 Practice on a slippery floor. Oftentimes the puppy's behind will simply slide into position.

- 🦴 Relax your expectations. It isn't necessary for your puppy to lie down in one session. Go with the flow.

- 🦴 Don't keep repeating the word if you're looking for reliability. Say it once and wait. If your puppy can't figure it out, go back to the point where she was successful.

- 🦴 If it's fun for you, it's fun for your puppy. So if your puppy stands around or seems bored, get happy! Dance around and use different vocal sounds from kissy sounds to howls. Pretend to eat food and exaggerate with "hmm-mmmm . . . look what I have!" Drop to the ground and pretend you found something interesting. Use a tennis ball or another of your puppy's favorite toys in order to generate interest.

☞ The Magnet Game is the biggest help for the down exercise (see page 177).

Lie Down—Grade School Level
In grade school level lie down, you will build on the puppy's previous success with this behavior, which leads to greater reliability.

☞ Gradually decrease the number of times you reward the down with a treat, in the same way you did with sit (see above). Integrate down into your puppy's daily routine as well, using life rewards with the Nothing in Life Is Free principle (see page 179).

☞ Practice having your puppy lie down from a standing position (instead of the sit position), using your voice signal only.

☞ Teach your puppy to sit from a down position. Imagine that an invisible string is attached from her nose to your hand. Begin with a treat in your hand and slowly move it straight up. Click and reward. Then practice "sit-ups": sit, down, sit, down. Click, praise, and treat.

Stand
Teaching your puppy to stand is really helpful for visits to the veterinarian, when wiping your puppy's paws, and for grooming and washing.

Stand—Kindergarten Level
Prepare: Begin in an environment that has few distractions or no distractions at all. Put a treat between your thumb and index finger. Hold the clicker in your other hand. Place your hands in the starting position on your chest.

Step One: Get the Behavior Using a Treat (Lure) and a Hand Signal

Place your puppy in a sit, facing you. Move the hand that's holding the treat from your chest to a position directly in front of and one inch away from your puppy's nose, palm forward (see Figure18-7). Slowly move your hand away from your puppy's nose, keeping it parallel to the floor (see Figure 18-8). This hand movement becomes the hand signal for "stand." As your puppy lifts his behind the least little bit, click, praise, reward. Repeat this a few times, and with each subsequent attempt, click and reward your puppy for lifting his behind a little more off the floor. Some puppies get this immediately and you don't have to go in baby steps ("approximations"). Repeat ten to fifteen times. When your puppy is successful eight out of ten times, you are ready to proceed to step two.

Figure 18-7

Figure 18-8

In step one of stand, place your hand one inch from your puppy's nose, palm forward.

Next, slowly move your hand away from your puppy's nose, keeping it parallel to the ground. As your puppy lifts his behind the least little bit, click, praise, and reward.

Step Two: Attach a Word to the Behavior Along with the Hand Signal

Put a treat between your thumb and index finger. Hold the clicker in your other hand. Place your hands in the starting position on your chest. Say "stand" immediately preceding the hand signal of moving your hand away from your puppy's nose as in step one. When your puppy stands, click, praise, and treat. Repeat ten to fifteen times. When you are sure that your puppy will follow your hand motion 80 percent of the time, you are ready for the next progression in which you put the treat in your other hand. Place your hands in the starting position on your chest. Say "stand" just before you move your empty hand away from your puppy's nose. When your puppy stands, click, praise, and treat from the other hand. Repeat five to ten times. When your puppy stands eight out of ten times, you are ready for step three.

Step Three: Use the Word Without the Hand Signal

Put your hands in starting position on your chest. Say stand without using the hand signal. Wait up to forty-five seconds. If he does it, click, praise, and jackpot; then repeat. If he doesn't do it, go back to step two.

Having Problems?

- ☞ Make sure the hand with the treat isn't more than an inch from his nose at any time.
- ☞ Reward approximations (baby steps). Reward your puppy for leaning forward, then reward again for leaning a little bit more forward, then again for slightly lifting his behind off the floor, and so on.
- ☞ Relax your expectations. It isn't necessary your puppy stands in one session. Go with the flow.
- ☞ Don't keep repeating the word if you're looking for reliability. Say it once and wait.

For this and all exercises, your attitude can help tremendously. If it's fun for you, it's fun for your puppy.

Stand—Grade School Level

Ask your puppy to stand, starting with him in a down position, on a vocal signal only. If your puppy doesn't stand immediately, wait forty-five seconds. If he still doesn't do it after forty-five seconds, first have him sit from the down position (see the previous Grade School Level) and then ask him to stand. Repeat three to five times. Now ask him again to stand directly from the down. If he does it, jackpot him. If not, repeat the down, sit, stand, as above, until he gets it.

As with sit and lie down, gradually fade out the treat rewards from 100 percent of the time, to 50 percent, to 25 percent, to every once in awhile. Replace treats with life rewards like praise, petting, attention, playtime, trips outside, and so on.

Stay

In the last chapter, you learned about the three Ds—duration, distance, and distractions. Stay is the signal used when asking your puppy to remain in position for any length of time—otherwise known as duration. It is the ultimate control position. Some trainers don't teach "stay" as a separate behavior. They feel that the sit, lie down, or stand signal has a built-in expectation that the puppy will remain in that position until released. The theory is perfectly sound, but we find most people forget to release their puppies from a behavior and the puppies end up releasing themselves. Signaling "stay" is not only a reminder to your puppy to remain in position, it is also a reminder to you that you have asked him to remain in position and will tell him when he can move around again.

You will also be adding the other Ds—distance and distractions—to your stay. Don't worry. It will all make sense as you zip along.

Practice stay with all of the behaviors you learned thus far: sit, lie down, and stand. Just because your puppy has learned sit-stay, that does not mean she will know down-stay or stand-stay. You must repeat the steps from the beginning for each of those positions. For example, your puppy may have mastered a three-minute sit-stay, but you will need to start at one second again when you start working on down-stay. Most puppies figure this out pretty quickly.

Stay—Kindergarten Level

At the kindergarten level of stay, you should be able to progress to a point where your puppy will stay for up to three minutes.

Step One: Adding Duration.

Ask your puppy to sit, lie down, or stand. Say "stay" and position the palm of your hand facing your puppy, fingers pointed up, as if you were directing traffic to stop. You are starting by using the hand signal and the word signal together since you already know your puppy can do the behavior. Say "stay" and count one second ("one thousand one") and, if your puppy stays, click, praise, and treat. Then you can release your dog and give him permission to move by saying "okay."

Ask your puppy to stay again. This time count two seconds ("one thousand one, one thousand two"). If your puppy stays, click, praise, and treat. Be sure that you bring your hand back to the starting position on your chest right after you say "stay," rather than holding it up for as long as your puppy is position. Otherwise you will be unintentionally teaching your puppy to stay for as long as you have your hand up—pretty inconvenient if you would eventually like to have a thirty-minute stay.

With each successful exercise, which means your puppy isn't moving from her position once you've asked her to stay, increase the length of time in five-second increments until your puppy will stay for up to three minutes at a time. That's usually the limit for a puppy, but as she gets older you can incrementally add more time to her stay.

Tips:

- Virtually every puppy will stay for a second or two. We are explaining these steps in a second-by-second manner to illustrate how the process works, but you can jump to five- or even ten-second time frames with each repetition if you are having success.

🦴 Some people don't like to use "okay" as a release word, since it is so common in conversation that someone around your puppy might say it when she is in the middle of a stay and inadvertently release her. You can use an alternate word or phrase like "free," or "that's all"—anything is fine as long as you are consistent.

🦴 The word you use releases your dog from the stay. The treat is not the release! Just because you have rewarded your dog with a click, praise, and treat, it doesn't mean the behavior is over.

Step Two: Adding Distance

Ask your puppy to sit, lie down, or stand. Say stay and position the palm of your hand facing toward your puppy as in step one. Move back a step and then return to your puppy immediately. Click, praise, and treat. At the kindergarten level stay you are working distance separately from duration, so don't count any seconds after you have stepped back from your puppy. Return immediately. Repeat three to five times.

Ask your puppy to stay. This time move back two steps, return. Click, praise, and treat. Repeat three to five times. With each successful attempt, which means your puppy isn't moving from her position once you've asked her to stay, increase the distance you are backing away to three feet, then four feet, and so on. Once again, make sure you return to your starting position right in front of her and reward her after each attempt. Continue adding distance until you can get her to stay in position with you moving and returning from thirty feet away.

Step Three: Adding Distractions—The Walk Around the Clock Exercise

Puppies are very sensitive to anything that comes up behind them and the Walk Around the Clock exercise will help desensitize your puppy to those surprises. It prepares your puppy for the real world, that is, when people are passing by, coming and going from all directions.

Have your puppy sit, lie down, or stand in front of you. Imagine your puppy is in the center of the face of a clock. Twelve o'clock is in front, three o'clock to the left side, six o'clock is behind your puppy, and nine o'clock is to the right side. Place your hands in the starting position on your chest. Ask her to stay.

Move your left foot and step to her side to the one o'clock position; return to the front of your puppy (at twelve o'clock). Click, praise, and treat. If she's successful in staying put, say "stay" and go one step farther (two o'clock) and then move back to the front. Click, praise, and treat.

Continue until you're able to walk all the way around your puppy. Each time you return to the start position, click, praise, and treat. Just go at your puppy's own speed. Once you get all the way around, give her a jackpot; that is, reward with four or five treats one after another, all the while telling her how great she is. Keep the sessions short.

Having Problems?

- Just because you are successful walking around your puppy in one direction that does not mean you will be successful walking around her the other way. If your puppy gets up when you walk around, go back to the point where she was successful. Then incrementally add more steps "around the clock."

- If your puppy is distracted, interrupt her with a sound such as "uh-oh," "oops," or "nope" and redirect her attention back to you with a motion such as waving your hand in front of her face (if necessary, with food in the hand).

- If your puppy moves as soon as you begin to move, try this tip. Have a friend stand next to you. With your puppy in position facing both of you, take a handful of treats and let her nibble them out of your hand while your friend walks around her. If your puppy is afraid of people moving behind her, this is a form of classical counter-conditioning. Your puppy is getting treats while the thing she's afraid of (person moving) is in play. Gradually she will change the way she feels about people moving because it will be associated with treats.

❧ A comfortable location often represents security to a puppy, so practice in a room where she is most at ease.

❧ If your puppy likes her bed, first practice stay on her bed, and then practice in other locations.

❧ Don't "stalk" your puppy by moving slowly or hesitantly. Walk at a relaxed, normal speed.

Stay—Grade School Level

Start combining the three Ds incrementally. Take one step back (distance) and count one second (duration) then return to your puppy. Click, praise, and treat. Then take one step back and count two seconds before returning. Click, praise, and treat. Now take one step back and count five seconds, and so on.

Once your puppy will stay in position for thirty seconds when you take one step away from her, increase the distance by taking two steps away from her. Incrementally increase the time she stays in position when you are two steps away, beginning at one second and working up to thirty seconds. Always return to her after each attempt and click, praise, and treat. Continue to combine distance and duration in this way, increasing your distance by a step, and gradually increasing the time that your puppy can stay in position with you at that distance.

Now continue adding distance and incorporate leaving the room. Begin with staying out of sight for one second and immediately returning to your puppy. If your puppy is eight to ten weeks old, progress to staying out of sight for one minute; ten to twelve weeks old, two minutes; twelve to sixteen weeks, three minutes; sixteen weeks to six months, four minutes; and for six months and older, five minutes and longer. If your puppy gets up, take him back to the location where you started.

Now you're ready for distractions. When you can walk all the way around your puppy while she is sitting, lying down, or standing in a stay, add these additional challenges:

🦴 Ask your puppy to stay and walk quickly around her. If she is successful, click, praise, and treat.

🦴 When your puppy is successful staying while you walk quickly, add an additional challenge by jogging around her. When she is successful, click, praise, and treat.

🦴 Then add the additional challenge of waving your hands and saying "booga, booga" in an excited voice as you run around your puppy.

🦴 Increase the number of times you can circle around your puppy at a normal pace. Then gradually increase your speed until you circle around the puppy three times saying "booga, booga" before stopping to click, praise, and treat.

For stay in all three positions (sit, lie down, and stand), you can fade out the treats by rewarding only the very best stays with treats. In other words, the longest stay (duration), or farthest away stay (distance), or stay in the most distracting environment gets a treat reward. Anything less than the very best gets lesser rewards, like petting and praise. As your puppy's skill level gets higher, you can raise your criteria for which stays are eligible for treat rewards.

Tip: Every exercise or behavior has a start and a finish. If you have asked your puppy to stay in any position, you must remember to "end" the behavior and give a signal that releases her. If you forget to release your puppy from a stay, she will eventually just release herself and leave. This makes for really unreliable stays.

Come When Called

The benefits of a reliable come when called, which is also referred to as a recall, don't really need to be enumerated. The key to its usefulness of course, is how consistent you are. There is simply no shortcut to reliability, which is based on three things: repetitions, consistency, and improvement through ever-increasing challenges. That's it.

The number one rule is: Never call your puppy to you unless you are 80 percent sure she'll respond; in other words, don't use the word "come" if there's a good chance she won't. Also, don't call your puppy to you if you're going to yell at her or if you're leaving for the day. (In positive training we don't yell anyway, so you should be okay.) If you do yell or leave her after calling her, your puppy will very quickly learn that there is a negative consequence whenever she hears the word "come"; hence, she won't come when called. Unless she's attained a strong grade school level come, never call her if she's running away. She might inadvertently learn that the word "come" is irrelevant or that "come" means run the other way (because that's the word she hears while she's running away from you).

Note: For this behavior, step three (use the word only) is not used. Always have your puppy touch your hand whenever you say "come."

Tip: If you find it difficult remembering to connect the word "come" with positive consequences, change the word to "cookie." Everyone remembers to be positive and give their puppy treats when they say "cookie."

Come When Called—Kindergarten Level

We teach come when called as a "targeting" exercise because it is so easy for both humans to use and dogs to learn. Targeting simply means teaching your puppy to touch his nose, paw, or other part of his body to a visible "target" such as a stick, a Post-it note, a light switch, a door handle, and so on. For come when called, you can use a target that is very easy to carry around—the palm of your hand.

In teaching come when called it's important to emphasize incremental training or teaching in baby steps. Your eventual goal is to have your puppy stop whatever he's doing and run to you as soon as you give the signal. He won't even think about it because it becomes an automatic response. The key to success is to do thousands of repetitions over a long period of time.

Step One: Get the Behavior Using a Treat (Lure) and a Hand Signal

Rub a highly valued treat on your fingers and hold the treat in your other hand. Put your hands in starting position on your chest (see Figure 18-9). Now bring the treat-smelling hand down to your side in front of your puppy's nose. The hand signal for come is your hand moving from your chest, down to your side. As soon as he touches it (see Figure 18-10), click, praise, and reward with the treat. Repeat ten to fifteen times and proceed to step two.

Step Two: Attach a Word to the Behavior Along with the Hand Signal

Say "come" immediately before presenting your hand. For each subsequent repetition, add an inch or two of distance (see Figure 18-11). Progress to a distance of twenty feet. The goal is that no matter how far away you are, your puppy will immediately rush over to you to touch your "magic hand." Always click, praise, and treat after every success.

Figure 18-9

In come when called, put your hands in starting position on your chest.

Figure 18-10

When your puppy touches your hand with his nose, click, praise, and treat.

Figure 18-11

As you progress in teaching come when called, continue to add distance.

Hints for Come When Called

Use everyday opportunities and life rewards to practice "come" such as:

🦴 Feeding time. Have your puppy touch your hand before you put the food down.

🦴 Going outside. Have your puppy touch your hand before you open the door.

🦴 When you take your puppy for a walk, periodically ask him to touch your hand (come).

Note: For this behavior, step three (use the word only) will not be used until you get to the Triangle Game on page 261. For now, continue to have your puppy touch your hand whenever you say come, before giving a treat.

Come When Called—Grade School Level

Grade school level come when called builds on the success of kindergarten level to develop greater reliability.

Step One

Form a square with other three other people, each about 6 to 10 feet apart. Ask your puppy to sit and stay in the middle. Have person "A" say with a happy, excited voice, "Jackson, come." As he arrives and touches her hand, click, reward with a treat, affection, praise and petting, and say, "What a wonderful puppy you are!" Then person "B" immediately calls, then person "C" calls, and then each person takes random turns calling "come."

Step Two

Repeat step one, but this time, ask your puppy for another behavior before rewarding. For instance, ask him to sit after touching your hand. When he does so, click, praise, and treat. Repeat five to ten times.

Step Three: Add Challenges and Distractions

🦴 Practice "come" with your back turned to your puppy.

🦴 Practice "come" while you're lying on the ground.

🦴 Practice "come" while you're sitting on the floor.

🦴 Practice "come" while you're in another room.

🦴 Form a longer behavioral chain. Ask your puppy to sit and stay. From a standing position ten feet away, say with a happy, excited voice, "Jackson, come." As he arrives and touches your hand, ask your puppy to sit again, then lie down, then, at the end of all these behaviors, click, praise, and reward him with a treat.

✏ Take it all outdoors. Remember, whenever you change environments, you have to go back to the beginning. So when you take your puppy outdoors, go back and repeat kindergarten level. Start in a relatively low-distraction environment like the backyard early in the morning.

✏ As with stay, reduce the number of treat rewards and give them only on the longest recalls, fastest recalls, and recalls in the most distracting environments. Always key your expectations to your puppy's learning baseline. So if your puppy is great at three feet recalls, but only good at six feet recalls, reward the six feet recalls with treats and the three feet recalls with lesser valued rewards like praise and petting. Or maybe your puppy is great at six feet recalls indoors, but not so great at six feet recalls outdoors. If that's the case, reward the outdoor recalls with food treats and the indoor recalls with other types of rewards. As your puppy improves, raise the bar for earning a treat.

Tip: Throughout the day, whenever your puppy is walking toward you, excitedly put your hand down and say come. This happens frequently, such when you are fixing meals, when you are at the door, when you play hide-and-seek, and so on.

Having Problems?

✏ Young puppies can't see really well at a distance, so crouch down and open your arms like a great invocation and with a happy, excited voice say, "Jackson, come."

Figure 18-12

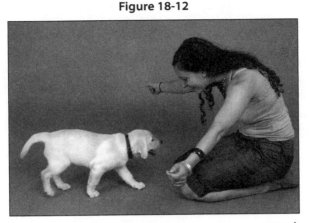

To encourage your puppy to come, you can crouch down and open your arms.

- If your puppy is skittish about facing people head-on, turn your side to him and crouch down when you offer your hand.
- Run the other way after saying "come" to make it a happy game.
- Play hide-and-seek (see the "Hide-and-Seek Game," page 259). Your puppy will always run to find you if you make it a game.
- Do a few repetitions with a treat in the hand that's signaling. Then go back to using a non-treat hand signal.
- If your puppy won't come at a certain distance, go back to the distance at which he was successful.

Heeling—Kindergarten Level

To many people, the term heeling means to walk on a loose leash. However, heel and walk without pulling are really two separate behaviors. (We'll cover walk without pulling after heeling.) Heeling means the puppy walks or stands by your side within an imaginary boxed area by your leg—not too far ahead of you, not too far behind you, not too far from your side, and not too close to you. The idea is that he stays within the perimeter of this imaginary box, without bumping your leg. Heeling is for situations when you want or need very strict control of your dog's movement while walking. It is terrific for circumstances like passing through crowds of people, passing by another dog that you don't want to greet, going through a narrow passageway, walking across the street, or going up and down steps. Most of the time on walks, however, you will want to allow your puppy to have a little freedom to move so he can sniff, go potty, greet other dogs, and so on. You just don't want him to pull your arm out of its socket while he's on the leash.

Heeling—Method One: Spontaneous Heeling

One of the easiest ways to teach your puppy to heel is spontaneous heeling, which is a variation of the Magnet Game.

In a non-distracting, enclosed environment, meander around with your dog off the leash. If you don't have an enclosed area in which to work, put him on a twenty-foot leash so he can't wander off. Whenever your dog happens to walk by your side, click, praise, and treat. You can encourage (prompt) him to do this more and more often by patting your leg, taking quick little steps, and praising even the slightest interest in staying by your side.

Every time he starts going off in another direction, abruptly turn and go the other way, being careful, of course, not to jerk him if he's on a leash. Every time he happens to come up to your side, once again, click, praise, and treat. If he stays there, continue to praise and treat.

Tip: Throughout the day, you will see your puppy start to show up more and more, walking by your side, inside the house and outside. "Catch" this moment with praise and a treat.

Heeling—Method Two: Traditional Heeling

This method is normally taught to puppies when they reach the age of four months or so. You won't follow the usual three-step process (get the behavior, add the word, then word only) because your puppy will figure this out quickly and, therefore, the 80 percent rule comes immediately into play—you are already 80 percent sure your puppy will be successful in doing the behavior.

Step One

In a non-distracting environment, have your puppy sit by your side. With your hands in starting position on your chest, say "heel" and, using the hand that is closest to your puppy, stick a treat in her mouth. Do not walk forward while you do this. Stay in place and don't move. Repeat this ten to fifteen times. The hand signal for heel is similar to the hand signal for come. Your hand will move from your chest down to your side. This works because both come and heel are targeting behaviors. In other words, wherever the target hand is, that's where your puppy is supposed to be. The only difference between come and heel is that in the come behavior your puppy is coming toward you and facing you. In the heel behavior your puppy is facing the same direction as you.

Figure 18-13

Step one of the traditional heeling method: With your puppy by your side, say "heel" and simultaneously stick a treat in her mouth.

Step Two

Your puppy will now be looking up at your hand anticipating another treat. At this point, begin to walk and treat at the same time. As you continue to walk, the hand next to your puppy brings the treat from your chest to your puppy's mouth. Just before you give it to your puppy, say "heel," click, and praise. Bring your hand back to your chest each time. Repeat ten to fifteen times.

Figure 18-14

Step two of the traditional heeling method: Begin to walk with your puppy by your side, say "heel," and stick a treat in her mouth while walking.

Step Three

Keep your hands on your chest. Say the word "heel" one time and begin walking. Take four or five steps, then stop and say "sit." (Use the sit hand signal—hand up over the puppy's head—if you need to.) When your puppy sits, click, praise, and treat. Begin again and each time gradually add more steps before stopping and asking your puppy to sit. For example, take eight or nine steps, then ask your puppy to sit. Then twelve or thirteen steps, and so on. If you practice this heeling exercise and add the distance of one additional house-length each day, you'll be around the block in a month or two with your puppy remaining in heel position.

Figure 18-15

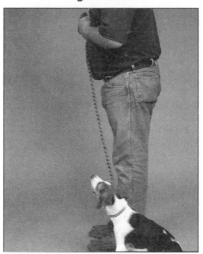

Step three of the traditional heeling method: Keep your hands on your chest, say "heel," and walk with your puppy. Take four or five steps, stop, ask your puppy to sit, and then treat.

Heeling—Grade School Level: Heeling with Automatic Stay

The automatic sit-stay or down-stay means that when your puppy is moving by your side, he will sit (or lie down) every time you stop, without being asked, and he will stay in that position until he is released. In essence, your stopping will become an additional signal for your puppy to sit (or lie down) and stay put. Automatic sits and downs are good substitute behaviors to teach your puppy so he doesn't jump on people or dogs when you meet them on walks.

Step One

Start in an environment with no distractions, like your back-yard. Keep your hands on your chest, with your puppy sitting at your side. Say the word "heel" one time and begin walking. Take four or five steps, then stop and say "sit" (or "down"). When your puppy does what you've asked, immediately click, praise, and treat. Repeat three to five times and proceed to the next step.

Step Two

Say "heel," walk a few steps, and then stop but don't say any-thing. Wait up to forty-five seconds for her to respond. When she sits (or lies down) without your vocal cue, jackpot her. Do a few more repetitions and call it a day.

Step Three

Practice this on walks, stopping every now and then and waiting for your puppy to sit or lie down without asking. Every time she does, click, praise, and treat her. When the sit or down becomes automatic every time you stop, you can fade out the treats—the continuation of the walk becomes the reward for sit-ting and staying.

You can also use the automatic sit (or down) to teach your puppy boundaries that he should not cross without permission, such as a curb or the edge of your yard. Walk up to the curb, say "sit" and treat. Instead of going into the street, back up and do it again. Repeat this three times. On the fourth time, stop at the curb and say nothing. Wait. If she sits, jackpot her, then say "okay" and cross the street. (If she gets up before being given permission, go back to the step where she was successful.) This is a good exercise to do because it teaches your puppy to auto-matically stop at curbs and to never go into the street unless she hears the word "okay."

Walk Without Pulling

Walk without pulling means just what it says. While the puppy is on a leash, he can go ahead of you, behind you, or to your side but he immediately backs up or returns to you the instant he feels the slightest tension in the leash. To teach your puppy to walk without pulling, we use a combination of four methods.

Note: For this behavior, the usual three-step training process is not applicable for methods one through three because, with those methods, the behavior is not "labeled" with a word or phrase. However, method four, the "get behind me method," is labeled with those words and therefore the three-step process is employed.

There is no clearly delineated line between a kindergarten and a grade school level—just keep practicing the various methods and watch your puppy improve. The four methods are:

1. The Start/Stop Method
2. The Voluntary Return Method
3. The Reversal Method
4. The Get Behind Me Method

All of these methods work fine by themselves but your progress can be greatly enhanced if you use two, three, or even all four of them. They are all powerful communications to your puppy that communicate: "Stay by my side (or close to it) without pulling and you'll be forever free to walk with me wherever I go."

Walk Without Pulling—Method One: The Start/Stop Method

Did you ever see a dog straining on a leash, pulling the human along? What's happening here is that the person has inadvertently taught his dog that the freedom to go forward is actually a reward for pulling. This is the exact opposite of what you want your puppy to do. In other words, you want to teach him that the freedom to move forward is a reward for keeping a slack leash.

Whenever your puppy pulls, creating a taut leash, stop in your tracks (see Figure 18-16). Your puppy will sniff for a while and eventually he'll wonder what's going on. When he turns his head to look back at you, you'll feel the leash slacken a bit (see Figure 18-17). Immediately praise and begin walking again. You are rewarding the relaxed muscle tension by walking forward.

This gives him the freedom to explore again. Now your puppy is learning that a taut leash (muscle tension) means stop and a loose leash (relaxed tension) means go.

Figure 18-16

In the stop/start method of walking without pulling, when your puppy pulls, creating a taut leash, stop in your tracks.

Figure 18-17

When your puppy turns back to look at you and the leash slackens a bit, immediately click, praise, and reward and start walking again.

Note: There is a critical juncture you must be aware of to make this method work. Within the first ten minute session, your puppy will figure this out. You have to be aware of his recognition. Here's what will happen. Let's say you've done a dozen or so stop-and-gos—there will now come a point where your puppy will back up or relax his shoulders as soon as he feels the leash go taut. This will happen so fast that you won't have a chance to come to a complete stop. This is the critical point where you effusively praise and, if possible, click, praise, and treat. He has figured out he can keep you moving if he doesn't feel any pressure, so he stops the pressure. That's the whole point of the method. If you don't acknowledge this recognition, he'll say, "Well, that wasn't it" and just keep pulling. I sometimes tell people to close their eyes so they can feel the tension rather that look for it. Just be careful you don't walk into a telephone pole.

Walk Without Pulling—Method Two: The Voluntary Return Method

You may find that while practicing method one, the start/stop method, your puppy voluntarily comes all the way back to you whenever the leash goes taut. If that happens, you can give your puppy an additional reward for being close to you. The first reward your puppy got for slackening the leash in the start/stop method was praise and the freedom to continue walking. In this voluntary return method, your puppy will get an additional, even greater reward if she happens to be by your side. To explain: Let's say that you are practicing the start/stop method and the leash goes taut, so you immediately stop. When the leash goes even a little bit slack, such as when your puppy turns her head to look at you, you praise her and immediately start walking again. (Tight means stop; loose means go.) But let's say that instead of pulling again when you begin walking, your puppy waits for you to catch up. Now she's by your side and you immediately click, praise, and treat her for being in that position. She will quickly learn that she can keep you walking as long as she keeps the leash loose . . . but she will also figure out that if she's by your side, she'll get an additional bonus of food treats.

Put simply, practice the start/stop method outlined above but now be ready to add an additional reward if your puppy:

1. Waits for you to catch up; or
2. Walks back to you a step or two.

This also works if your puppy happens to investigate something. You keep walking and quickly pass her. As she finishes her sniffing and quickly catches up to you, click, praise, and treat her the moment she is at your side. This is a form of the Magnet Game as you didn't ask her to walk by your side, but you "caught" her doing it with a click, praise, and treat.

Walk Without Pulling—Method Three: The Reversal Method

If you have a more challenging puppy, start out with the start/stop method but add another twist. Your new rescue puppy, for example, with his desire to walk ahead of you, will constantly try to shoot out in front of you. Anticipate his frolic to the front and just as he passes you, turn and walk the other way, being very careful not to jerk him (see Figure 18-18).

He will now be behind you, wanting to catch up. Now, just as he gets to your side on his way to the front again, click, praise, and treat. This click once again marks the position you're looking for. This method works because dogs really don't like to retrace familiar ground as much as they like to explore new territory. So he learns he can keep you going forward if he doesn't walk ahead of you. And he also learns that he intermittently gets treats if he stays by your side.

Figure 18-18

In the reversal method of walking without pulling, just as your puppy passes you, turn and walk the other way, being very careful not to jerk him.

Note: For those puppies who are really strong pullers, I recommend using a bungee leash combined with either an anti-pulling harness such as the Easy Walker or Gentle Leader by Premier. The leash will help communicate what you want and the harness will give you more control and help avoid any unintentional jerks on your puppy's neck.

Walk Without Pulling—Method Four: The Get Behind Me Method

This is one of the easiest methods to practice and is super effective.

Step One: Get the Behavior Using a Treat (Lure) and a Hand Signal

With your puppy by your side (either side is fine), slowly walk forward and simultaneously throw a food treat behind you. As your puppy goes back to retrieve the treat, click, and praise (see Figure 18-19). Whatever side your puppy is on, that's the hand you use to throw the treat. When you throw the treat behind you, throw it in the space between you and your puppy, not out to the side. Repeat five to ten times. When your puppy is successful 80 percent of the time, go to step two.

Figure 18-19

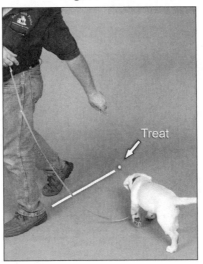

When practicing the get behind me method, throw the treat behind you, in the space between you and your puppy.

Step Two: Attach a Word to the Behavior Along with the Hand Signal

With your puppy by your side, slowly walk forward and simultaneously say "get behind me" or "get in back" and throw the treat behind you. In this case, the hand signal is the motion of your hand throwing the treat behind you. Repeat this five to ten times. Do several sessions of this behavior a day for up to a week until your puppy really knows what you're asking for when you say "get behind me." Then proceed to step three.

Step Three: Use the Word Without the Hand Signal

When your puppy attempts to get in front of you say "get behind me" without the hand signal and without throwing the treat. Your puppy will begin searching for the treat behind you. When he does, click and then treat him. You are now rewarding the behavior rather than luring him with the treat. Over time, he will begin hanging back in anticipation of the occasional treat.

Hints for Successful Walk Without Pulling

We've mentioned the use of life rewards, which include anything your puppy wants other than food, such as going for rides, coming in the house, being petted, chasing a ball, and so on. You can use three ready-made life rewards to help teach your puppy to walk without pulling:

1. Investigating the neighborhood
2. Marking the neighborhood with urine
3. Saying hello to other dogs or people

If your puppy has a strong desire to sniff and investigate every bug, bush, and bottle, use these puppy desires as rewards for not pulling. Instead of a food treat, use his desire as a reward. For example, if your puppy wants to leave a calling card for his pals in the 'hood, or if your puppy really wants to greet his pals who are also on a walk, use these as rewards for not pulling. The moment your puppy stops pulling and turns to look at you, expecting a food reward, instead (or in combination) say "okay" and let him investigate or mark the hydrant he was eyeing or let him say hello to his friends.

Take It and Drop It

Teaching your puppy take it means he will wait for permission before picking up a toy or food. Drop it teaches him to happily give up a toy or favorite chewie when asked. Since puppies have an instinctual drive to protect what's theirs, both of these behaviors are critical for safety, especially if your puppy grabs hold of something "illegal." We teach take it and drop it as one behavior with two separate parts. Take it is taught first and then drop it.

Take It—Kindergarten Level

Most puppies love to chase things and readily will pounce on anything you throw and then grab it with their mouth. This is the easiest way to teach take it. Take out a ball, squeaky toy, Frisbee, or rope tug toy and show your enthusiasm about it. Then throw the toy for your puppy to chase. If your puppy takes the toy in her mouth, click, praise, and offer her a treat. If she stays away from you, you can get her to bring the toy back to you by running away from her. When she catches up to you, offer her a treat and say "drop it." In order to eat the treat she has to drop the toy. Repeat five to ten times and end the session. You want this play experience to be really fun and end it while your puppy wants more. If you notice your puppy is picking up the toy eight out of ten times you throw it, begin saying "take it" just before the throw.

For those puppies who have little or no interest in chasing a toy, use the step-by-step protocol below to teach him to take things in his mouth.

Note: Some breeds, like retrievers, may immediately put certain toys in their mouths as soon as you start. That is, of course, your ultimate goal. If you have such a puppy, just skip over all of this and start with step five, "holding the object longer." But even these puppies may be hesitant to pick up some objects, in which case you'll still have to follow this step-by-step protocol.

Steps One and Two: Get the Behavior and Attach a Word to the Behavior

These steps are combined since it's more than 80 percent likely your puppy will give you the behavior you are looking for on the first try. Rub a piece of chicken or cheese on the object you want your puppy to take, such as a squeaky toy, a ball, or a Frisbee, and then hold the object in your hand one inch away from your puppy's nose. As you do this, say "take it." As your puppy comes forward to examine the object and touches it with his nose, click, praise, and treat with a $10,000 treat. Repeat five to ten times. Once your puppy is touching the object whenever you present it, progress to the next level (see Figure 18-20).

Note: At this point, your puppy is not actually "taking" the object, he's just touching it with his nose.

Figure 18-20

In steps one and two of take it, hold the object in your hand one inch away from your puppy's nose and say "take it."

Step 3: Say "Take It"

Do not click or praise or reward when your puppy touches the object as you were doing in steps one and two. Wait for an escalation. This means wait until your puppy really nudges or licks or mouths the object. When he does, then you will click, praise, and treat. Repeat five to ten times. Here's what's happening: Up to this point, the object has been used as a target similar to the process you used to teach your puppy to come when called when he had to touch your hand. In this case, when your puppy touches the object and is not rewarded, he will try to figure out why the reward did not follow. In essence, he's thinking to himself, "Wait a minute, we had a deal! You're supposed to give me a treat every time I touch the object. Well, I'll show you!" He will then naturally escalate his intensity by nudging, licking, or mouthing the object (see Figure 18-21). Wait for that to happen. It is that escalation that you are now rewarding. Repeat five to ten times. Do several sessions over several days so your puppy really understands that you are now only rewarding the escalated behavior.

Figure 18-21

In step three of take it,click, praise, and treat when your puppy takes the object in his mouth.

Progressions: If your puppy is nudging the object, reward that behavior for a day or two, then wait for the next escalation, which is licking. Then click and reward that behavior. Reward only the licking for the next session or so and then wait for the next escalation, which is mouthing. Reward only the mouthing for the next session or so and then wait for the next escalation, which is your puppy holding the toy in his mouth.

Now begin to lower the toy toward the floor each time you present it and say "take it." Lower the object an inch closer to the floor with each presentation. When you get to the point that you're holding the object on the floor when you say take it, proceed to step four. This may take one or more sessions, but most puppies figure it out within two days.

Step Four: Use the Word Only

Place the object on the floor and say "take it" without pointing to it. Give your puppy forty-five seconds to figure out what you want. When she picks up the object, click, praise, and reward with a treat. Repeat five to ten times and do several sessions over a period of two days. When your puppy picks up the object eight out of ten times, proceed to the next step.

Step Five: Holding the Object Longer

Place the object on the floor, say "take it," and teach your puppy to hold onto it for longer and longer periods of time by rewarding each subsequent success. This is done by delaying the click and reward, first for one second, gradually progressing to two seconds, then gradually progressing to three seconds, and so on. Do not immediately ask your puppy to hold the toy for longer periods of time. In session two, you might work for a two-second hold, then going to a three- or four-second hold in session three. When your puppy is holding the toy for three seconds before releasing it, you are ready to add the word "hold." Place the object on the floor, say "take it," and then say "hold." Count to three and click, praise, and offer her a treat.

Hint: Take out a ball, squeaky toy, Frisbee, or rope tug toy and start playing and throw it for your puppy to chase. If your puppy takes the toy in her mouth click, praise, and treat. If your puppy starts picking up the toy every time you throw it, begin saying "take it" just before the throw.

As you teach take it, be sure to use the same object until your puppy is reliably picking it up and holding it whenever you ask. Then you can begin to teach your puppy to take new objects. When you do that, go back to steps one and two and follow the same step-by-step protocol with each new object. Eventually you won't have to repeat all of these steps because your puppy will "generalize" and learn that "take it" means take whatever object you are pointing to. Some objects are more difficult for puppies to put in their mouths, such as metal objects like soda cans or eating utensils. You may have to spend more time with steps one and two with those types of objects.

Naming the Objects

Once your puppy knows that "take it" means to pick something up, you can begin assigning names to the objects. How many objects can a puppy learn to recognize? German media recently reported on a puppy who could identify 200 different objects. Simply point to the toy and say its name, immediately followed by "take it." For example, say "Ball, take it." Repeat this five to ten times each session and within one or two sessions your puppy will anticipate you are going to say "take it." Now eliminate the "take it" signal and just say the word for the object. Ta da!

Drop It—Kindergarten Level

The kindergarten level of drop it introduces your puppy to this behavior, which really means, "open your mouth when I ask you to."

Steps One and Two: Get the Behavior and Attach a Word to It

Steps one and two are combined here because it's more than 80 percent likely your puppy will give you the behavior you are looking for on the first try. Once you've asked your puppy to "take it" and your puppy is holding the object in his mouth for three seconds or longer, say "drop it" as you present a $10,000 treat. When he drops the object from his mouth, click, praise, and reward him with the treat. Repeat five to ten times. In other words, you are asking your puppy to take the toy, then hold the toy, then drop the toy.

Step Three: Use the Word Only

Now use the word only. As your puppy is holding the object, say "drop it" without presenting any food. When your puppy drops the object, click, praise, and treat. Repeat this sequence a few times, saying your verbal signal without showing a treat, yet giving a treat reward after the fact. If it doesn't work right away, don't worry; simply go back to offering the treat and saying "drop it" a few more times. Then periodically say "drop it" without holding the treat until your puppy gives you the toy when asked, without having to see a treat "up front." If at any time he shows more interest in the treats than in the toy, and therefore stops playing, put the toy away for awhile and work on "drop it" at the next play session.

Note: To speed the process, whenever you see your puppy carrying a favorite toy in his mouth, present him with a treat and say "drop it." Then always give the toy back to him. If your puppy is holding an illegal object, like your slippers, offer the treat and say "drop it." When your puppy drops the object, interject another behavior, like sit, before giving him the food treat. This is important because you want to reward the puppy for sitting and not let him get the idea that you are rewarding him for bringing you the slipper.

Step Four: Using the Reward Only

The next time you ask for the toy back, simply say "drop it" without holding a treat in front of your puppy's nose. If your puppy gives you the toy, in anticipation of a reward, say "good boy" (or click) and jackpot him. Repeat this sequence a few times, saying your verbal signal without showing a treat, yet giving a treat reward after the fact. If it didn't work, don't worry; simply go back to offering the treat and saying "drop it" a few more times. Then periodically say "drop it" without holding the treat until your puppy gives you the toy when asked, without having to see a treat "up front." If at any time he shows more interest in the treats than in the toy, and therefore stops playing, put the toy away for awhile and work on "drop it" at the next play session.

It shouldn't take too long before you have taught your puppy Rule Number One of Playing: Give back the toy when asked. In fact, you may notice that he automatically relinquishes the toy without waiting to be asked. Now is the time to change the nature of the reward. If your puppy gives up the toy, the reward is that you keep playing! Throw the ball again, or let him grab the toy in his mouth, as the prize for letting go of it. Ask for the toy back many times during a play session, as "payment" for the continuation of play, like putting another quarter in a parking meter. If at any point he refuses to let go when asked, stop playing. He will learn quickly that if he wants you to play with him, he has to follow the rules. If your puppy hasn't yet learned to bring the toy back when you throw it, now is the time to throw it farther, as he should now be eager to return it to you for the continuation of the game. When you decide you would like to end the play session, you can reward the final giving up of the toy with a treat.

Note: If your puppy shows any aggressive behavior when you ask him to relinquish an object, review the exercises to prevent resource guarding in the socialization chapter and call an expert.

"Emergency" Drop It

If you have to open your puppy's mouth in an emergency situation, gently cup one of your hands around his upper or lower jaw. Then, with your fingers on one side of the jaw and your thumb on the other side, gently push up and roll his lips over his back teeth (see Figures 18-22 and 18-23). Most puppies will open their mouths when they feel the skin on their teeth. Say "drop it" while you are doing this and reward your puppy even though he was forced to let it go. You do not have to use a lot of strength to open your puppy's mouth. Always be gentle.

Figure 18-22	**Figure 18-23**
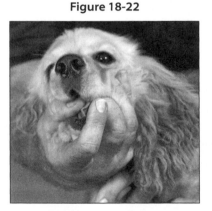	
In "emergency" drop it, one option is to gently cup one of your hands around your puppy's lower jaw. Then gently push up and roll his lips over his back teeth.	In "emergency" drop it, the other option is to gently cup one of your hands around your puppy's upper jaw. Then gently push up and roll his lips over his back teeth.

Go to Your Spot

Go to your spot is the most useful behavior you can teach your puppy; it can solve virtually every problem behavior inside the house. Go to your spot can help in many different situations, such as when your puppy barks at the mail carrier, nudges you while you're on the phone, races to the door when the doorbell rings, begs at the dinner table, or acts fearful about the gardener or the handy man. It's a great behavior to teach a puppy for safety reasons, such as whenever a baby or small child enters a room. Also, by designating your puppy's bed as his "spot," you can take the bed with you on trips and then tell him to stay there for as long as you want. When you tell your puppy to go to his spot, you are redirecting his attention and giving him something to do. This can help calm him if he's nervous or distract him when he's doing something you don't want him to do. Also, a puppy in a relaxed down on his bed will bark less. There's also a very practical use of this behavior when your puppy is in your way. For instance, you can avoid tripping over him when you have a heavy laundry basket in your hands by asking him to go to a specific place.

Teaching your puppy to go to his bed, blanket, mat, go outside, get in the house, and so on are exactly the same as teaching him to go to his kennel. For instance, you could refer to the kennel as "kennel," or "get in your house," or "go to your den" but, whichever one you pick, always use the same word or phrase for the kennel. Going step-by-step, most puppies will pick up this behavior in up to three short sessions. Don't rush it, keep the sessions short, and end each session on a high note.

Go to Your Spot—Kindergarten Level

In kindergarten level go to your spot, your puppy will learn the basic behavior and be able to go to his spot in a nondistracting environment.

Step One: Get the Behavior Using a Treat (Lure) and a Hand Signal

Stand beside the place you want your puppy to use as a "spot" and make sure you are no more than one foot away from it. The "spot" can be a bed, blanket, or any other place you want to teach him to go to. Start with your puppy in a sit position facing you. Put your hands in the starting position on your chest (see Figure 18-24).

Let your puppy see you throw a $10,000 treat onto the "spot" (see Figure 18-25). The hand that is throwing the treat is the hand that is closest to the spot. In other words, don't throw the treat across your body with the opposite hand. For this behavior, the hand pointing to the spot and then immediately returning to your chest is the hand signal for "go to your spot." As soon as your puppy gets to the spot to get the treat, click and praise. Repeat three to five times. Therefore, since you are already 80 percent sure your puppy will be successful, as the puppy always goes for the treat, you can quickly proceed to step two.

Step Two: Attach a Word to the Behavior Along with the Hand Signal

Say "spot" (or "place," or "bed," or "kennel," or whichever word you have chosen) and use the same hand motion you used while throwing the treat. (Your hand started on your chest, you threw the treat, and your hand returned to your chest.) Use a different word for each new spot or location you are teaching your puppy to go to. When your puppy is successful 80 percent of the time, move on.

Now you're going to increase the distance of the reward by putting the treat in your other hand. Give the verbal request and use the same throwing motion with the now empty hand, as you pretend to throw the treat. Simply move your hand from your chest and then back again. Wait up to forty-five seconds. If your puppy goes to his spot, click, praise, and treat when he gets there. The difference here is that you're no longer using the treat as a lure or target. It is now used only as a reward. When your puppy is successful eight out of ten times, proceed to step three.

Figure 18-24

In step one of kindergarten "go to your spot," start with your puppy in a sit position facing you. Put your hands in the starting position on your chest.

Figure 18-25

Next, let your puppy see you throw a $10,000 treat onto the "spot."

Step Three: Use the Word Without the Hand Signal

Keep your hands on your chest. Say the word once. Wait up to forty-five seconds. If your puppy puts a paw on the bed, click, effusively praise, and jackpot him with several treats. Repeat ten to fifteen times. If your puppy doesn't go to his spot within forty-five seconds, return to step two.

Go to Your Spot—Grade School Level
In grade school level go to your spot, you will build on the puppy's previous success with this behavior, which leads to greater reliability.

Step One: Add Distance
Move one step away from the bed. Keep your hands on your chest. Say the word once. Wait up to forty-five seconds. If your puppy puts a paw on the bed, click, effusively praise, and jackpot. Repeat ten to fifteen times. If your puppy doesn't go to his spot from one step away within forty-five seconds, return to standing right next to the bed and do a few repetitions. Whenever your puppy is successful, increase your distance a step at a time. Click, praise, and treat with every success. If your puppy doesn't know what you're asking, it's a good bet you've gone too far too fast. Go back to the point at which you both were successful and work at that distance a little while longer before increasing the distance.

Note: Once you have begun to move farther from the spot (adding distance) you never throw the treat as a lure again. You only use the vocal signal. The only time you use the treat as a lure is at the very first step when you are next to the bed. After that, the treat is only used as a reward.

Step Two: Add Distractions
Once you've reached a point where your puppy will go to his spot from virtually anywhere, you can begin adding distractions. Remember, any time you add a new element to the training process, you will start the training process all over again from the beginning. For example, let's say the distraction is someone knocking on the door or ringing the doorbell:

1. Stand by the door and tell your puppy to go to a spot right next to you by saying the word of your choice, "spot,"

"bed," "blanket," or whatever, using the treat as a reward, not as a lure. (This means you are not throwing the treat to get your dog to go to the spot; he only gets the treat after he does the behavior.) When he gets there, click, praise, and treat. Repeat five to ten times.

2. Now knock or ring the doorbell and, as before, send your puppy to his spot. Click, praise, and treat each time he is successful. Repeat ten times. If he doesn't go to his spot when asked, go back to using the treat as a lure. This means each time you ring the bell or knock, you will throw the treat and say the word simultaneously. Once again, try to send your puppy to his spot without the lure.

3. Knock or ring the bell and say nothing. Wait up to forty-five seconds. If your puppy goes to his spot without you saying anything, click and give him a jackpot.

   Knocking on the door or ringing the doorbell has now been installed as a signal for your puppy to run to his spot. With several days, weeks, and months of practice, your puppy will automatically go to his spot whenever someone knocks on the door or rings the doorbell. You can now start asking him to lie down and stay when he arrives at his spot.

   Note: If your puppy does nothing after forty-five seconds, go back to step two.

4. Gradually move the spot farther away from you and the door, one step at a time. Knock or ring the bell, send your puppy to the spot, and click, praise, and treat each success. Work up to being able to send your puppy twenty feet away from the door to his spot after you have knocked or rung the bell.

Having Problems?

🦴 Leave treats on the spot throughout the day. Within a very short time, your puppy will actually go to the spot and search for the treat. When that happens, use the Magnet Game. Instantly click, praise, and throw an extra treat to your puppy the moment he places a paw on the spot.

☞ Look at the spot after giving the signal. Puppies have a tendency to follow your gaze.

☞ Make sure you wait a full forty-five seconds for your puppy to figure out what you want.

Get off the Couch

There are three choices you have regarding your puppy and your furniture:

1. Puppy will always be allowed on all the furniture;
2. Puppy will be allowed on specific furniture; or,
3. Puppy will never be allowed on furniture.

If you never want your puppy on the furniture you must be vigilant about allowing access. This is a real consideration if you are concerned about doggy hair getting on guests and also if you have a baby.

If your puppy is allowed on specific furniture, you must be vigilant about allowing access and teach your puppy to actually get on the permitted chair, bed, or sofa, and only that piece of furniture. This training normally starts around twelve weeks of age. For little dogs, you can purchase lightweight, foam stairs so they can climb up.

If your puppy is allowed on all furniture, there are two rules she must adhere to:

1. She can only get up with your permission.
2. She must always get off when you say "off."

To teach your puppy to get "off" (or "on") the couch, a chair, bed, or any other object, use the exact same process as go-to-your-spot, but instead of saying "spot," you would simply replace the word with whatever you are teaching, like "up" for getting on the furniture; "off" for getting off the furniture; or "chair" for getting on the chair, and so on.

Hints:

- ⌘ Practice prevention and management so your puppy can't get on any chair you don't want him to be on. To keep your puppy off the chair when you are out of the room, a simple preventative measure is to put sheets of aluminum foil across the chair or couch cushions as puppies dislike the feel and sound of aluminum foil. Your puppy will soon learn to avoid the foil-covered furniture and you can discontinue using it.
- ⌘ If you see your puppy about to get on a chair or couch that is forbidden, you can interrupt him with "ah-ah" and redirect him to the acceptable chair or spot.
- ⌘ We also suggest you keep a short cable (tether) on your puppy when he is in the house so if you ever have to move a stubborn puppy off the furniture, you can simply grab the tether he's wearing and gently pull him off. It's okay to pull a puppy if necessary as long as you are gentle and don't jerk him. Gently pulling him off avoids any possible negative association of being grabbed by the collar. Note: Never let your puppy wear a leash (tether) if you are not around to supervise!

Leave It

"Leave it" means: "Puppy, turn away from whatever you are eyeing." This could be the Thanksgiving turkey, your shoes, the children's stuffed animals, the TV remote (God forbid), the puppy's poop, road kill, or Paul's Portuguese water dog's favorite—dead fish. You can also use "leave it" to keep your puppy from approaching other dogs, cats, and people.

Leave It—Kindergarten Level

The kindergarten level of leave it introduces your puppy to this behavior. As with all behaviors, you'll want to teach kindergarten level in an environment that is as distraction-free as possible.

Step One: Get the Behavior Using a Treat (Lure) and a Hand Signal

Put a treat in your hand and close your fist. Put your fist, fingers facing your puppy, at your puppy's nose level about two inches away. Your puppy will start mouthing and licking your fist. Stay still (see Figure 18-26). Within ninety seconds, your puppy will either back up and turn her head to the side *or* lower her head beneath your fist. The instant your puppy takes her mouth off of your hand, even if it is only an inch away, click and immediately give her the treat from your fist (see Figure 18-27). Repeat this ten to twenty times. Your puppy will have a "wait a minute, something's happening here" moment somewhere between ten and twenty repetitions. You will present your fist but your puppy will hesitate and not come forward. This hesitation may only be for a fraction of a second but when it happens, click, treat, and really praise your puppy. You have rewarded your puppy for avoiding the treat. The hand signal in this case is your closed fist. Now proceed to step two.

Figure 18-26

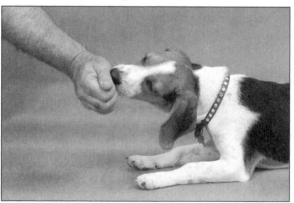

In step one of leave it, put a treat in your hand and close your fist. Then put your fist, fingers facing your puppy, at your puppy's nose level. She will start licking and mouthing your fist.

Figure 18-27

The instant your puppy takes her mouth off of your hand, even if it is only an inch away, click and immediately give her the treat from your fist.

Step Two: Attach a Word to the Behavior Along with the Hand Signal

Say the words "leave it" and present your fist as before. If your puppy makes no movement toward your fist, click, praise, and treat. Repeat this ten to fifteen times. When you get to this stage, lower your hand and inch or so closer to the floor with each presentation. Progress to the point where you can place the treat on the floor with your hand covering it. Say "leave it" as before and give your puppy the treat if she avoids moving toward it (see Figure 18-28). When your puppy is successful eight out of ten times, you're ready to move on.

Now place the treat on the floor, covered by your hand as before. Now uncover the treat and say "leave it," but keep your hand close to the treat in case your puppy decides to try and grab it. If she does, snatch the treat away. Try again. If she stays put for a fraction of a second, click and give her the treat. Now progress to uncovering the treat for two seconds, then three, and so on. Once your puppy will leave it for ten seconds, go to the next step.

Figure 18-28

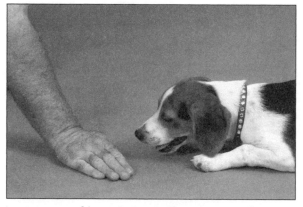

In step two of leave it, you will progress to the point where you can place the treat on the floor with your hand covering it. Say "leave it" as before and give your puppy the treat if she avoids moving toward it.

Hint: Ask your puppy to lie down before you say "leave it." When you put the treat on the floor, make sure it is at least two feet from your puppy.

Step Three: Use the Word Without the Hand Signal

Drop the treat on the floor instead of placing it. Say "leave it" and drop the treat from a height of two inches off the floor and at a distance of two feet from the puppy. Count one second, click, and give your puppy the treat that you dropped. Gradually increase the height from which you drop the treat—from two inches, to three inches, to six inches, and so on—until you can drop a treat from a standing position and your puppy will "leave it" when asked. Now drop the treat without saying anything. Your puppy should stay put and wait for you to give her the treat.

Note: Do not release your puppy and allow her to get the treat herself. Always pick up the treat that you dropped and then give it to her. This method will really help when you accidentally drop a piece of food on the kitchen floor. Your puppy will have a powerful habit installed that she can never touch something unless you give it to her. (By the way, the reason you went back to one second in this step is because you changed the context. You hadn't previously taught her to "leave it" with the food being dropped. Remember, the rule is, every time you change the situation, you have to start over.)

Leave It—Grade School Level
Once your puppy is reliable at the kindergarten level of leave it, you can advance to adding duration, distance, and distractions.

Step One: Add Duration
Say "leave it," and drop the treat on the floor, then count two seconds before picking up the treat and giving it to your puppy. Progress incrementally to saying "leave it" and then waiting ten seconds before letting your puppy have the treat.

Step Two: Add Distance
Say "leave it," drop the treat, take one step away, then return, click, and give your puppy the treat that you dropped. Then move two steps away, return, and so on.

Step Three: Add Distractions
You may have noticed that up until now you have asked your puppy to "leave it" while in a stationary position, yet many times you will want your puppy to turn away from something forbidden while she is in motion. Prepare for this situation by putting your puppy on leash, then place a treat on the floor. Walk past the treat, four to six feet away from it, just out of reach of your puppy's mouth. As you approach the treat, say "leave it." If your puppy moves away from the treat or turns toward you, click, praise, and treat from your pocket. If your puppy strains on the leash toward the treat, stop moving, so that your puppy cannot reach the treat, and wait forty-five seconds. If your puppy moves away or turns toward you within forty-five seconds, click and give her a jackpot. If she is still straining after forty-five seconds, try again at a greater distance from the treat, until she is successful. Your puppy can now do a "moving leave it."

Practice leave it when your puppy is moving, such as on walks, where she'll have low-level distractions like blowing leaves, mild smells in which she's interested, and so on. If she's straining toward something, ask her to "leave it." If she moves away from the distraction or turns toward you, either reward her by letting her go investigate it or giving her a treat, or both. If she continues to strain against the leash, wait forty-five seconds—if she gives up in any way from trying to get to the distraction, let her investigate it or give her a treat, or both. If she doesn't turn to you, increase your distance.

Note: Until your puppy becomes reliable with leave it, you may find her climbing up to steal food from the table or kitchen counter. To interrupt this behavior you can startle her with a sound intense enough to get her to stop what she's doing and get her back on all fours. Whistle, shake a can, or clap loudly— but startle, don't scare! Then take this opportunity to teach her what you want her to do. Practice leave its to remind her that she'll be given the treats if she lies down and waits. Until she figures this out, use prevention and management by using tethers or baby gates to keep her from stealing food and hence being self-reinforced!

At this point, you can begin introducing the objects you don't ever want your puppy to touch. Simply show her the object, your slippers for example, say "leave it," and place them on the floor. Here's what will happen: Your puppy will stare at the slippers and eventually glance at you. Capture this glance by clicking and/or saying "good" and jackpotting her. You are rewarding her for turning away from the object. Repeat this thousands of times in the months to come.

You can also set up the environment to test her and further strengthen this "avoidance" behavior. Put a slipper on the floor while your puppy is out of the room. When she enters the room and moves toward it, say "ah-ah" to interrupt her. Watch closely. She will look at the slipper and then glance at you. Jackpot her!

"Commercial" Puppy Training—A Last Word on Getting Your Practice In

When we say "commercial" puppy training, we mean as in when you're watching TV. Paul coined this term to illustrate how stress-free and easy daily training can be. As we mentioned earlier, several short training sessions throughout the day are better than two or three longer sessions. What better times to train your puppy than during TV commercials? They normally last two to three minutes and you can practice ten repetitions of several behaviors during that time . . . and you don't even have to get off the couch! Ten downs, ten stays, ten come (touch my hand), ten go to your bed, ten take its and drop its, and so on.

Congratulations! You've read a lot. Treat yourself to a movie, a novel, or a concert, then come back to the next chapter on games and tricks you can teach your puppy for even more fun.

Chapter 19

Games and Tricks: Combining Play, Training, and Exercise

Here are some games, tricks, and other fun ideas that can actually teach your puppy life skills. Putting behaviors in the context of a game helps keep training light and fresh, and helps satisfy the play needs your puppy has as well. Puppies should care little about whether you are asking them to down-stay, chase a toy, or do a high-five. Everything is a trick and that is the attitude to have in training. Tricks help keep us interested in training and keep puppies mentally stimulated. As you'll see, some of these games and exercises require previously trained skills, while others do not.

Adding games and tricks to your puppy's repertoire is another way to bond with your puppy—and perhaps impress a few friends with your training prowess. In addition, teaching your puppy games and tricks helps to build your confidence as well as your puppy's. Another benefit is that you will raise your puppy's stress-management threshold, which will help her cope with life's challenges. In turn, this will strengthen her immune system which will keep her healthier and help her to live longer. And, as you know, how you treat your puppy is linked to how you treat yourself and others, so you, too, will reap all of these same benefits. The other great thing about teaching your puppy any new behavior is that they also have practical uses.

There are many ways to teach games and tricks:

The Magnet Game: If you use the Magnet Game, simply wait for your puppy to do something and as soon as she does, click, praise, and treat. (See "The Magnet Game," page 177.) Paul taught his Portuguese water dog, Molly, to sneeze on cue using the Magnet Game. Whenever she would sneeze, he would immediately praise her and give her a treat. Then he added a vocal signal, "gesundheit!" and, thereafter, she would dutifully sneeze on cue.

"Shaping" the Behavior: Shaping is the process of forming a behavior using baby steps, otherwise known as increments or successive approximations. Each approximation is a successful behavior in and of itself which ultimately leads to the final position you are looking for. A good example of the use of shaping is teaching your puppy to play dead.

Luring: Luring entices a puppy to do something without touching him, such as a puppy following a treat to lie down or come when called. Most of the behaviors in this book are obtained through luring, the Magnet Game, and shaping.

Find It

Just like it sounds, "find it" means tracking down a treat, toy, or other hidden object.

Find It—Kindergarten Level
Age: Eight weeks and up. Prerequisite: None.

This game utilizes your puppy's keen sense of smell and desire to hunt. Once your puppy masters find it, this game becomes an excellent source of employment and, at the same time, it's extremely useful for you. Imagine your puppy running around the house hunting a dozen or so pieces of "buried" chicken, cheese, or turkey bits while you read the newspaper, go take a shower, or have breakfast.

Step One

Place a $10,000 treat—like a piece of turkey—on the floor right in front of your puppy and simultaneously say "find it." Repeat five to ten times, progressively moving the treat farther off to either side of your puppy, but still in plain view.

Step Two

Hide the treat behind the leg of a table or chair or behind a footstool as you say "find it." Let your puppy see you place it (not too far away), but put it out of sight. He'll probably look at you as if you're kidding and it may take him a second or two to figure out what's going on. He now has to find the treat with his nose instead of his eyes. Give him up to forty-five seconds to figure it out. When he finally locates the treat and gobbles it up, praise him to high heaven for being such a brilliant puppy. Now run across the room and as soon as he looks at you, say "find it" and let him see you hide another treat. Continue this game of moving about the room and hiding treats until you've shown him a dozen or so hiding places. Continue this treat-hiding game for a few weeks, running around and showing him hiding spots.

Find It—Grade School Level

Age: Four months and older. Prerequisite: Kindergarten level sit-stay and down-stay.

At the grade school level of find it, you can actually improve your puppy's reliability with other behaviors by linking them together in a behavioral chain. This chain of behaviors will help you to wean your puppy off treats, as well as improve your puppy's reliability in the stay behavior.

Step One

Have your puppy sit, then lie down, then stay. Leave your puppy, walk into another room, and hide a treat in that room. Return to your puppy and say "find it." At this level, you no longer show your puppy where you are hiding the treats, you only have to give him the words for this behavior and he'll know what you mean. If he is successful, gradually make it more and more challenging by hiding treats in more than one place each time you leave the room. Now your puppy has to concentrate for longer periods of time.

Note: Because your puppy hasn't learned yet that "find it" means there may be treats in unfamiliar places, you must hide the treats in the same locations you showed him in step two of kindergarten level.

Step Two
Age: Four months and older. Prerequisites: Kindergarten level sit-stay, down-stay, go to your spot, and come when called.

A more challenging behavioral chain is accomplished by adding even more behaviors before rewarding your puppy. As in the previous step, have your puppy go to his spot, sit, lie down, and stay. Then leave your puppy and walk into another room and hide the treats. Return to your puppy. Now, instead of saying "find it," say "come" and have your puppy touch your hand. Then say "find it" and let your puppy search for the treats.

Within a week or two, your puppy will figure out that "find it" means there's always a treat to be found so you're ready to hide treats in areas you haven't shown him before. Send him to his bed, ask him to sit, then lie down and stay. Go to another room and put a big pile of really yummy treats in an unfamiliar location. Return to your puppy and say "find it." He'll eagerly search for the treats in the familiar hiding spots. Not being able to find any, he might pause and look at you. Say "find it" again if necessary, and walk toward the pile of hidden treats. His nose will soon pick up the scent and, voilà, he will successfully complete his hunt.

Hint: You can use a treat-filled Kong or a long-chewing treat such as a bully stick as one or more of the hidden treats. Then, for the next twenty minutes while your puppy is occupied with his reward you can take a shower or have breakfast. Have fun!

Hide-and-Seek Game (Peek-A-Boo)
Hide-and-seek builds on the skills developed in find it and applies them to seeking out people rather than objects.

Hide-and-Seek Game (Peek-A-Boo)—Kindergarten Level
Age: Ten weeks and older. Prerequisite: None.

This game is similar to the hide-and-seek we all played as children. It is a combination of several different behaviors and it's one of the best ways to obtain an even more reliable stay as well as a more reliable come when called.

Step One

Ask your puppy to sit or lie down and stay.

Note: For a puppy who has not learned to stay for any length of time, have someone hold her while you run behind a chair, wall, or other obstruction.

Step Two

Now run bchind a chair and hide.

Step Three

Stick your head out and let your puppy see you. Enthusiastically say "peek-a-boo!" and hide your head again. When your puppy finds you, really praise and treat her and make a big deal out of how clever she was in finding you (see Figures 19-1, 19-2, and 19-3).

Figure 19-1

In step two of hide-and-seek, you hide from your puppy.

Figure 19-2

Once you are hidden, your puppy will start looking for you.

Figure 19-3

In step three of hide-and-seek, stick your head out and let your puppy see you. Enthusiastically say "peek-a-boo!" Then hide again. When your puppy finds you, praise and treat her.

Note: You may have noticed that you are using "peek-a-boo" as an alternate release word here. If your puppy has learned your usual release word so well (example: "okay") that she doesn't move without hearing it, say "okay" right after "peek-a-boo" and encourage her to come to you. With a few repetitions of this she should easily learn that "peek-a-boo" is also an acceptable release word. A variation on the game can be that you say "come" instead of "peek-a-boo," thereby practicing your puppy's response to the recall signal. As a rule, your puppy can be released from a stay in one of two ways—either with a release word, or with a signal for another behavior (like "come," "stand," "get behind me," and so on).

Hide-and-Seek—Grade School Level

Gradually make the basic game more challenging by asking for longer "stays" and hiding in your bedroom or in a closet. To make it easy at first, keep the door open a few inches. Get other people involved and have them say, "Find Jane! Where's Jane?" Even more of a challenge, jump up—gingerly, of course—on a chest of drawers. Challenge your puppy to find you "up in the air."

The Triangle Game

The Triangle Game is composed of several behaviors; it is a more advanced game for a puppy who already has some basic skills. Why is it useful? Imagine this: Your puppy escapes from your yard and you see him chasing a squirrel. You run out the door and see the squirrel dart into the street with your puppy close behind. You yell "Come!" or "Down!" or "Leave it!" and, because of your consistent training, your puppy does so immediately. How do you get your puppy to be this reliable? The triangle game is the easiest and simplest way to acquire high levels of reliability. It is comprised of the behaviors sit, down, stay, leave it, come when called, and find it.

The Triangle Game—Kindergarten Level

Age: Four months and older. Prerequisite: Kindergarten level sit-stay or down-stay, kindergarten level come when called, and completion of step one of grade school level leave it. In other words, before attempting the triangle game, your puppy must have mastered leave it to the extent that you can drop a treat on the floor and he doesn't move for at least ten seconds.

We suggest you read through all of these steps before actually trying it. Once you understand the concept, it is very easy to practice. Pay attention to the distances we've suggested. The more consistent you are, the quicker your puppy will learn this. If you have any problems with the individual behaviors, go back and review those sections. It can help to start teaching your puppy the triangle game when you are low to the ground. You can teach this game from on your knees, while you're sitting on the ground, or in a chair if you like.

Step One
Ask your puppy to sit or lie down and stay.

Step Two
Say "leave it" and place a treat off to your side about three feet from your puppy.

Step Three
Place your hands in starting position on your chest. Say "come" and move your hand from your chest to about two inches to the side of your puppy's head so your puppy has to turn away from the treat to touch your hand. As soon as your puppy turns his head and touches your target hand, click and say, "Good! Find it!" or "okay" and let him get the treat. Now you are teaching your puppy that if he turns his head away from the treat and comes to you first, then and only then will he be given permission to get something on the floor or ground.

Note: The major difference between this exercise and the leave it behavior is that now you are giving your puppy permission to get the treat. Previously, once you told him to leave it, you did not allow your puppy to get the treat. If he stayed put, he had to stay in position and then you picked up the treat and gave it to him as a reward. Now you are teaching your puppy that if he turns his head away from the treat and comes to you first, then and only then will he be given permission to get the treat himself.

Step Four
Now repeat the same exercise. Ask your puppy to sit or lie down and stay, then place the treat off to your side about three feet from

your puppy. Place your hands in starting position on your chest, say "come," and move your hand from your chest to a position an additional inch away from your puppy's nose. If he touches your hand, click, praise, and allow him to get the treat. The next time, place your hand four inches away, then five, and so on. After each exercise, click, praise, and allow him to get the treat.

Step Five

Progress to the point where your target hand is as far away as the treat, but on the other side of your body. This is the triangle. Your puppy is at one point of the triangle, your target hand is at one point and the treat is at one point (see Figure 19-4). Once your puppy will do this three times in a row—touching your hand when you say "come" and then allowing him to get the treat when you say "okay"—it's time to add another challenge, which you will do by standing up while you teach the behavior.

Figure 19-4

In the triangle game, your puppy is at one point of the triangle, your target hand is at one point, and the treat is at one point.

The Triangle Game—Grade School Level

In grade school level of the triangle game you will be adding greater distance.

Step One
Ask your puppy to sit or lie down and stay.

Step Two
Say "leave it" and drop the treat about six feet from your puppy.

Step Three
Move the other point of the triangle so that you are six feet from the treat and six feet from your puppy (an equilateral triangle).

Step Four
From a standing position, place your hands in the starting position on your chest.

Step Five
Say "come" and present your target hand as before. If your puppy comes to you and touches your hand, click, praise, and allow your puppy to get the treat. Repeat ten times.

Hint: If your puppy starts toward the treat instead of your hand, quickly step between your puppy and the treat and say "ah-ah," then do it again. This time, put your puppy back in position but instead of standing six feet from your puppy, stand three feet from your puppy along the same line of the triangle. If three feet is too far and your puppy is still going to get the treat when you say come, move to a distance of two feet or one foot. In other words, find the distance where the puppy will come to you and touch your hand. At that point of success, gradually add more distance until you reach six feet. Gradually increase your distance until you, your puppy, and the treat are equidistant.

When you ask your puppy to "come," use the hand that is on the other side of your body, away from the treat. If you signal "come" with the hand closer to the treat, your puppy will be more tempted to veer off and snatch the treat.

Play Dead—Also Known as Go to Sleep, Relax, and Gotcha

Age: Ten weeks and older. Prerequisite: Kindergarten level down.

Practical Application: Teaches a puppy to relax and builds trust.

Step One: Get the Behavior Using a Treat (Lure) and a Hand Signal

Face your puppy and have her lie down on her hip. Place a treat an inch from her nose. Move your hand with the treat a couple of inches around to the side of her head. Click, praise, and treat. Next, move your hand a little further so she turns her head a bit more toward her back end. Click, praise, and treat (see Figures 19-5 and 19-6).

Figure 19-5

Figure 19-5. In step one of play dead, you will place a treat an inch from your puppy's nose.

Figure 19-6

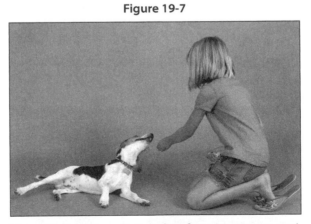

Move your hand with the treat a couple of inches around to the side of her head.

At this point, you should see that her opposite shoulder (the one on the floor) is more relaxed. Now move the treat in a straight line from its current position and continue over her nose to the floor. Her head will follow the treat and lay on the floor. Click, praise, and treat (see Figures 19-7 and 19-8). Repeat five to ten times.

Figure 19-7

Move the treat in a straight line from its current position and continue over her nose to the floor.

Figure 19-8

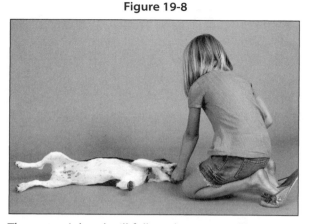

The puppy's head will follow the treat and lay on the floor. Click, praise, and treat.

Step Two: Attach a Word to the Behavior Along with the Hand Signal

Say your selected word such as "gotcha!" and simultaneously move the treat, starting from her nose, around to her back, up in a straight line and continue over her nose to the floor as you did in the previous three steps. Her head will follow the treat and lay on the floor. Click, praise, and treat. Repeat five to ten times.

At some point, your puppy may not come all the way back to her original down position but will hesitate a second or two in the relaxed position or maybe just lift her head. Reward that with many treats and then go to the next step. This will teach her to stay in the position longer.

Step Three: Use the Word Without the Hand Signal

Put your hands in the starting position on your chest and say "gotcha!" or the word you chose. Wait forty-five seconds. If she only moves a little—as if to say "Is this what you're looking for?"—click, praise, and treat. On each subsequent attempt, reward any moves she makes that are closer to the final position.

Finally, after you've said the word or given the signal "gotcha!" and she's completely relaxed laying on her side, with both head and body on the floor, add the word stay to keep her in that position. Ask for a one-second stay, click, praise, treat. Then progress to two seconds, and so on.

Hints: Whatever side your puppy is on, that's the direction you want her to go. Don't "go against the grain" and try to get her to shift over and play dead on the other hip.

Position your body so your treat hand and arm don't get in your puppy's face. If your puppy is on her left side to start, use your left hand to do this. If your puppy is on her right side to start, use your right hand.

Having Problems?

If your puppy refuses to roll on her shoulder and gets up the moment your hand gets close to her back, or if her leg is so planted she refuses to roll onto her side, you'll have to shape this position in micro-mini steps:

- Click, praise, and treat a head turn of two inches. Next time, click, praise, and treat a turn of three inches, and so on. When you get to the point where you know she won't go any further, click, praise, reward that position five to ten times and end the session. In the next session, do the same. You will notice that within three days, she will relax a little more each time and you'll finally be able to complete the behavior.
- In between sessions, whenever you see her on her side resting, go over to her a stroke her and talk with her softly. Her body will remember these experiences and help you when you practice.
- Also, you might want to practice this exercise after she has been very active, and she is a little more tired and relaxed.

Spin—Also Known as Twirl
Age: Five months and older. Prerequisite: None.

Note: The steps below are for a left spin. Repeat the same protocol on the other side when teaching a right spin.

Step One: Get the Behavior Using a Treat (Lure) and a Hand Signal

1. Stand with your puppy facing you.
2. Position your left hand with the treat in front of your puppy's nose, no more than two inches away.
3. Begin moving your arm to the left and leading your puppy to turn her head and body around in a circle. As your puppy follows the treat, move your arm in a complete 360-degree circle maintaining your hand position at your puppy's nose level. The movement of your hand in a 360-degree circle over your puppy becomes the hand signal for spin. Complete the circle and click, praise, and reward. Repeat five to ten times.

Step Two: Attach a Word to the Behavior Along with the Hand Signal

Now simultaneously say "left turn" or "left spin" (emphasizing the word "left") while you lead her around in the circle. Repeat five to ten times and click, praise, and reward after every completion.

Step Three: Use the Word Without the Hand Signal

With your hands in starting position say "left turn." Wait up to forty-five seconds. If your puppy makes an attempt—as if to say "Is this what you're looking for?"—click, praise, and treat. If she simply stands there or walks away in frustration or boredom, return to the previous step.

Chapter 20

Resolving Puppy Problem Behaviors or "What Do I Do When My Puppy. . . ."

"What happened to my remote control?" "It's 3 A.M. . . . why is that puppy barking so much?" "Oh, no! What did I just step in?" Puppy behavior does not fit into a nice, neat package. Despite your best efforts, your puppy's behavior will sometimes drive you up the wall. In this chapter, we'll give you solutions to the most common puppy behavior problems. The keys to success are consistency, timing, and repetition, repetition, repetition.

Before you deal with problem behaviors, review Chapters 8 to 15 to determine any imbalances in areas such as diet, play, socialization, quiet time, exercise, employment, rest, or health care. For example, too little play time or exercise can lead to problems such as attention nipping, stealing, and chewing stuff, or barking. If you have identified and corrected the cause of the problem, the problem behavior usually disappears. If the problem persists, employ one or more of the Six Strategies of Nonviolent Puppy Training, presented in Chapter 16:

1. Reward what you want your puppy to do. (Substitution)
2. Practice prevention through management. (Prevention)
3. Play the Magnet Game. (Magnet Game)
4. Make your puppy earn good things, aka "Nothing in Life Is Free." (NILIF)
5. Interrupt and redirect your puppy's behavior. (Interrupt)
6. When all else fails, apply a negative. (Negative)

271

Note: For each solution below we'll identify the specific principle that applies.

Mouthing and Nipping

Veterinarian, trainer, and behaviorist Ian Dunbar did a long-term study of behavior development in puppies, from which he was able to determine that puppies learn acquired bite inhibition by playing with littermates in the first three to four months of life. Acquired bite inhibition is the ability of a dog or puppy to modulate the degree of pressure she uses in her jaws when she bites. When the puppies in a litter play wrestle, they lay their mouths on each other and give each other mock bites. Even though the game is not an actual fight, sometimes a puppy squeezes her teeth on one of her sisters a little too hard. At this point the littermate squeals out a "yipe!" and stops playing. The offending puppy has just learned a crucial lesson—if she presses too hard with her jaws, her playmate gets upset, and the fun stops. In this way, puppies learn that it doesn't take much pressure for a bite to hurt, and that if they are going to bite, biting softly is the socially acceptable way to do it.

It's important to teach your puppy bite inhibition and playing games is a great way to do this. Puppies get excited when playing and naturally use their mouths a lot in the middle of a play session. You are bound to feel your puppy's needle-sharp teeth on your hand as she grabs for the ball or tug toy. You will notice that some "mouthings" are harder than others. Use the opportunity of one the harder mouthings to act like a puppy and squeal "yipe!" Try to sound as much like a puppy as you can by using a high-pitched voice. Stop playing. Resume the game when your puppy relaxes. After a few of these incidents, your puppy will start putting her mouth on your hand more softly. The strategies you have employed here are interruption ("yipe!") and applying a negative (stopping the game). By using these strategies you are teaching your puppy to control the pressure of her jaws when playing with you. These rules should be followed by anyone who plays with her.

Once your puppy is using her mouth "softly," you can teach her to avoid putting her mouth on you altogether. Whenever she puts her mouth on you, squeal "yipe!" (interruption) then declare "game over," and put the toy away (negative). Do not resume playing again for at least a few minutes. When she has calmed down you can resume playing. By introducing bite inhibition exercises into your play sessions, you are teaching your puppy to use her mouth only on toys—not on humans. This lesson is an essential safety measure for unforeseen circumstances, such as an accidental step on a tail, when your puppy might reflexively nip at someone.

Once your puppy has learned to wait patiently for toys, to give up toys when asked, and to keep her mouth off you at all times, "game over" can be used to maintain all the rules of play. If your puppy grabs a toy out of your hand without permission, for example, now you can say "game over," stop playing, and put the toy away. You can do the same if your puppy does not give you back the toy on request, or if she puts her mouth on your hand. You will find that your puppy studiously avoids "game over" by playing in a mannerly way. And once you have all the rules necessary to make games with your puppy safe and enjoyable, you can start having fun!

Here are some other solutions to mouthing and nipping:

- Chew on a toy. Mouthing in puppies is often an expression of teething needs. Make a list of the times of the day and/or situations in which your puppy tends to mouth or nip you. Then, before she has a chance to nip or mouth, give her a stuffed Kong toy, a Nylabone, or a bully stick to chew on instead. You can also give your puppy an ice cube or frozen piece of canvas, or freeze the stuffed Kong toy. In addition to making the Kong last longer, freezing a chew toy helps numbs the gums for a while, alleviating the discomfort of emerging teeth. (Substitution)

- Lick your hand. You can teach your puppy to lick you instead of nip you. Rub some turkey, peanut butter, or cream cheese on your hand. As your puppy licks it off, say "lick." Then click, praise, and treat with turkey. After your puppy has learned this trick, you can say "lick" whenever she starts to nip you, or, better yet, before she starts to nip you, and then reward her with attention and petting. Another variation of this is to lick the palm of your hand and then let your puppy lick your saliva. (Substitution)

☞ Sit or lie down. If your puppy nips your ankles or feet while you are walking, have her sit or down whenever you approach, before she starts nipping, and reward with a treat once you have passed by. (Substitution)

☞ Walk away from you. This is another good alternative behavior for puppies who like to nip moving feet. As you approach your puppy, toss a treat to your side, so that she follows the treat away from your path of movement. If she comes back toward your feet, toss another treat off to the side. You can add a cue for this behavior by saying "excuse me," or "find it," just before you toss the treat. Soon your puppy will start anticipating the thrown treat and start hanging back so she can get to it sooner. Eventually, you will be able to say "excuse me" whenever you are walking by or toward your puppy and she will move out of your way. You can then reward with a tossed treat after you have passed by. (Substitution)

☞ Look you in the eyes. This is a good alternative for puppies who tend to nip when being petted, touched, groomed, or held. Hold a small piece of turkey in one hand, in front of your nose, while you pet or brush with the other hand. If your puppy is looking at the treat in your one hand, she is also looking in your eyes, which means she isn't nipping your other hand, right? Now click and give her the treat for such good behavior. Repeat this sequence. You can add a cue by saying, "look" or your puppy's name, just before putting the treat in front of your nose. Over time, as your puppy gets good at this, remove the treat from your hand and ask for longer and longer periods of eye contact before rewarding. (Substitution) Also see pay attention, page 197.

🦴 Put your puppy in a kennel or exercise pen or behind a baby gate (preferably in a social area) so nipping can't occur. (Prevention)

🦴 Tether your puppy so nipping can't occur. (Prevention)

🦴 Any time you catch your puppy chewing on appropriate toys or licking your hand, click, praise, and treat. (Magnet Game)

🦴 You can interrupt nipping or mouthing in situations other than play with the "yipe!" training described above. When you feel so much as a tooth for whatever reason, immediately make your high-pitched "yipe!" If your puppy backs off, give praise. You can then ask for one of the alternate behaviors listed above, such as sit, down, lick, and so on, and reward that behavior. Note: Puppies all have different temperaments. If your puppy gets more excited and nippy when you do this, this is not the technique for her. Don't do it. (Interruption and Substitution)

🦴 Interrupt nipping or mouthing with the "aaaah!" method. Lower your vocal pitch and make a quick "aaaah" sound. To some puppies this is perceived as a low-intensity growl and they will back off. Again, praise if your puppy does back off and ask for an alternate behavior, then reward. Some people just yell "ow," which is also effective. Note: As with "yipe," if your puppy gets more excited and nippy when you do this, this is not the technique for her, so don't do it. (Interruption and Substitution)

🦴 If your puppy sits quietly at first, but then starts to mouth you after you begin to pet her, immediately stop petting and ignore her until she relaxes or grabs a toy, licks you, and so on. (Negative)

🦴 When your puppy nips, immediately hold her gently but firmly until her body relaxes. (See Figure 10-2 in the socialization chapter on page 123.) Then say "okay" and release. Note: If your puppy gets more excited and nippy when you do this, you'll want to do more handling exercises as described in the socialization chapter before using this technique. (Negative)

✑ Whenever a nip occurs, leave the room. You can mark the unwanted behavior by saying "time out" as soon as you feel the nip. This method has the advantage of not having to touch the puppy in order to get her to her time-out "spot," which sometimes intensifies the nipping behavior. This method requires, of course, that you are able to place something between you and your puppy, like a gate or closed door, in order to prevent her from following you out. The time out should last two minutes, with no hard feelings when it's done. (Negative)

✑ When your puppy nips, immediately put her in a short, two-minute time out in her kennel or behind a baby gate in another room. You can combine the principles of interrupting the nipping with a "yipe" or "aaaah" and, if the puppy doesn't stop nipping, say "time out" and put your puppy in the time out. This combination can be very powerful. The difference between this time out and the previous time out is that now you are removing your puppy from the room, rather than removing yourself. (Negative)

Note: Some people worry that using the puppy's kennel for a time out will make the kennel itself an unpleasant place and that the puppy will be unwilling to go to the kennel in any situation. If your puppy already hates being confined this is true, so don't use this method. We like to point out that sending a child to his room is a common time out used by parents. Yet nobody ends up hating his room. On the contrary, a child's room tends to be his "safe" place. The same is true of kennels. The unpleasant aspect of the time out is not the kennel itself, but rather the social separation at a time when the puppy wants attention. So if you've done your work at making the kennel a pleasant place to begin with, a time out there is as fine as anywhere else.

Chewing and Destruction of Property

🦴 Chew on appropriate toys instead (Kong, bully stick, Nylabone, and so on). Make sure your puppy has something attractive, rewarding, and challenging to chew on. Most destructive chewing in young puppies is a result of them finding shoes and furniture legs more tasty or more available than chew toys. The Kong is a great solution to this problem as it is designed to be stuffed with yummy food that your puppy gets nowhere else. The Kong can be stuffed in "layers"—a layer of liver paste, a layer of peanut butter, and a layer of cream cheese, for example—and then its hole can be plugged with something hard and crunchy like a carrot or dog biscuit. The result is a toy that is tastier than the sofa leg, which will make your puppy gravitate toward chewing on the toy and away from chewing on the furniture. In addition, the Kong gives your puppy a fun challenge as he works to empty it of its contents and it will keep him focused on that task for an extended period of time. If your puppy chews when you leave him alone, make sure to give him the Kong when you leave. If he chews when you are at home, try to predict which times of day he needs this kind of employment and give him the Kong during those times. You can prepare several Kongs in advance and put them in the freezer overnight, which makes them last even longer. Lots of good Kong recipes can be found on the Kong Web site at *www.kongcompany.com*. (Substitution)

🦴 Leave it—teach your puppy to turn away and ignore prohibited objects (see "Leave It," Chapter 19.) (Substitution)

🦴 If destructive chewing tends to take place when you are away from home, train your puppy to stay in a kennel while you are away (see Chapter 5). In a kennel, it is impossible to chew on the sofa, or your shoes, or your CD collection. (Prevention)

Note: If your puppy chews on the bars of his kennel, tries to bend open the door to escape, chews through walls around doorways to the outside, or destroys windows and blinds in an attempt to get out of the house, do not kennel him! His destructive behavior is likely the result of severe separation anxiety and needs the attention of a qualified trainer or behaviorist. Continued kenneling will likely result in serious injury to your puppy.

- Tether your puppy when you are home so chewing can't occur. (Prevention)
- Puppyproof the home. Make sure you keep forbidden objects like shoes, pens, and so on out of reach in closets, drawers, or above jumping level. (Prevention)
- You can try spraying furniture legs with a deterrent such as a mouthwash or citronella, which is available at pet stores. Sprays such as this are usually poor substitutes for good management and supervision, and are unnecessary if the measures outlined above are followed consistently. Don't spray your puppy with these products! (Negative)
- Make sure you give lots of attention when he's chewing on something legal. Come over to him, pet him, praise him. (Magnet Game)
- Make your puppy earn the freedom to move around the house, which is a privilege. He must earn that privilege by keeping his teeth confined to approved objects and surfaces. Have him sit, lie down, go to his spot, and so on before giving him anything to chew on. (NILIF)
- Interrupt him by whistling loudly, blowing a whistle, clapping, yelling "ah-ah," or any other such distraction in order to stop the behavior. Your goal is to startle him, not scare him. Then ask your puppy to find his toy or have him come, sit, stay, and then give him an appropriate chewy. (Interrupt and Substitute)
- If you catch her in the act, apply a negative by putting your puppy in a time out. You should only have to do this two or three times. If you are doing this more than that,

the other principles are not being applied consistently or correctly. Call a trainer. (Negative)

Barking

When dealing with excessive barking, the first thing is to determine why the puppy is barking. Is the puppy barking at you, neighbors, guests, other dogs, or the cat? Does he bark when left alone, outside, inside, in the kennel, while playing, or when the doorbell rings? Is the barking high or low pitched, continuous or distinct, rapid fire or slow? The answers to these questions will affect the way you deal with the barking.

If your puppy is barking at you in a high-pitched, distinct (one bark at a time) bark while you are not paying attention to him, he is most likely barking for attention. If your puppy barks rapidly in a high pitch when playing, or when you first come home, that is probably excitement barking. If your puppy is barking in a low-pitched, rapid-fire bark at guests when they enter the house, and the bark is accompanied by either lunging or backing away, the underlying problem is aggressive behavior, which is rare for puppies. It's most probably rooted in fear and, in such a case, you should see a qualified trainer or behaviorist.

- For attention barking: Make eye contact, have your puppy sit, lie down, and relax. (Substitution)
- For excitement barking: Provide a toy or other chewy. (Substitution)
- For alarm barking: Have your puppy come when called, down, and stay. This is a good sequence of alternate behaviors if your puppy barks at neighbors, passersby, or other dogs, while in the yard or through the window. (Substitution)
- Be "quiet" on cue. (Substitution) This one is a little tricky, so follow closely:
  1. Whenever your dog barks, click and treat. Yes, you read right—you are rewarding the barking to begin with.

2. Now start saying "speak" just before you think your puppy is about to bark, and reward with a treat when he does.

3. Now only reward barking if you have asked for it with "speak" and ignore all other barking.

4. The final step is to practice asking for "speak," then, without giving a treat, say "quiet." Count five seconds. If you get five seconds of quiet, reward your puppy with a treat. From now on, reward only "quiet" followed by five seconds of quiet.

5. As "quiet" becomes reliable, gradually ask for longer periods of quiet before rewarding.

Keep your puppy away from whatever is triggering his barking. Distance very frequently does the trick. Gauge the distance between your puppy and whatever he normally barks at and consider this your baseline. For example, if your puppy barks at passing dogs from a distance of ten feet, but can generally sit quietly at a distance of fifteen feet, always keep him at a fifteen foot distance from other dogs and reward quiet sits. As he gets very good at this, start rewarding quiet sits at fourteen feet, then thirteen feet, and so on. Eventually you should be able to get quiet sits or downs right next to whatever he barks at. (Prevention and Substitution)

Reduce the motivation for the barking. Frequently, barking is an expression of an unmet need, primarily insufficient exercise, attention, and play. (Prevention)

If your puppy is constantly barking at other dogs, it may be because he doesn't have enough exposure to them. The answer in this case would be to increase his socialization opportunities with other dogs, so that seeing another dog is more "ho-hum" and not quite as rare and extraordinary. (Prevention)

Block your dog's ability to see and/or hear whatever is triggering him to bark. Pull down blinds, close doors, put him in a kennel, take him inside, and so on. This is especially important for puppies who tend to bark at movement and sound outside the house when they are alone. If your puppy continues to bark when you are not there to redirect it, the barking will only become more of a problem. Ask your neighbors if they hear barking when you're away, or leave home and take a secret trip back to hear for yourself. If barking when alone seems to be a problem, position your puppy's kennel away from outside doors and windows. (Prevention)

🦴 You can also limit your dog's ability to hear outside noise by turning a radio on. (Prevention)

🦴 Give your puppy something like a stuffed Kong to work on and keep him busy. (Substitution)

🦴 Put some peanut butter on the roof of your puppy's mouth in situations which tend to trigger his barking. (Prevention)

🦴 Be on the lookout for any of the alternate behaviors listed above, or for any quiet behavior at all, particularly in the situations where the barking tends to be a problem. As soon as your dog stops barking, count one-thousand-one and praise and treat. If he starts barking again, turn away. (Magnet Game and Negative)

🦴 If barking happens during play, catch your puppy before he barks at you as a request to play with her. As soon as he picks up a toy, reward him for picking it up by playing with him for five minutes. In this case, you have rewarded him for taking the toy in his mouth, rather than barking. (Magnet Game)

🦴 If your puppy barks for attention and petting, catch him anytime he's sitting or lying down quietly and reward him with tons of affection. (Magnet Game)

🦴 If your puppy tends to bark at other dogs and people, catch him being quiet in the presence of another dog or person and reward him with a treat. (Magnet Game)

🦴 For attention barking: Speak to, pet, and look at your puppy only when he's sitting quietly, laying down quietly,

or doing another quiet behavior that you have identified as desirable. Ignore your puppy at all other times.
(NILIF)

🦴 For excitement barking during play: Throw a toy only
when your puppy is sitting quietly. Otherwise hold on to
the toy and ignore your puppy. (NILIF)

🦴 For barking to go outside or get out of the kennel: Open
the door or gate only when your puppy is doing a quiet
alternate behavior. Otherwise, wait patiently and ignore
your puppy's barking. (NILIF)

🦴 Whenever your puppy barks for attention, give him a
short time out in his kennel or another room. You can
give a warning signal like "knock it off" or "quiet" after
the first bark. If he barks again, after the warning, say
"time out" and put him in a time out for two minutes. If
you teach your puppy these signals well, he will eventually respond to the "knock it off" warnings in order to
avoid the time outs, and you won't even have to carry
through with the time out itself. (Negative)

🦴 If your puppy barks for you to throw the toy you have in
your hand, immediately declare "game over," stop playing, put the toy away, and ignore him for a few minutes.
This will help reinforce the concept that barking is not a
behavior to use whenever he wants to. (Negative)

🦴 Hold your puppy firmly but gently until quiet. When
you feel his muscles relax, even slightly, say "okay" and
release him (see Figure 10-2 on page 123). (Negative)

Jumping

🦴 Teach sit, lie down, move away, or go to her bed. These
are the simplest and most effective alternatives to jumping. (Substitution)

🦴 Tether your puppy to something solid and immovable,
within sight of the door but out of reach of your guests as
they enter. (Prevention)

🦴 With your puppy tethered at high-excitement times, click, treat, and pet every time she happens to sit without being asked. Ignore her at all other times. Eventually, as she gravitates toward sitting and away from jumping at high-excitement times, try the same routine without the tethering. (Prevention and Magnet Game)

🦴 With your puppy tethered, instruct guests to refrain from greeting your puppy until she sits. If she starts to jump again once they approach, tell them to move back out of reach until she sits again. Make a rule: Puppy only gets petted if she is sitting. (Prevention, Magnet Game, and NILIF)

🦴 Voice your displeasure with an "ahhhh" and combine that with turning away. (Interruption and Negative)

🦴 If your puppy is jumping on someone else, you can clap, "ah-ah," whistle, or do anything else you can think of to startle her. Once she's on all fours again, you can direct her to sit, find it, lie down, and so on. (Interruption and Substitution)

🦴 If she jumps again, give her a two-minute time out in her kennel or another room. (Negative)

Bolting Out the Door

If your puppy tends to bolt out the door, safety and well-being are at stake so management is all-important. Keep your puppy on a leash, behind a baby gate, or in a kennel. Even after your puppy is reliably trained, remember that no behavior is 100 percent. We suggest that you never let your puppy off leash in an outside area, unless the area is fenced and dogs are allowed off-lead. Otherwise, not only do you risk harm to your puppy, but in most places it is illegal. We suggest putting a note on the door to remind people to "Look out for the puppy before opening!" It's also a good idea to put a folding exercise pen outside the door as an added barrier in case your puppy scoots through your legs. That way, he won't get far! (Prevention)

🦴 Teach your puppy to sit or lie down and stay.

🦴 Never let your puppy pass through any door without staying and waiting for your okay. Going through the door becomes the reward. (NILIF)

🦴 If you see your puppy following someone who is about to leave, get his attention by clapping, whistling, yelling . . . or anything that startles him and stops him from going forward. Just be careful you don't scare him, as that might cause him to quicken his pace to the door! (Interruption)

Practice the "Door Fan" Method: (NILIF)

1. With your puppy on a leash for safety, open the door two inches and let your puppy think he's going out. When the door doesn't open all the way, he'll back off and perhaps walk around a little. As he backs off, open the door wider. He'll scoot back, ready to bolt, but as he moves toward the door again, quickly close it back to the two-inch mark. Be extremely careful not to catch your puppy's nose in the door!

2. Repeat over and over until your puppy sits while the door is open two inches. Then say "okay" and open the door wide and let your puppy go outside.

3. Progress to opening the door further and further before you say "okay."

4. Finally, progress to you going through the door first, coming back in the house, and saying "okay."

5. Practice having your puppy sit and wait for permission to enter the pet store, exit the vet's or groomers, enter the park gate, and so on.

Stealing and Playing Chase

Stealing and chasing are often related. For example, your puppy may steal your shoe and then try to run away with it. So the first thing to do is keep your environment puppyproofed. (Prevention)

Never chase your puppy and don't scream or yell. If she is running away, follow her but not in a direct line behind her. Run parallel or at an angle if possible. When your puppy glances back your way, drop to the ground and pretend that you found something really interesting. In many cases, your puppy will turn around and come to back to you to see if what you've got is more interesting than whatever is in front of her. When she's close to you, face her and offer a treat (if you have one with you), and then smoothly and calmly take her by the collar or pick her up. Do not make sudden motions; otherwise, she may run away again. (Substitution)

Here are a few other tips:

- Teach a reliable come, lie down, stop, or hide-and-seek so that she will respond when asked. (Substitution)
- Teach a reliable drop it (see page 238). (Substitution)
- Let your puppy drag a tether around when allowed free time in the house. If she steals something, simply step on the tether so she can't run away with it. (Prevention)
- Keep the puppy tethered (when supervised), behind baby gates, or in an exercise pen. (Prevention)
- Reward your puppy every time she comes to you or brings something to you. (Magnet Game)

Index

About the Authors

Paul Owens is nationally recognized as a leading proponent of nonviolent training who promotes kindness, respect, and compassion. His DVD, *The Dog Whisperer,* a companion to his best-selling book, has been rated as the best family dog training DVD on the market. He lives in Los Angeles.

Terence Cranendonk apprenticed as a trainer with Paul Owens and is a Certified Pet Dog Trainer (CPDT), as well as a Certified Dog Behavior Consultant (CDBC). In addition to dog training, he is a professional actor and university instructor. He lives in Akron, Ohio.

Norma Eckroate writes on the holistic care of humans and animals. She produced the companion DVD to *The Dog Whisperer.* She lives in Los Angeles.